Praise

GETTING OUT OF SAIGON

"Captivating. . . . It's hard not to admire [White] for his pluckiness in the face of bureaucratic indifference as well as his growth from a risk-taking adventurer into a humanitarian with genuine compassion for the Vietnamese whose lives depended on him."

—*The Washington Post*

"Gripping. . . . White's persona seems like something out of a Terry Southern or Ian Fleming novel—as does his writing. White tells his inspiring story with wit, panache, humility, and a captivating sense of time and place. A fantastic read."

—*Kirkus Reviews* (starred review)

"[White's] story is one of courage, resolve, and determination born from challenge."

—*The Christian Science Monitor*

"An edge-of-your-seat, too-insane-not-to-be-true story."

—OprahDaily.com

"A must-read for those of us who were there, for those of us who watched the fall of Saigon on the six o'clock news, for all those who lived through that dark period of American history, and for a younger generation who have seen the documentaries and read the books. Ralph White's *Getting Out of Saigon* opens old wounds, but also heals. An amazing tour de force and a stunning human drama set against the cataclysm of a lost war."

—Nelson DeMille, bestselling novelist and
former U.S. Army first lieutenant in the
First Cavalry Division, Vietnam 1967–1968

"By turns harrowing, enchanting, and leavened with a humor as dark as Saigon's quayside alleys, Ralph White's *Getting Out of Saigon* belongs on your bookshelf between Graham Greene and Neil Sheehan."

—Bob Drury and Tom Clavin, coauthors of
*Last Men Out: The True Story of
America's Heroic Final Hours in Vietnam*

"[An] enthralling story."

—*Library Journal* (starred review)

"[A] stirring debut. . . . A propulsive and suspenseful narrative. . . . What [White] modestly refers to as his 15 minutes of fame is made more resonant by his deep humanity."

—*Publishers Weekly*

"Thrilling. . . . White has succeeded in transforming his own Profile in Courage moment into an inspiring and timeless story that is particularly relevant today, when many in government, politics, and business have been called on to decide whether or not to take great risks and follow the dictates of their consciences."

—Thurston Clarke, author of *Honorable Exit:
How a Few Brave Americans Risked All to
Save Our Vietnamese Allies at the End of the War*

"In the history of the Chase Manhattan Bank, one event stands out as clarifying the bank's responsibility to its employees. In 1975, Chase sent Ralph White to rescue its Vietnamese employees before the fall of Saigon. Only in retrospect do we now know how desperate those employees were, or how extraordinary were the obstacles White faced in rescuing them."

—Anthony Terracciano, former vice chairman of the
Chase Manhattan Corporation

GETTING OUT

OF SAIGON

How a 27-Year-Old American Banker
Saved 113 Vietnamese Civilians

RALPH WHITE

SIMON & SCHUSTER PAPERBACKS
New York   London   Toronto   Sydney   New Delhi

Names and identifying characteristics of some individuals
have been changed. Dialogue has been recreated.

An Imprint of Simon & Schuster, LLC
1230 Avenue of the Americas
New York, NY 10020

First Simon & Schuster trade paperback edition April 2024

SIMON & SCHUSTER PAPERBACKS and colophon are
registered trademarks of Simon & Schuster, LLC

Simon & Schuster: Celebrating 100 Years of Publishing in 2024

For information about special discounts for bulk purchases,
please contact Simon & Schuster Special Sales at 1-866-506-1949
or business@simonandschuster.com.

The Simon & Schuster Speakers Bureau can bring authors to
your live event. For more information or to book an event,
contact the Simon & Schuster Speakers Bureau at 1-866-248-3049
or visit our website at www.simonspeakers.com.

Interior design by Kyle Kabel

Manufactured in the United States of America

1   3   5   7   9   10   8   6   4   2

Library of Congress Cataloging-in-Publication Data has been applied for.

ISBN 978-1-9821-9517-5
ISBN 978-1-9821-9518-2 (pbk)
ISBN 978-1-9821-9519-9 (ebook)

For the former employees of the
Chase Manhattan Bank's Saigon branch,
and their families and descendants in America

CONTENTS

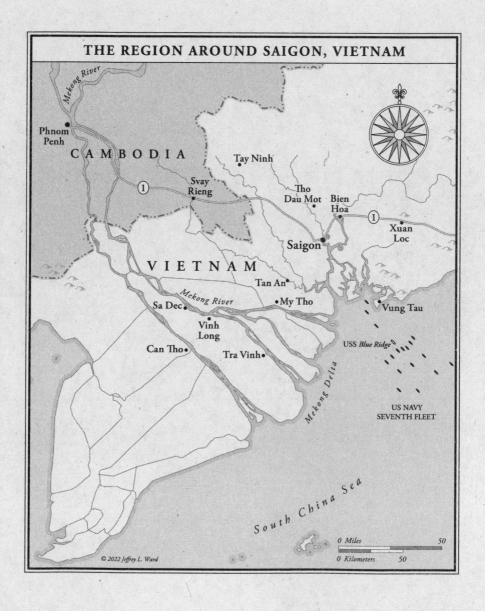

THE REGION AROUND SAIGON, VIETNAM

Mekong River

Phnom
Penh

CAMBODIA

Tay Ninh

Svay
Rieng

Tho
Dau Mot

Bien
Hoa

Saigon

Xuan
Loc

VIETNAM

Tan An

Mekong River

Sa Dec

My Tho

Vung Tau

Vinh
Long

USS *Blue Ridge*

Can Tho

Tra Vinh

Mekong Delta

**US NAVY
SEVENTH FLEET**

South China Sea

© 2022 Jeffrey L. Ward

0 Miles 50

0 Kilometers 50

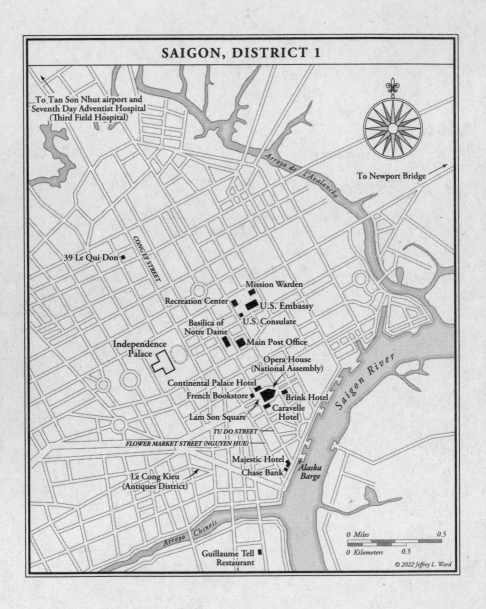

SAIGON, DISTRICT 1

To Tan Son Nhut airport and
Seventh Day Adventist Hospital
(Third Field Hospital)

Arroyo de l'Avalanche

To Newport Bridge

CONG LY STREET

39 Le Qui Don

Mission Warden

Recreation Center
U.S. Embassy

Basilica of
Notre Dame
U.S. Consulate

Main Post Office

Independence
Palace

Opera House
(National Assembly)

Continental Palace Hotel

French Bookstore
Brink Hotel

Lam Son Square
Caravelle
Hotel

Saigon River

TU DO STREET

FLOWER MARKET STREET (NGUYEN HUE)

Majestic Hotel

Le Cong Kieu
(Antiques District)
Chase Bank
*Alaska
Barge*

Arroyo Chinois

Guillaume Tell
Restaurant

0 Miles	0.5
0 Kilometers	0.5

© 2022 Jeffrey L. Ward

AUTHOR'S NOTE

In my depiction of events, I adhere to the conventions of memoir, which hold me to a high standard of truthfulness while permitting creative license in reproducing dialogue. The words in quotation marks were spoken in my presence. The events related herein are entirely true.

GETTING OUT
OF SAIGON

LAST CABLE WITH CHASE MANHATTAN BANK, SAIGON BRANCH

THIS IS CHASE REGIONAL OFFICE CLG CHASE SAIGON IS
ANYONE THERE

YES MR WHITE

WHAT ARE YOU DOING THERE AND WHY DID YOU NOT LEAVE
TERMIJN WHO IS THERE NOW

THIS IS WHITE STOP SAIGON IS STILL FAIRLY QUIET AND
SECURE AND ADDIONALLY

ARE ANY OTHER PEOPLE STILL THERE

YES MANY PEOPLE ARE HERE STOP

HOW MANY HAVE LEFT

SIXTY TWO SIR AND HAVE FIFTY SIX FOR TODAY STOP ALL
OTHERS HAVE ELECTED TO STAY STOP THERE SEEMS TO BE
NO PROBLEM IN THIS REGARD STOP ELLERMAN EXTREMELY
CONCERNED ABOUT HOW DEPOSITORS WILL GET THEIR FUNDS
STOP HE DOES NOT WANT CUSTOMERS PENALIZED FOR HAVING

1

DONE BUSINESS WITH AMERICAN BANK STOP RIGHT NOW
RECORDS AND KEYS ARE AT FRENCH EMBASSY PER YOUR
INSTRUCTIONS STOP WOULD YOU LIKE ME TO GO TO GOVERNOR
OF NATIONAL BANK WITH ELLERMAN AND TRY TO TRANSFER
ACCOUNTS TO OTHER BANKS STOP I BELIEVE THAT I HAVE THE
TIME TO DO SO WITHOUT JEOPARDIZING THE OTHER OBJECTIVE

PLS STOP THIS NONSENSE AND YOU ARE HEREBY INSTRUCTED
TO LEAVE VIETNAM TOGETHER WITH THE OTHER GROUP TODAY
STOP HEAD OFFICE WILL INSTRUCT NATIONAL BANK WHAT TO
DO STOP I REPEAT GET OUT OF THERE TERMIJN

YESSIR MY PLEASURE STOP IS THAT ALL

MESSAGE FROM MR KLIMM TO MR WHITE PLS MAKE SURE
TESTKEY DESTROYED AND ALL AVAILABLE MICROFILMS WOULD
BE HAND CARRIED BY YOURSELF TONIGHT STOP

MAY I SEND MICROFILM AND LAST DAYS WORK THROUGH
DIPLOMATIC POUCH

ONLY IF YOU CAN NOT CARRY YOURSELF NONE OF THE PRIOR
POUCHES HAVE REACHED US YET STOP

OK WILL CARRY STOP ANY MORE

TKS AND PLS TELEPHONE OR TELEX ADVISE US FROM YOUR
ARRIVAL POINT STOP OVER BYE BYE

BYE BYE CAM ON

> —*Telex Exchange between the author and Cornelis Termijn
> at Chase Manhattan Bank's Asia Pacific Regional Office
> in Hong Kong, April 25, 1975*

Chapter One

SUNDAY, APRIL 6—MONDAY, APRIL 14, 1975

It took me longer than it should have to spot what had changed since I had lived in Saigon four years earlier. In my defense the place was a study in sensory overload. In 1971, I had managed the American Express Bank in Pleiku, South Vietnam, my first job out of college. Now, in April 1975, I had returned for a temporary assignment with the Chase Manhattan Bank. Just how temporary, nobody knew.

Much of Saigon remained familiar: the high-pitched whine of small, two-cycle motorbikes, the fearsome shards of broken glass topping the walls around residential compounds, the tortured phonemes of spoken Vietnamese. The heat and humidity felt like heavy outer garments. I checked into the Majestic Hotel and was relearning the waterfront when it hit me: in 1971 there had been a perpetual, chest-high cloud of dust suspended throughout the city. Now the dust was only ankle deep. I wondered how many others had noticed.

The military situation in early 1975 was in the public domain. The North Vietnamese communists had used the cover of the 1973 peace treaty to infiltrate seventy thousand troops into South Vietnam. These were highly disciplined, well-trained, and well-supplied North Vietnamese Army troops. These guys wore uniforms, which the local guerrillas, the Viet Cong, usually didn't. They were the varsity

3

team. As they flooded across the Demilitarized Zone, the DMZ, separating North Vietnam from the South, they were unopposed by our South Vietnamese allies, and when the southern troops did stand and fight, they were slaughtered. Their retreat became legendary for its disorder and dishonor. On the day I arrived, North Vietnamese tanks idled within a leisurely one-day drive outside Saigon. No rational person thought Saigon could hold out much longer. That U.S. ambassador Graham Martin thought it could made his sanity a popular topic of discussion. The Chase Manhattan Bank didn't have an exit strategy for Vietnam, unless you counted me.

We had fifty-three Vietnamese employees and we had to assume that they would be executed if we left them there. That's what had happened to the employees of foreign enterprises in Cambodia when the Khmer Rouge took over. Moreover, our Saigon branch manager, Cornelis Termijn, carried a Dutch passport and couldn't be persuaded that the American government would evacuate him if things got hot. Officially, we were still saying *if*. Chase needed an American to keep its Saigon branch operating for as long as it was feasible. The bank's ideal candidate to relieve Termijn would preferably be nearby, young, single, and not to put too fine a point on it, expendable. Previous Vietnam experience, like mine, would be icing.

Chase's senior executive in the Asia-Pacific Regional Office was John Linker, headquartered in Hong Kong. John had initially approached another Chase officer, Gael Blake, about relieving Cor Termijn in Saigon, and his answer had been a nervous chuckle, likely reflecting the proposal's expendability feature. The name Blake is derived from the Old English word for black. Linker's second choice was a guy named White.

John Linker was trim and handsome, bright and confident, a natural leader and a real up-and-comer in the bank. I hadn't met John before he showed up in Bangkok to recruit me for this assignment; I doubt he'd even heard my name. Nor was I easy to find. If his intel on me had been better, he wouldn't have begun his search at the onset of a weekend. As usual, I was in the coastal village of

Pattaya, sailing and diving by day, and immersed in intensive Thai language study into the night.

I had just been assigned to Chase's Bangkok branch a couple of months earlier as an entry-level corporate banking officer. A yearlong training program in New York had taught me just enough accounting and financial statement analysis to distinguish a robust commercial borrower from a dicey one. The objective of the academic training was to weed out the bad credits, but local management in Bangkok took a more holistic view. They told me you couldn't swing a cat in Bangkok without hitting some questionable enterprise more than happy to pay up for the privilege of doing business with Chase. They also pointed out that bonuses were paid for putting loans on the books, not for keeping them off. I was still looking for a cat to swing when North Vietnamese General Dung Van-Tien heard his call to destiny and marched his crack troops across Vietnam's undefended DMZ.

*   *   *

It was late afternoon on Sunday, April 6, 1975, when Amat, one of the bank's drivers, knocked on the solid teak door to my apartment in Bangkok. I'd already conscripted Amat into my notions of cultural immersion and he knew to speak to me slowly in his native language. *"The big boss says take you to his house right now."*

The big boss would be Hendrik Steenbergen, one of the Dutch nationals, like Cor Termijn in Saigon, who ended up employed by Chase after we'd acquired the Southeast Asian banking licenses of Nationale Handelsbank in 1962. With a few exceptions the Dutch managers were mostly duds. By and large they were the second and third sons of tulip farmers, consigned to some of the planet's most obscure time zones to seek their fortunes after the eldest brother inherited the family farm. These generally older Dutch guys made big money for the bank when local economies were booming, and gave up those gains in downturns. Chase's new business plan called for less profit volatility, ushering in the first wave of Ivy League MBAs to the Asia Pacific. We had to stop calling it the Far East when locals pointed out that they weren't far from anything. We expatriates might be, but they were home.

Most of the Dutch country managers used Chase as a kind of assisted living facility in their quiet years before an honorable retirement. Large staffs of servants provided the assistance. In addition to chauffeurs, they had guards, cookboys, poolboys, gardeners, housekeepers, and caregivers for visiting grandkids. They also had fixers on retainer, often retired police officers with wide networks and meticulously kept accounts of favors receivable. Need an appointment with the finance minister? Call your fixer. Crash your car? Fixer. Gonorrhea? Fixer.

Henk Steenbergen was blessed with a strong Thai economy and a couple of world-class cat swingers in his branch. No one, including Henk himself, needed to know where he would have stood on the competence spectrum absent good fortune and a robust economy.

Amat pulled up to the country manager's driveway and a servant squeaked open the cast iron gates to Paradise. Paving stones set in a manicured lawn followed the contours of a curvy swimming pool surrounded by coconut palms. A path so close to the water would be unsafe for someone unfamiliar with the potency of Thai beer, much less Thai *ganja*, stumbling home in the moonlight.

Henk Steenbergen, aged fifty-one, and another man, less than seven years my senior, rose from their poolside seats when I emerged through the palms. Dutch is one of those accents that imparts its distinctive character depending on the speaker. It can come across as sexy or wise or slippery or friendly. It's a truly versatile accent. Steenbergen's was bumbling. The contrast between him and John Linker, the other man by the pool, could not have been more vivid.

John surveyed me so keenly, thoroughly, and deliberately that I guessed there wasn't much to tell him about myself that he hadn't already heard, read, or intuited. He continued his examination during our handshake and afterward as we took seats around an outdoor table. When I recall John, it is his eyes that I see most clearly, often disembodied, like the smile of the Cheshire Cat.

A servant provided me a tall glass of limeade and I asked discreetly in her language if it was with or without salt, knowing that local lore conferred a health benefit to salt as yet undiscovered by Western civilization. Her: *With.* Me: *I prefer without.* Her: *Back in a minute.* It was a seven-second conversation, conducted within the constraints of a very rudimentary vocabulary.

John said, "That's impressive. How long have you been here?"

"Two months."

"Very impressive. How's your Vietnamese?"

"Couple hundred words, three hundred maybe." In retrospect it should have already been obvious where this meeting was going, but in real time it was just introductory chatter under the rustling clicks of palm leaves.

"Say something in Vietnamese."

My salt-free limeade arrived and I took a sip. "Sure." Random phrases acquired years ago in the Central Highlands came back to me. *Just one kiss. I go home. Two canned beers. I'm shy. Eat corn. I do not know. Handsome. Spring roll with fish sauce. Ten thousand piastres. Philanderer. Sorry.* I took another sip of limeade, now seized with anxiety that John might know some Vietnamese and realize how delinquent a student I'd been.

Along with the retrieval of the disused words came associated sensory images from those days. Massive clouds of butterflies floating over a field. Antique Renault sedans roaming the streets. Thieves on motorbikes. The stinky-sweet flavor of durian fruit. Card games interrupted by the rumble of distant B-52 bombing runs. An old woman sitting on the ground obsessively scrubbing the soles of her feet. The long crack in the surface of the pool table at the Pleiku officers' club, creating an uneven playing field for both players.

"I understand you have a pilot's license and a marine master's certificate."

John had done some homework. I could pilot a plane. I could helm a vessel. I could say *eat corn* in a language understood only by people who wore flip-flops to work. I wondered what else he knew. Did he know that it took me five years to get through college, or that my father had lost his medical practice because he preferred Demerol to fatherhood? It had not been chance that deposited me on the side of the globe opposite my father.

Pale blue water rippled in the pool. Servants glanced surreptitiously toward us as they puttered around the property. And always, palm fronds crackled overhead.

"Do you know Cor Termijn?" John's eyes were back in X-ray mode.

"Only heard of him. Country manager at Saigon branch. Good guy, I hear." In fact, I had it on good authority that Cor was a man of steady habits and quiet competence. One of the good Dutchmen.

Steenbergen piped up. "Former colleague of mine at Handelsbank." It was a flawlessly noncommittal endorsement.

At that point I knew perfectly well why I'd been invited to Steenbergen's limeade party. I beckoned the servant over, handed her my empty glass, and assembled the first complete sentence I'd ever spoken in Thai, *Please add a double shot of Mekong whiskey to my next limeade.* These bastards were sending me to Vietnam! The communists were sending General Dung in from the north and the capitalists were sending me in from the south. I called out to the departing servant, *Make that a triple!*

Even General Dung's enemies conceded that he was a strategic genius. My best friends knew that I'd cheated to get my pilot's license. When the clerk at the Federal Aviation Administration told me to cover my one good eye and read the chart on the wall, the one with the big E at the top, I said I'd start with the fine print on the bottom line. "P-E-Z-O-L-C-F-T-D." I had memorized it after being blinded in my right eye in a tennis accident. General Dung would have been proud. When the draft board asked me to read the same chart, I'd said, "What eye chart?" I'd be the first to admit there's something unsavory about simultaneously holding a pilot's license and a draft deferment for blindness.

The servant returned with my Mekong sour. I'd invented a damn fine drink.

John said, "Cor is leaving Saigon at the end of this week. His wife has already left and his household goods are being shipped out."

"So I suppose the branch will be closing."

I couldn't imagine Chase would leave a branch open without an expatriate country manager. This was a bizarre conversation for the lowest-ranking officer Chase employed in Southeast Asia to be having with its senior-most executive. It was the equivalent of a lieutenant shooting the breeze with a general. The softly padding servants and the glamorous poolside setting enhanced the absurdity. The Mekong whiskey sour helped, but not nearly enough.

"We have very competent local staff there," John said. "The branch runs itself day to day. Problem is that all of the remaining employees are Vietnamese. If Cor were to leave, they'd have no incentive to keep coming in to work. They'd believe we had abandoned them and they would try to get out on their own. That would cause a de facto closing of the branch, and probably an embarrassing one at that. I'm the one who's going to decide if and when that branch closes, not truant employees."

I was tempted to point out to my commanding officer that that's exactly the kind of stuff that happens in wartime. Then again, John Linker hadn't invited me to hear my views. He'd be looking for a *yes* or *no*. I wasn't quite there yet. I said, "I'm listening."

John called the servant over and pointed to my drink and said, "I'll have one of those."

That wasn't going to happen. I told her, *"Make his a virgin."* When she giggled, I realized that Thais didn't use the word in its nonalcoholic sense. She understood though. John's limeade would be unsullied by Mekong whiskey.

"What did you say to her?"

"To hold the salt. They typically make it with salt." John needed to be brought back on message. "You need an American to sit behind the country manager's desk for the duration." *Duration* was military slang for *until the end of the war.* Since 1965 it had been used interchangeably with *in perpetuity.* General Dung planned to refine that definition.

John said, "That's the idea."

"You want me there to encourage the staff to stay on the job . . ." On the tip of my tongue was . . . *by giving them a false sense of security.* Neither of us needed to say it. John knew I knew, and I knew he knew. Who knows what Henk knew? John hadn't articulated his plan because it didn't amount to much more than sending me in as a hostage. With me there, the Vietnamese employees wouldn't bail out and Saigon branch would continue to operate—for some newly defined duration.

I drained my sour and the servant came right over. She was a shapely forty-something, light on the feet and heavy on the makeup. She gave me the eye.

"Another?"

"Yeah."

"A sexy one?"

"Yes, please."

Missing in John's strategy so far was how exactly he planned to imbue his hostage with the unfounded security that was supposed to rub off on the locals. Then it occurred to me. He hadn't asked me to do anything. He'd just visually imprinted the mission into me. I'd practically volunteered. At Gettysburg, General Longstreet had probably given General Pickett the same look John Linker had just given me. It was a look that said, *I won't be there, Pickett, so you'll have to figure things out on the fly.* Try as I might I could not identify with General Pickett.

Still, I was excited by the proposition. It was vaguely complimentary. I had a primitive affection for Saigon. I'd be following in the footsteps of Somerset Maugham, Graham Greene, Joseph

Conrad. The Vietnamese were an attractive, pleasant people. The café in the courtyard of the Continental Hotel served delicious, buttery croissants. I bobbed my head and said, "I'll do it."

I wasn't exactly clear on what I'd agreed to do, other than babysit some employees. John was visibly relieved. He'd be able to tell head office that he had taken charge of the situation. He was parachuting in a young American with previous Saigon experience to replace the defecting country manager in order to keep the employees from closing the branch. John would oversell my fluency in Vietnamese. He might also mention that I had yet to contribute much at Bangkok branch. Telling head office that Henk Steenbergen could easily spare me would be the most truthful part of John's report.

*   *   *

Someone was going to miss me though—Oie, my girlfriend. Thais all have nicknames since even to them their names are excessively multisyllabic. In Thai the word *oie* is a raw sugarcane snack, and she truly was a sweetie. She was a Chinese-Thai and her English was perfect because she'd attended college in the States. She had an exceptionally pretty face and, in her thickly padded brassieres, was a real head-turner. Bright too. She worked as a journalist. She was a respectable girl, more so than anyone expected to see me with.

It was Oie who gave me my Thai nickname, *Seua Cao*, or White Tiger. It never really caught on, though my colleagues at the bank sometimes used it derisively. Oie thought going to Vietnam while it was in free fall was insane but also swashbuckling. I neglected to tell her it was just a babysitting assignment or that my corporate title would be hostage.

*   *   *

The standard wait for an American to get a Vietnamese visa in Bangkok was two weeks. Time to call in Chase's fixer. His name is lost to history but he was a dapper, wrinkled, and soft-spoken old gent whose police specialty had been handwriting analysis. Thai is written phonetically, with forty-four consonants, a dozen vowels, five tones, a sprinkling of diacritical marks, and regional orthographic standards, all providing a rich, multidimensional puzzle for the handwriting analyst. It's no wonder he was so highly regarded. Our guy was the quintessential fixer. In quid pro quo for my Vietnamese visa, he promised the Viets a no-questions-asked Thai visa for whomever they might designate, and I got my visa in three days. It was a far better deal for the Viets since there was considerably more demand to flee Vietnam than to enter.

*   *   *

I was a light traveler. I packed a small toiletries bag, a shirt, and a pair of pants. I'd be wearing a shirt and pants so that made two of each. Extra-wide bell bottoms were the style and mine were eleven inches wide. Socks and underpants. That took up about half of the space in my small leather briefcase. That left plenty of room for the one bulky commodity that the bank wanted me to take, and for another personal item which I added under my own responsibility.

There is justifiable sensitivity about corporate executives handling large quantities of money. A lapse in integrity was a serious offense at Chase, as it had been in my upbringing. In my childhood I'd had the backs of my legs belted mercilessly for relatively small infractions. When John Linker gave me a bag of cash to be used for exigencies, I briefly considered declining it. Ultimately I decided that if unaccountable money might help Chase employees escape execution, it would be justified. I didn't sign for it; there was no documentation of any kind. In packing for my Saigon assignment, I tucked the twenty-five grand in with my underwear and socks.

To put that $25,000 in perspective, it cost only $100 to take out a contract to have someone murdered in Thailand. A Bangkok branch colleague had researched the matter after one of the cat swingers in our branch had mistreated his wife. One of my scuba guides in Pattaya had been killed for the can of baht coins he kept in his truck. A baht was worth a nickel. His throat was slit and he was thrown facedown in a sewage ditch. Nice kid. Good diver. Killed for about two bucks in American money. If I were killed for the contents of my briefcase at least my friends would know my value. *Say what you will about Ralph, but by definition he was worth twenty-five grand.*

A little background explains that other personal item in my briefcase. We always had firearms around the house when I was growing up. I would come home from school and head out into the woods behind our house for an hour or two with our beagle and bring home rabbits, squirrels, and partridge. I'd butcher them myself, and my mother would lead me through one of her game recipes. The guns were kept in an unlocked closet along with other sporting goods like ice skates, baseball mitts, and fishing equipment. Hunting was just another facet of country life. It produced free food. I contributed to the family table.

One of my guns was a Smith & Wesson Chief's Special, a five-shot revolver. I shot thousands of rounds at homemade bull's-eyes tacked to trees down in the woods. I kept the gun cleaned and oiled. I became as comfortable with my revolver as I was with our shotguns and rifles. I'm sure most kids in my high school had hunting arms in the house, and I knew several who had pistols too. I doubt, though, that many of my friends trained as hard as I did. My mother had to install a bell on the back porch to summon me out of the woods at dinnertime.

When the Chase Manhattan Bank assigned me to Southeast Asia, I stuffed my .38 Special into the bottom of a ski boot and packed thick wool ski socks into the cuff to cover it. I dumped a full box of bullets into the bottom of a blue Maxwell House coffee can with a snap-on plastic lid. I covered the bullets with an assortment of screws, bolts, nuts, and washers. I'd have preferred to take my rifle, but it didn't fit into my ski boot.

The leather briefcase I carried with me from Bangkok to Saigon had a small interior pocket which made a perfect holster for my revolver. If needed I could bring it out as though I were producing my passport. Of course, it was inconceivable that I would ever find a use for a gun on an international banking assignment with the Chase Manhattan Bank.

*   *   *

Oie wasn't the only one who thought I was nuts for agreeing to go to Vietnam. My American friend, Larry, counseled against it. "You're plumb loco, amigo." My friends at the Royal Varuna Yacht Club in Pattaya just shook their heads. "I wouldn't go," one said. My scuba diving buddies said, "Wouldn't get me over there." But nobody had asked any of them to go. Aside from my Chase colleague Gael Blake, whose refusal elevated me to the top of John Linker's list, nobody else had been asked to go. You can't turn something down unless it's offered to you. I don't think my Thai colleagues cared if I went or stayed. I was the enigmatic new guy. Amat, the driver, was the only one who wished me good luck, which he did in Thai, adding that phrase to my vocabulary.

My Bangkok assignment came with an apartment, and the apartment came with a live-in servant named Nawa. She told me to be careful, adding another new word. Nawa had shown me how to negotiate the price of vegetables in the farmers' market. I should push just hard enough to show that U.S. dollars hadn't softened my brain, but not so hard as to insult the vendor's produce. One of her most useful lessons was the Thai technique for cutting up a pineapple. Nawa was also thrilled that I had such a nice girlfriend, knowing as she did that the downside with expatriate bachelors was infinite. She genuinely wanted me to return from Saigon safely.

*   *   *

Cor Termijn flew in from Saigon and gave me a three-day briefing on the mission while the Vietnamese consulate milked my visa application for additional favors. I admired Cor incredibly. I wanted to be Cor Termijn when I grew up. He knew stuff I needed to know and he doled it out in ample portions of hard facts and droll humor. His was an elegant iteration of the Dutch accent, cannily self-aware. He ran through a long list of people with whom he'd already set up appointments. A few were diplomats; others included journalists and businessmen. One was a restaurateur.

Cor adopted a different tone when he and I were alone from the one he used when our boss, John Linker, was around. With me he was collegial and conspiratorial. For instance, if I was going to become his alter ego in Saigon, I'd need to know where to exchange currency on the black market. When John was with us, Cor would climb the respectability ladder, offering to introduce me to an intelligence operative at Air America or the bureau chief at *Time* magazine.

Cor also had a fixer I would need to know about, and John would not. Cor would be on the record now, off later. Over beer and sausage at a bar on Sukhumvit Road called the Bierstube, Cor told me that his surname, Termijn, which he coached me to pronounce *Ter-MANE*, derived from the same Latin root as the English word *terminus*. With an impish Dutch smirk, he said it was a fitting name for the last manager of Saigon branch. I suppose he meant the last on-the-record manager.

*   *   *

John, Cor, and I departed for Saigon from Bangkok's Don Mueang Airport. Like Saigon's Tan Son Nhut Airport, it now did double duty, serving both military and civil aviation. From windows in the departure lounge I could see F-4 Phantom fighter jets, tricked out in jungle camouflage, lined up on the far side of the airport's parallel runways.

Third World airports on the Asia Pacific rim were having a lively competition at the time for the dingiest departure lounges. Down in arrivals, the competition was for the most breakdowns of luggage conveyer belts. Don Mueang was celebrating its fiftieth birthday and they had been hard years. The United States Air Force had taken one look at Don Mueang and decided to sugar-daddy six other airports in Thailand to support the Vietnam War. Don Mueang had been passed over for refits for a half century and now had the ambience of a filling station at Half Moon Lake, Georgia.

In the airport restaurant, John Linker skillfully moderated the conversation among the three of us. He'd ask Cor a question and Cor would hold court with a flow of colorful details. Cor also went over a list of his Vietnamese employees and selected the dozen or so who were the most vulnerable to communist reprisals. They would be my top priorities for evacuation. If I could only get twelve employees out, it would be them. I also knew the ones who would have to be left behind. It sickened Cor to think he might have their blood on his hands.

In hindsight, I believe John purposely kept the conversation lively and engaging so that I wouldn't have any time to consider defecting. His call to Head Office would be very different if his hostage had given him the slip.

*   *   *

Once in Saigon, Linker and I checked into the Majestic Hotel, located where Tu Do Street discharged into the Saigon River. John took the presidential suite on the top floor and I got a standard room on the third facing Tu Do Street, not the river. Cor still had enough furniture in his house to support a bachelor so he kept the cab and headed off into the humid night.

John planned to fly back to Hong Kong the next day, which gave us only a few more hours that night to wrap up. He summoned me to his penthouse suite, and when I arrived I saw that he'd set up two straight-backed chairs facing one another, separated by a small coffee table. He set two bottles of 33 Export beer on the table.

"John, I'm not a beer snob but I draw the line at 33," I said. "Trust me, you wouldn't like it either."

Five minutes later a lovely young Vietnamese cocktail waitress sporting a disarming smile and a form-fitting ao dai, the traditional Vietnamese dress, delivered two oversized bottles of Tuborg beer. I noted her nametag for future reference. Then I noticed her wedding ring and stopped fantasizing. I was still fairly principled in those days. After the waitress left, John asked me, for the first time since we met, if I had any questions about my assignment. This might possibly be my final chance for the elephant-in-the-living-room question I'd been afraid to ask in case the answer should have been obvious.

Carefully pouring some Tuborg into a tilted glass I said, "Now that you ask, I do. Why can't we just shut Saigon branch down now? Tomorrow morning? The situation here, just being realistic, isn't getting any better. Instead of risking a nightmarish disaster later, why not close the branch in an orderly fashion while we have the chance? Commercial airlines are still operating here so we could easily evacuate any employees who want to leave. Customers could be notified to close their accounts and move their funds wherever they wanted. It would be hard for the host government to object; let's face it, they couldn't even defend the northern provinces. No one but Ambassador Martin thinks Saigon can hold out much longer, and the consensus is that he's . . ." I searched for the politic word. ". . . squirrely."

John's gunmetal eyes came at me like incoming missiles. He belted out his explanation rapid-fire. "There's a very simple explanation which you couldn't be expected to know. Chase Saigon has to stay open because of a lesson we learned in Hong Kong during the Korean War. After Red Chinese troops overran North Korea, senior management was worried that Hong Kong would be next, so Chase erred on the side of caution and closed the branch. It turned out the Chinese didn't invade, and to this day Chase has a reputation in Hong Kong for being a fair-weather friend to local businesses." Upon completion of his sermon John's volume dropped for his benediction. "The British banks stayed open throughout the Korean War and now they flaunt their unbroken commitment to the Hong Kong business community. Not a week goes by that I don't have some obnoxious British banker say, 'Oh, is Chase back?' It permanently damaged our franchise there. I will not let our Saigon branch close prematurely."

I could understand John's point and still distinguish between prudence and cowardice. I wondered how he weighed fifty-three employees' lives, fifty-four including mine, against the reputation of a bank already enjoying global esteem. After all, these were the Rockefeller years. My eyes were no match for John's and I left my remaining reservations unaddressed. In the coming days I'd have plenty of time for introspection. Maybe my thinking would somehow catch up to his.

All I could manage was, "That leaves the question of how I'll know when the jig's up. It must have crossed your mind that Saigon might very quickly become the communists' next domino. Looking at some frankly realistic scenarios, I might not only fail to evacuate our employees, but I could get caught in the undertow."

"You'll be in daily contact with the U.S. embassy. You'll have some very senior contacts there and they're going to keep you very well informed. Cor will stay here for a few more days to complete his introductions, and after that he'll coordinate from Hong Kong Regional. You'll relay whatever intel you pick up and I'll evaluate it."

"Well, guess what, John! I've already got some intel for you. Did you notice the layer of dust hanging over the streets and sidewalks on our way in from Tan Son Nhut? When I worked here in '71, that was a static, four-foot-high cloud. Getting through it was like skiing deep powder on the Haute Route. Now it's down around your ankles, like a slushy New England bunny slope. It was America's massive military presence in Saigon back then that kicked up that cloud. Three years ago it started to settle after peace was declared and our military started pulling out. John, there's nobody left. We're defenseless. South Vietnam can't defend its own people. They're not going to help us; they think America abandoned them. For them it's already over. They're waiting for General Dung to show up so they have someone to surrender to."

"You may be reading too much into that dust out there."

"Honestly, John, I don't believe I am."

Chapter Two

TUESDAY, APRIL 15, 1975

I'd been under the impression that John Linker had booked an early return to Hong Kong, so I was surprised to find him and Cor Termijn having a leisurely breakfast at a window table in the Majestic's spacious lobby. John saw my confusion. "Cor got us an appointment today with the defense attaché, General Homer Smith, so I put off my departure. I'll stay all day if we can get back in with Ambassador Martin. He personally assured D.R. that our staff would have the same priority in any evacuation as his own embassy staff. So as far as the bank's senior management is concerned all you will have to do is call the U.S. embassy and they will reserve a plane for us. I'd like him to repeat those words to you."

D.R. would be David Rockefeller, the chairman of the board of directors of the Chase Manhattan Bank. I thought I found something ragged in John's logic.

"John, I'm not getting how the ambassador's gazing on my face enhances an oath he's already given to D.R."

"Martin wouldn't lie to your face."

"John, the North Vietnamese negotiator, Le Duc Tho, looked into Henry Kissinger's eyes and lied about the peace treaty. Ambassador Martin's adoptive son was killed in the war. And because of that he's more gung-ho than the most battle-hardened sergeant. Doesn't want his kin to have died in vain. Meeting me isn't going to change that." It was too late for John to change his mind about conscripting me. He was stuck with me. That I was even more stuck worked to his advantage.

Still, it was instructive that, at this incipient moment in my assignment, John was openly mulling the ambassador's integrity.

Time was short and it was going to be a busy day. I needed to get some food into me. I caught the waiter's eye and pointed toward Cor's plate. My gesture said, *I'll have the same.* I wanted to know what a worldly-wise Dutchman ordered for breakfast on the banks of the Saigon River in the middle of a war. End of a war. Whatever. I hoped it wasn't brined minnows. The Dutch are wide-spectrum omnivores.

The breakfast conversation I'd interrupted was about our schedule for the day. Cor had tapped into his old Saigon hands network to set up a gap-free agenda. John said, "We want everyone we meet to know that we're keeping the branch operating as long as possible. They don't need to know anything about our embarrassment in Hong Kong twenty-five years ago, only that we're committed to serving the American business community here."

Cor said, "Yet we do not want them to think we're naive about the gravity of the situation. We want to come across as both committed and well informed."

As much as I liked Cor, I didn't like the sound of that. I thought that being well informed argued against a commitment to stay open. I deserved a say since I was the one who would face a firing squad if John and Cor were wrong. I said, "If half of what we know is true, we're in an unstable position. Last month Hue and Da Nang fell to the North Vietnamese Army. Qui Nhon fell on April Fool's Day. Nha Trang fell four days later."

"Ralph!" It was Linker.

"Okay. On the third of this very month South Vietnamese prime minister Tran Thien Khiem resigned and left for Paris. On the fourth, the Australians closed their embassy and evacuated their staff. On the eighth a South Vietnamese pilot, a so-called *friendly,* bombed the Presidential Palace, though regrettably President Nguyen Van-Thieu survived."

"*Ralph!*"

"On April 9 the North Vietnamese army attacked Xuan Loc, just forty miles from where we are sitting. Xuan Loc is defended by one of South Vietnam's most able generals, Dao Le-Minh. He commands one of the best fighting units in the South's army, the Eighteenth Infantry Division. If the charismatic General Dao and his heroic Eighteenth are defeated, Saigon could be overrun by the enemy within hours. If there's going to be a bloodbath it would start then."

John didn't stop me so I continued. "Four days ago President Ford proposed a billion dollars in military and economic aid for South Vietnam, and it was rejected by Congress."

I couldn't compare the current situation with the one Chase Hong Kong faced during the Korean War, but how could that possibly have been as dire as what we now faced in Saigon? Despite Linker's solemn invocation of precedent, the two situations were not remotely comparable. I didn't think I needed to repeat my objection to keeping the branch open. The cascade of facts ought to have settled the matter. On the other hand, facts had often been casualties in Vietnam.

With both the North and the South having arrayed their forces as best they could, the final stakes of the Vietnam War were set. As the roulette croupiers said, "*Les jeux sont faites.*" Actually, the odds were much better in roulette than for Saigon.

It was too late now for Linker, or Chase, or America to change their bets, but not necessarily too late for me. Privately I adopted a very simple, one-dimensional decision criterion. I'd stick with Linker's program as long as the 18th Division held at Xuan Loc. If the 18th were defeated, then I'd get the hell out of Saigon, with or without the employees. With that decided I could keep my mind on my job at the bank without constantly agonizing about the security situation. General Dao would make my decision for me. I wished him luck.

*   *   *

My first impression of Embassy Saigon, as our diplomats called it, was of a teeming crowd of Vietnamese civilians outside a high white wall. I wouldn't exactly describe it as a mob, though it was only a few decibels removed. Cor explained that they were visa applicants lined up for the consular section, which was to the left of the main gate, with the massive concrete honeycomb of the embassy proper set well back to the right. As marine guards parted the crowd for the bank's black sedan, it was clear to me that there was in fact no line whatsoever; it was a terrified, lawless throng.

I imagined every person there having a distinct story, carefully prepared for the consular officers, but I wouldn't bet on any of them getting a chance to finish it. What was there to say? "I have skills." "I have a friend in Texas." "I have some gold." "The Viet Cong will kill me." The wall echoed with their collective whimper.

From the get-go I liked James Ashida, the embassy's commercial attaché. At fifty-six he was fit, helpful, and friendly. He was an army veteran, as were a lot of careerist foreign service officers assigned to Saigon. He came across as a friend. He was there to help. "All I can say is thank God for Chase Manhattan," he said.

That triggered my first question. "Do I have counterparts at the other American banks? Are their American managers still here?"

"Neither Bank of America nor First National City Bank has expatriates here anymore. They'll fly in from Bangkok or Hong Kong for a few hours, and always leave the same day. They're relying on local nationals to wind down their business. The defeat of military regions one and two sent them packing. When one bank manager came in to say goodbye, he showed me clippings from a U.S. newspaper with North Vietnamese fighter aircraft parked on the runway in Pleiku. *The Saigon Post* didn't see fit to carry those pics. If civilians knew MiGs were in Pleiku they'd panic."

For my benefit Cor explained. "The government censors the press here. The war is theoretically democracy versus communism, but the good guys aren't angels."

I didn't have to wait long for John Linker to bring up one of his pet issues. "Ambassador Martin told us last week that there was ample room in embassy quarters for Cor and Ralph. Chase is keeping its end of the bargain by staying open. The embassy could show its appreciation by letting my officers move into the residential compound."

Ashida said, "You'll have to get the DCM on board with that. It'll be his call."

Cor translated for Linker, "That's Wolfgang Lehmann, the deputy chief of mission. We have him on our agenda this afternoon."

"But the ambassador already committed."

"Trust me, John," said Ashida, "Martin would have intended his comments as conceptual. That's his style. In the real world, only the DCM can get you into Pittman, our Pittman Apartments." He wished he could help, but it was entirely out of his hands. Ashida had picked the right career. He was a really good diplomat. I liked the guy, but if I could have magically conjured an ideal contact at the embassy, I might wish for someone other than by-the-book James Ashida.

*   *   *

Our second appointment was with Shepard Lowman, forty-six, Harvard Law, blandly handsome, clear-eyed and clean-cut, who headed up the Internal Political Affairs Unit, and who was located alongside the highest-ranking members of the U.S. mission on the third floor of the embassy. I wondered who his counterpart might be in the Thieu regime. To meet with the prime minister, Lowman would have to fly to Paris. I was initially surprised that he'd even agreed to meet with us; Chase had nothing to do with politics—or did we?

As it turned out, Shep, as he invited us to call him, had been given a very special, very ad hoc mandate, to get *at-risk* Vietnamese (his words) out of the country. Rare for a foreign service officer, he preferred *Vietnamese* to *local national*, possibly because his wife was one of them. He explained the challenge, "The host government requires what they're calling an *exit visa* to leave the country. They're hard to get, even for the embassy's local employees. The regime fears a mass exodus. Probably reasonably. Saigon could flip from a tropical paradise to Dante's Inferno very quickly."

Linker said, "So it's the Thieu regime that's making it difficult to get people out?"

I never did discover why Nguyen Van-Thieu was always called by his given name rather than his family name. Maybe because Nguyen was so common.

Lowman was patient. "I'd be less than candid if I didn't say that President Thieu is fortunate to have a U.S. ambassador perfectly in tune with his thinking. Ambassador Martin is only too happy to help Thieu block the stampede. The only people I'm currently able to exfiltrate are local intelligence assets who would get tortured if they were left behind. I can't say any more than that."

Cor said, "We don't want our employees to leave yet either. But they need to know that we'll help them get out before it's too late."

"Sorry, but you really can't tell them that. How many are we talking about?"

Cor looked toward heaven thoughtfully, then returned to earth. "It's hard to say because it includes, in addition to fifty-three employees, their spouses and children. For discussion, let's say a hundred."

It was the first I'd heard anything close to that number.

"Sorry, Mr. Termijn," Lowman said. "That's just not in the cards now, but I can offer you one assurance. When and if the embassy discovers a way to get its own Vietnamese employees out, we'll give Chase's employees the same priority as our own."

"I'll shake your hand on that, Shep, if you don't mind," Linker said. He rose and extended his hand. "And I'll find a quiet way to get that assurance to David Rockefeller, who has taken a keen interest in Ralph and his mission here."

It had to be the first time that my name and any Rockefeller's had ever been coupled in the same sentence.

*   *   *

Our next stop in this chock-a-block day of introductions was with minister-counsellor, economic affairs, Denny Ellerman. The State Department attracted some astonishingly good people, especially young professionals kicking off their careers with a résumé-enhancing stint in government service. At thirty-four Ellerman was on his third assignment to Vietnam. The first had been as a marine. The second as an economist assigned to the Defense Attaché Office (DAO) in 1973, armed with a Harvard ABD, his way of saying his economics PhD was complete—all but dissertation. When I met Ellerman he was still in the first thirty days of his third assignment, but it had been an eventful month. Ban Me Thuot had fallen to the communists four days after he arrived. When I met him, he had just sent his family on a shopping trip to Hong Kong. I wondered if the ruse of a shopping trip had been for the benefit of Ambassador Martin, who might have interpreted the family's departure as shading toward disloyalty.

But if Martin had favorites, Ellerman was likely one of them. When he had worked at the DAO his economic reporting had been optimistic about the regime's capacity to stand on its own. Ambassador Martin probably found in Ellerman's reports an upbeat outlook, one that supported his own.

Another entry on Ellerman's résumé would have stood out; he had just completed a five-month gig at the National Security Council, where he had enjoyed an office in the Executive Office Building, next door to the White House. The young man's presumed political network would have been catnip for Martin.

His business card read *A. Denny Ellerman*. He was energetic and wiry, not uncommon for marines, with chiseled features, Ivy

League glasses, and a trim, playful mustache. For a guy at the top of his game he was cautious. "Who've you talked to so far?" He'd know how much we knew based on whom we'd met.

John Linker answered, "Ashida and Shep."

"Good," he said. "You'll need them both. Protocol stipulates that the commercial attaché be your main contact, and if anything, protocol will get tighter as security deteriorates. Ashida has to be your eyes and ears, and if need be your voice inside this building. If I were you, I'd keep him in line of sight, like a scuba buddy. Shep is theoretically our political affairs guy, but with politics overshadowed by military events, his mission has morphed to helping locals exfiltrate, though as I'm sure he told you, there are some obstacles."

John Linker asked, "Is Ambassador Martin one of them?"

"Martin is misunderstood and misportrayed. He's trying to implement policies that were devised by Washington long before the North's invasion and are now obsolete."

Cor Termijn said, "John's leaving for Hong Kong tomorrow. I'll follow on Friday. We're pretty comfortable with the American embassy helping Ralph get out. He's American. We're here to find out if the embassy is going to help us evacuate our employees. You're the marine. You know better than any of us how badly the North Vietnamese Army treats civilians."

Ellerman said, "We're here not just to support Americans but, more broadly, to support American interests. That includes business interests, and that includes the Chase Manhattan Bank, and that includes its employees."

Emboldened by the cause and undaunted by the venue, Chase's lowest-ranking officer in Asia asked the minister-counsellor, economic affairs, the all-but-dissertation Harvard PhD, the marine combat veteran, the National Security Council insider, "You really are going to help us, aren't you?"

The patron saint of financial institutions soon to be overrun by communists answered, "Yes, I am. You can put that in the bank."

I hoped Ellerman meant it figuratively and not my bank, the Saigon branch of the Chase Manhattan Bank, which was absolutely doomed.

*   *   *

Cor informed us that the next stop was with the Central Intelligence Agency, though the guy's card didn't say CIA; it said Office of the Special Assistant. The name on the card was Conrad LaGueux. Cor must have known him; he called him Conny. Somehow Cor knew that LaGueux was the deputy CIA station chief. Cor was a savvy country manager. I truly did admire him.

If the best spooks look like fifty-three-year-old insurance sales-men, Conny LaGueux was an ace. He had receding hair, heavy-framed tortoiseshell glasses, and an enigmatic pursed-lip smile. Cor told us that LaGueux had been a commando behind the lines in France and had trained teams of commandos in China. It was absolutely inconceivable. This iteration of Conny LaGueux was gracious, gentle, wise. Surely it had been decades since he'd killed a man. Nonetheless, I pitied any Saigon thief who tried to steal LaGueux's watch.

Conny LaGueux had been the first American to understand what the loss of Hue, Da Nang, and Qui Nhon implied for American foreign policy. At the end of March, he had commandeered an Air America helicopter and soared up the coast over Route 7, doing his own reconnaissance. Had it not been for him, the United States government would never have discovered that the Army of the Republic of Vietnam, the ARVN, had put up no resistance in those cities. Entire army divisions, along with their dependents, were in headlong flight, southward on Route 7, their command structure obliterated. Calling it a retreat would have dignified it. Even when the ARVN had outnumbered the enemy, they had turned and run. With his training, LaGueux could tell from a thousand feet in the air that the U.S. policy of *Vietnamization* of the war had gone belly-up.

LaGueux said, "I'm giving you information President Ford got only two weeks ago. You watch. Kissinger will offer to return his Nobel Peace Prize."

I said, "We honestly do appreciate your being candid with us, Mr. LaGueux." I wasn't calling a fifty-three-year-old man Conny. "It would be fascinating if it weren't so frightening. So forgive me asking the obvious. If it's common knowledge the war is over, why isn't everyone here shredding documents and packing files into cardboard boxes? Why aren't evacuation flights taking off one after the other at Tan Son Nhut? Why is everyone here still sitting behind their desks?"

Sitting there in the deputy CIA station chief's office I realized that John Linker's strategy of keeping the bank open as long as possible—which barely made sense—was consistent with the embassy's policy of downplaying the desperate security situation—which made no sense whatsoever.

LaGueux was the calmest person in the building, maybe in the city. "Why are we still at our desks? That's a perfectly fair question. I think it comes down to the nature of leadership. There's only one person who can order the abandonment of the embassy, and he's not there yet. Here's how Ambassador Martin frames the issue. As long as the embassy stays open, we retain the option to close, but once we've closed, we lose the option to open."

John Linker said, "That's how the Chase Manhattan Bank frames the issue. An expired option has no value."

I resisted pointing out that an expired person has no value either.

"So tell us, Mr. LaGueux." I thought I knew the answer to this one too, but I wanted to hear him say it. "What's the basis of Ambassador Martin's optimism? Is he seeing what everyone else is seeing and processing it differently, or is he onto something we don't know?"

"I think it's fair to say that Martin believes that if the American flag is lowered on this building, it could impact the South's morale and turn a marginally hopeful cause into a lost one."

I couldn't constrain myself. "We had two and a half million troops here. Three hundred thousand were wounded. Fifty-eight thousand were killed. Now our ambassador thinks a flag waving over this building will make a difference?" I avoided Linker's glare.

LaGueux's response was a smile and a quip. "If he turns out to be right, he'll be called visionary."

I didn't buy it, and I couldn't believe LaGueux did either. Back in America they put people who think like that in padded cells to keep them from hurting themselves—and others.

*   *   *

When I'd worked for American Express Bank in Vietnam four years earlier, the military side of Tan Son Nhut airport had been called MACV, for Military Assistance Command, Vietnam. Its nickname, which even appeared on maps, was *Pentagon East*. The 1973 Paris Peace Accords required America to reduce its military headcount to fifty, and MACV became the Defense Attaché Office, or DAO. The incumbent defense attaché, next on our itinerary, was General Homer Smith. He was America's commanding general in Vietnam—in charge of exactly fifty American troops.

On the fifteen-minute ride out to meet him at Tan Son Nhut, Cor gave us some background. "General Smith is a logistics guy, exactly the person you'd want as defense attaché at this point in the conflict, since America's mission is now restricted to providing military and economic aid to the Thieu government. Smith knows his stuff; his first assignment in the army was logistical support for D-Day."

When I'd worked in Vietnam earlier, MACV had been bustling. It had looked like a country club with its manicured lawns; there were more colonels than privates on the walkways. Now it was a ghost town. Buildings were empty and the sidewalks were over-grown with weeds, and the open areas were cluttered with debris.

Following introductions, John Linker asked General Smith, "So, is it over, General?"

Smith was the first two-star general I'd ever met, a major general. He wore a chestful of ribbons and the brave face of a man contemplating a firing squad. "Ask Senator Sparkman. Foreign Relations Committee. Just turned down President Ford's request for seven hundred twenty-two in military aid and two hundred fifty in economic. Our Senate's a lifeguard sitting there while the swimmer drowns. We're the greatest country in the world militarily but politically we've become weak. Twenty-two million souls are about to be lost to communism over here because of American politics."

Linker again, "You don't give the South Vietnamese Army any chance then?"

"Two possibilities there. The first is try to defend a *trunc-u-ated* South Vietnam." My notes captured General Smith's mispronunciation. "Comprising just tactical regions three and four. The second is that the 18th kicks butt at Xuan Loc and the commies give up and go home. In my opinion neither is going to happen, so yeah, it's over, and no, the South can't win, certainly not with Congress standin' in its way."

The junior guy in a meeting isn't supposed to speak unless spoken to. I broke the rule. "All due respect, General Smith, but are you okay? You don't look well. I'm sure this whole thing has got to be stressful."

"I got a sad day coming up, when I get on that last chopper heading out of here. I dread it worse than death."

Linker must have seen the general's encroaching melancholy as ending the meeting. He asked, "Realistically, how much time has Saigon got left?"

"Two weeks, max. Say, what the hell's your bank still open for? That's just one more thing for logistics to mop up in the end."

Linker took General Smith's question as a dismissal.

General Smith, the man, left me unmoved, but General Smith, the allegory, intrigued me. Here was a soldier whose career was launched with America's greatest victory, D-Day, and whose career was about to end in a hellish debacle. He'd been there at the beginning when America's determination was at its zenith, and Fate had placed him here at the end, when, if you accepted his own analysis, America's will had faltered.

It was now the afternoon of April 15. If Ambassador Martin had called General Smith right now and asked how long it would take to get every American out of Vietnam, and as many compromised Vietnamese as possible, how would Smith have answered Martin's question? Maybe two months? Smith was absolutely the best qualified person in the world, and certainly the best positioned, to make that estimate, and he'd just confided that the place couldn't survive two more weeks. Not everyone the Americans wanted to get out was going to make it. The North Vietnamese Army had forty thousand troops just thirty-six miles away, and seventy thousand in total south of the Demilitarized Zone. The 1973 Paris Peace Accords, abided to by only one of its signatories, limited us to fifty troops. Even a victory at Xuan Loc wasn't going to save Saigon.

It was becoming hideously clear that Ambassador Martin's stress-induced psychosis was making an epic humanitarian disaster inevitable. Unless he were to authorize an immediate, massive airlift for Vietnamese tainted by their involvement with the Americans, like our Chase employees, they would suffer terribly under a bloodthirsty enemy. The conclusion was inescapable. There just wasn't enough time. The exit visa business, the Thieu regime's refusal to negotiate, the disgraceful collapse of the South Vietnamese Army, Ambassador Martin's irrational refusal to authorize an evacuation, and the closeness of overwhelmingly superior enemy forces, all these factors foretold a blunt and brutal outcome.

*   *   *

On our return to the embassy, Cor Termijn prepped us for our next meeting. "You might think that a guy who miraculously escaped Nazi Germany as a thirteen-year-old would have learned something about getting out when the getting was good, but in the case of Deputy Chief of Mission Wolfgang Lehmann you'd be wrong. If he had been in charge of evacuating Jews from Germany, Hitler's body count would have been a lot higher. Lehmann sat in on our meeting last week with Ambassador Martin and, if you listen to the two of them, there have been no military setbacks in the north, the Demilitarized Zone is holding, and the South has the North right where they want them. Lehmann's fifty-four now and he's just as delusional as his ambassador."

I asked Cor, "Why do we think that?"

"It's easier to understand in Martin's case since, as you pointed out, his nephew, whom he adopted, was killed in action, but Lehmann's harder to explain. He's a combat-decorated World War II veteran so he knows war. He's a Haverford College graduate so he's incredibly bright. He's had a distinguished foreign service career, which would get badly tarnished if he screws up the endgame in Saigon. Yet here he is, one of only two people outside of Washington who thinks there's a pony under all this horse shit."

I wanted Linker on record. "John, what did you think of Lehmann?" The problem was that although Linker was perfectly rational, his objective of keeping the Chase branch open played smack into the hands of the embassy's delusionaries.

"It hardly matters, Ralph. We are one hundred percent reliant on him to get our people out. We have to listen very carefully, read between the lines, and above all, stay on his good side."

*   *   *

Wolfgang Lehmann, Wolf to his peers, though never to his subordinates, had a command presence. He brandished a handsomely rugged face, more ski instructor than diplomat, and below it a physique that glided with balance and economy. His receding hair was light brown, with silver overtaking his temples. His chin was especially square, with a pout in its middle where a dimple might have served him better. When his facial muscles relaxed his smile remained expectantly amused. John and Cor had met with Lehmann two weeks ago.

"Back so soon, gentlemen?" If he thought he was rid of the Chase Manhattan Bank he'd underestimated its regional executive. If the two of them had been in opposition Linker might be Lehmann's match, but it was beginning to appear as though they had become aligned.

John Linker pitched our agenda. "We're back to introduce Ralph White, who will be replacing Cor to provide expatriate continuity. He'll keep the Chase Bank running as long as possible and he'll evacuate the Vietnamese staff if necessary. We'd appreciate the U.S. mission's support in both phases of that assignment."

I loved John's phrase *expatriate continuity*. I wasn't just some rural urchin whom Chase had cycled through its Global Credit Training Program as cannon fodder for its far-flung International Department. I was an *expatriate*. Ernest Hemingway, F. Scott Fitzgerald, Ralph White. Exotic drinks, white linen suits.

"Good for Chase!" It was as though Lehmann was applauding a brilliant performance. "The other banks' managers have gone missing. And IBM is trying to run their operation out of Guam."

What did they know that we didn't? What were we falling for that they hadn't?

Lehmann settled into his chair, steepled his fingers, and said, "Maybe you understand better what's going on here."

That was highly unlikely, though Chase's institutional bravado had at least earned us a more sincere version of the Lehmann smile.

"Watergate and Paris, that's all you need to know." The wily diplomat leaned forward in his chair, as did the earnest young expatriate facing him. "Congress took advantage of a weakened Nixon administration to halve U.S. assistance to Vietnam. Without that botched Watergate break-in, Congress wouldn't have been able to undercut foreign policy the way it has. The peaceniks wouldn't be getting the press coverage they are, and the enemy wouldn't be reading about America's depleted resolve."

He adjusted his necktie. He needn't have; it was already perfect. "The Paris Accord was absurd. Kissinger told me as much. The North signed it intending to break it. The so-called Provisional Revolutionary Government doesn't even exist; it's a complete fiction."

I've always hated it when something gets maligned as fiction. I rather like novels. Once a character like Ahab or Kurtz is introduced into our consciousness he is every bit as real as any renaissance pope. The Provisional Revolutionary Government might be artificial, contrived, bogus, but it hardly rose to the level of fiction.

Lehmann hadn't stopped talking during my reverie. When I caught up he was saying, "That type of agreement is useless unless there is sufficient political will to enforce it, which America lacked. Some may say we still lack the will, but I believe that with restored funding, augmented by tactical bombing, the South could still win."

Every rational soul on the planet knew that neither the funding nor bombing was going to happen.

Lehmann continued. "Both of which are still possible. And I'm glad the Chase Manhattan Bank agrees with me that leaving now would be premature."

If we had taken a vote on that it would have been a 2–2 tie, with Cor and me for bailing out, and John Linker and Wolf Lehmann for tempting fate. At least Lehmann would be voting his own fate. John would be proxy-voting mine.

Lehmann was still talking. "The Thieu regime is a stable, democratic ally, and not at all the despotic, corrupt regime depicted by the activists and the media."

This always happens when you don't check someone's illogical trajectory early enough; they think they've hooked you. Before you know it everyone's dancing around bonfires and chanting gibberish. People like Wolf Lehmann take the absence of objection as full-throated support.

If the moment hadn't decisively passed, I'd have asked Lehmann why he thought that an enemy army that had just swept away every obstacle in its path would miraculously stop on the doorstep of its objective. What motivated such willful delusion? Was it solidarity with the Thieu regime? Had 58,000 American lives and 150 billion American dollars counted for nothing? Did Lehmann want to stand shoulder to shoulder with President Thieu in the surrender photos?

Cor was sympathetic to my view. I furrowed my brow at him while jerking my head toward Lehmann, willing the wise Dutchman to ask the obvious.

"Wolf," he said. "When will you know when it's time? How will that get communicated to Ralph?" God bless Cor.

"I fought at Anzio. I'll know when it's time. If we retreat too soon, we might demoralize our host country, quite possibly creating panic. If we make our move before it's time, we could make things worse. We can't even talk about leaving; they might hear us. That's why we haven't cut down that banyan tree in the courtyard to make it safe for helicopters to land there. That tree is visible from the street and it would signal our loss of confidence in the regime. The South would take it for abandonment."

Was Lehmann even listening to himself? It was the enemy that was demoralizing the regime by kicking its ass; not the Americans for noticing. Make things worse? Worse than what? Losing their country? More than half of South Vietnam had already been abandoned to the communists. The Army of the Republic of Vietnam had panicked at Quang Tri, bolted at Hue, retreated at Pleiku, hightailed it at Qui Nhon, and been routed at Da Nang. Who in their right mind expected Saigon to be any different? North Vietnam's General Dung would cruise to victory whether or not we whispered our doubts, lowered the flag on the roof, or turned the embassy courtyard into a lumberyard.

*   *   *

Cor had scheduled dinner with the bank's four Vietnamese officers at an inexpensive, second-floor restaurant on Tu Do Street. Cuong Vu-Huy was the deputy general manager, responsible for the overall administration of the branch. He was extremely competent and the main reason Cor could leave on trips for weeks at a time. He was thirtyish, with black hair, a slender build, and a perpetually somber expression. The other three officers were women. Ho Thi Bach-Mai, in her late twenties, was the assistant manager for credit. She was quite pretty, and all business. Nguyen Hong-Lien was the assistant manager for customer service. Possibly in her thirties, she had a cherubic face and shorter hair. Tran My-Nga was the assistant manager for operations. She had long, silky hair and wholesome, Earth Mother looks.

In Vietnam, the family name comes first. In my previous incarnation in Vietnam with American Express I'd learned that about 40 percent of Vietnamese use the surname Nguyen. It was the name of the last imperial dynasty. It is pronounced in a single syllable. The *ng* phoneme is present in English at the end of words like running. The trick to pronouncing a name like Nguyen that begins with *ng* is to start with the back of the tongue touching the roof of the mouth, the palate. Or say *running* silently and leave your tongue where it ends up before aspirating the vowel. Same trick for the name Nga, which is one of the most common female names. Vietnamese appreciate it when an American makes the effort. They are accustomed to having their names butchered.

Having skipped lunch, Linker, Termijn, and I were famished and we ate gluttonously. It was the staff's first impression of me and I must have looked primitive to them. At least I knew how to handle chopsticks. In the present circumstances my dexterity allowed me to eat even faster. I couldn't have looked very gentlemanly chugging my beer either.

Cuong spoke for his team. "We are completely dependent on Chase to get us out of here. It would be hard to explain how desperate we are. When the communist Viet Minh conquered North Vietnam, they slaughtered the Vietnamese who worked with the French colonial administration. We fear the same kind of bloodbath when the NVA comes to Saigon." Cuong was perfectly articulate in English and he'd deliberately said *when* the North Vietnamese Army comes to Saigon, not *if.*

General Dung's forces had so far shown forbearance in the northern provinces, but I couldn't contradict Cuong; he could be right. Civilians had been slaughtered when Hue fell during the '68 Tet offensive. Moreover, Chase didn't need an ideological reason to help these four officers and their dependents. They were loyal Chase employees; they were us.

I would have preferred to hear more from Bach-Mai at this initial meeting but she did more listening than talking. With so few of her words to go on, she left more of a visual impression. Her face was sad and her skin sunstruck. Cor inadvertently explained Bach-Mai's reticence when he said that her husband was the chief engineering executive for Air Vietnam, the country's flagship air carrier. Her family would be able to fly out anytime they wanted, papers or not. She wasn't reliant on Chase.

I also learned that Bach-Mai's high-profile husband, Cau, had flown to Da Nang to rescue his parents and been trapped behind enemy lines when the defending forces had fled. If the communists were to capture a man with his skills, they'd never let him go. He was five hundred miles away and she hadn't heard from him for ten days. No wonder she wasn't feeling talkative.

I was glad to have met the bank's senior staff. Now I had faces to associate with the names printed on Cor's briefing documents. They were decent, bright, hardworking folk. They had families. Their English was as good as the average American's. They were under no illusions about how ill-fated they were, and they struggled to believe that I might alter that fate. Then I remembered Shep Lowman forbidding us from promising to help.

*   *   *

As with the previous night, Cor headed home, and John and I returned to the Majestic. Up in his penthouse suite John again set up the facing straight-backed chairs with the little table between them. Instead of beer, he ordered snifters of cognac. We marveled at Cor Termijn's ability to put together such an impressive itinerary: James Ashida, the commercial attaché, Shep Lowman, the political attaché, Denny Ellerman, the minister-counsellor, economics, Conrad LaGueux, deputy station chief for the CIA, General Smith, the defense attaché, and topped off with Wolfgang Lehmann, the deputy ambassador. John wondered if any of his other country managers in Asia could have done what Cor did on such short notice.

I asked, "Any eleventh-hour changes to the plan?"

"Nothing substantive, really," said Linker. "I feel vindicated in choosing you for this assignment. We're both fortunate to have Cor Termijn. Cuong looks very capable. The team of officers here is strong. Now you've got six senior people inside the American embassy who should return your calls. Don't give up trying to meet with Ambassador Martin. You're to keep the branch open as long as possible, then get the key staff out. There's no manual of procedure for this. It will call for street smarts. I'll be briefing the seventeenth floor multiple times a day."

The seventeenth floor at One Chase Manhattan Plaza was Chase's executive lair. The building itself was located in New York City's Wall Street district, between the Federal Reserve and the New York Stock Exchange. The walls on seventeen were paneled in dark mahogany. The lighting dim. The board of directors met in a sumptuous boardroom on the south side of the corridor, with a twenty-mile view that included the Statue of Liberty. The offices of executive vice presidents and vice chairmen lined the north-facing facade. None of this is what Linker meant when he invoked the seventeenth floor; he meant David Rockefeller. Linker was going to be providing daily briefings to D.R. on Ralph White's progress at the insane asylum known as Embassy Saigon. I sipped my cognac. It had the pleasant bouquet of fresh spar varnish.

"Now, Mr. White, give me your impressions of the day. Speak your mind."

"First, we agree about Cor's high marks. Overall I'd say that we heard a lot of predictable grumbling about how America's checks and balances clipped the war hawks' wings. I also think the embassy is secretly pleased that the South Vietnamese government blocks its citizens from leaving, since if it didn't, Chase and other American companies would have closed long ago. You and I differ on the Korean War precedent, but your vote counts more than mine."

John asked, "How about Lehmann? I noticed you drifting during his presentation."

"Ahh, mea culpa. There's one thing he said that I've been grappling with. At first I didn't understand the business about how the departure of Americans would aggravate security, make things worse, create panic, that kind of thing. Lehmann offers this as a reason for not wanting Chase to close, not cutting down the banyan tree, not reducing his own staff. The thing is, once Americans were gone they'd be safe, and the turmoil left behind couldn't harm us. The only way that Lehmann's stay-for-the-sake-of-security argument makes any sense is that he's worried about friendlies turning on us as we depart. Lehmann's more worried about getting shot by a friendly general than being targeted by enemy artillery."

John was unconvinced so I tried another explanation. "I'm sure you've heard the Chinese expression *riding a tiger*. It's a terrifying place to be, but falling off the tiger is even worse. Martin and Lehmann are riding a man-eater, and they aren't going to help us evacuate our employees until they fear our North Vietnamese enemies more than they do our South Vietnamese allies. It's fear of the Thieu regime, not General Dung's hordes, that immobilizes Martin and Lehmann. Saigon has the potential to devolve into a massive humanitarian disaster, and if that does happen it won't be the enemy's fault—it will be our own ambassador's."

John looked tired. I finished off my snifter of varnish and headed back downstairs to the cheap rooms.

Chapter Three

WEDNESDAY, APRIL 16, 1975

"You'll need local currency." Cor Termijn would know. He said, "You'll want to meet Raj Singh."

Cor didn't have to tell me not to change money at the bank, where I'd get only 755 piastres per dollar, but I laughed when I saw where Cor's black market dealer had set up shop. It was exactly under the window of my room. A dark, suspicious Indian face about my age peered out from the recesses of a newspaper kiosk. Cor said, "Good morning, Raj. Meet my friend."

Raj said, "Hello, friend of my friend." A pleasant smile replaced the scowl. Currency was much more fun than newspapers. The raw material of both commodities was paper; it was the printing on the surface that produced the smile.

I said, "Selling dollars."

"I am buying dollars today at nine-fifty."

That was a lot better than 755 but my Thai maid, Nawa, had trained me to probe. "Raj! Nine-fifty? Come on, make it a thousand."

"Sorry, my new friend, but it's nine-fifty today. Please come around to the side door."

In the shade of his kiosk, I handed Raj a hundred-dollar bill. The piastres he handed back were 25 percent more than if I'd changed my money at the Chase bank. Black market indeed!

"Say, Raj!"

"Yes, my new friend?"

"Wasn't the piastre defeated along with the French at Dien Bien Phu? How come we still call Vietnamese money by its French name? The Vietnamese call it dong. Shouldn't we call it dong in English too? Selling dollars; buying dong?"

Raj's face displayed amusement. He had what would be called range in the acting business. The two sides of his business showcased that range. "Very, very happy to sell you dong anytime, new friend."

*　　　*　　　*

Chase's Saigon branch was at 27-28 Ben Bach Dang, about three doors south along the waterfront from the Majestic Hotel. The main banking floor was a frenzy of activity. A line of anxious customers stretched out the doors. The bank staff was harried. It was hard to see any order to it. Cor carefully surveyed the scene like a naval commander on the deck of a ship locked in close combat. "Busy," he pronounced it. I found it chaotic. I followed him up the stairwell to his second-floor office.

Cor sat behind his desk and waved me to the chair in front of it, saying, "I recommend you change money every day. The rate will be a proxy for the security situation. As Saigon goes further down the tubes there will be less demand for a currency soon to be obsolete."

I knew that. I was green but not bright green.

"Hey, Ralph, I need a little time to make a call. I just learned my household goods haven't been shipped out yet. The freight forwarder went home to Australia, leaving everything I own sitting in a warehouse. I've spent half my life in Asia and have a huge collection of art and antiques." He busied himself with the phone.

I couldn't see much through the windows of Cor's office facing the river because of some sort of metal slat assembly outside. I speculated on the purpose and thought it might be there to block sunlight. But surely there must have been a better way to shade the room without obstructing what must be a dramatic view of the harbor. The way the slats were angled downward, I could see a growing line of customers on the street, some in uniform and some carrying rifles. Colt M-16s were a fairly common fashion accessory in Vietnam and it was easy to stop noticing them. Still, a surly customer with a rifle will quicken one's pulse. It was scant comfort that I was the rare Chase Manhattan banker prepared to return fire. I carried my revolver in my leather briefcase, and I took it everywhere.

Cor got off the phone. "Buggers! I should have listened to my wife and packed up earlier. Now I'm going to have to go down to the docks and find someone to bribe. Trouble is, finding the right person."

He'd seen me looking through the slatted window. "Had to install that paraphernalia after we got hit by a 122 millimeter rocket in January. It's the North Vietnamese Army's way of informing us that they've managed to get within ten miles. That's the rocket's range. When the rockets fall short, they hit this row of buildings."

It just so happened that *this row of buildings* included my current residence, the Majestic Hotel. Mental note: move to Caravelle Hotel ASAP.

"Now we have to get over to the Mission Warden." It must have been obvious to Cor that I had no clue. "That's the loosely structured civilian security force under the Defense Attaché Office. The top guys are security professionals contracted by the embassy and others are effectively deputized civilians. They'll play some role if there's an evacuation. Sorry, forgot who I'm talking to; *when* there's an evacuation."

It was reassuring that Cor counted me among the realists. The wishful thinkers were delusional at best and some were beginning to look psychotic. I could foresee a scenario where, as the realists departed, the more sway the delusionaries would have. The sane could quickly become outnumbered.

*   *   *

The Mission Warden meeting was at the Brink BOQ, the main bachelor officer's quarters, located in the throbbing heart of the old city. Four years ago the Brink had been a raucous testosterone mill. I couldn't imagine a more delightful overseas billet for a young army officer. It was right behind the Opera House, a building whose design I'd heard called Beaux Arts. I'd also heard it called the National Assembly, though that implied a civil government, for which there was scant evidence. There was a scenic plaza in front, called Lam Son Square, with the venerable Continental Palace Hotel on one side and the Caravelle Hotel on the other. The Continental, as it was universally known, had the best croissants outside of Paris, and the Caravelle had a rooftop restaurant overlooking the mystique of Southeast Asia. The French bookstore was just the other side of Tu Do Street, and Nguyen Hue Street, called Flower Market Street, was straight ahead. For the bachelor officer unimpressed by opera, croissants, Beaux Arts, French literature, or fresh flowers, there was the neon-lit fleshpot of Tu Do Street. Saigon truly did offer something for every taste.

Cor guided me the length of Tu Do, from the bank to the Brink. It was about a quarter mile of gaudy paintings, antique Zippo lighters, and street food, including pho, the traditional Vietnamese noodle soup. At the entrances of bars young women tried to entice passers-by. I hoped none of my former language instructors would recognize me, though by now they had probably set up shop in Denver and Marseilles. The air was charged with fresh diesel exhaust, stale garlic, and cheap perfume. Today's layer of dust was still ankle-high, though perhaps an inch thinner than a day earlier. If it could have been accurately measured the dust might be as predictive of Saigon's fate as the exchange rate.

There was another predictor too, though it took Cor to point it out. As we passed Raj's newsstand, I noticed that *The Saigon Post*, the English language daily, had blank patches on its front page. The tops of some of the columns were vacant of text. Stories started two or three inches below their bold font titles. Cor said, "That's the work of government censors. The government's retreat from the northern military regions has turned into an all-out rout. I doubt you'll find anything about the battle for Xuan Loc unless the 18th Infantry wins. The paper's not allowed to report defeats. White space in *The Saigon Post* is bad news. I'd keep an eye on that if I were you."

"How about other English language newspapers, or French?"

"Sorry, the government prohibits their importation."

*   *   *

Expatriate civilians who hang around war zones have always been a motley crew. I should know; that was me when I'd worked for Amex. The lobby of the Brink was packed with American civilian hangers-on from every walk of life. Contractors were well represented, as were former soldiers who had nothing to go home to. There was no ventilation in the space, other than the open front door, and the air was stagnant. It takes very few unwashed men under such circumstances to create atmosphere.

"Listen up, gents." The speaker looked like a lumberjack and sounded like a cowboy.

"This meeting's about the emergency evacuation procedures set up by the Special Planning Group. As many of y'all know, SPG has chosen thirteen buildings leased by Americans as chopper evac points. Selection criteria include obstacle-free roof space, proximity to American housing, and roof strength to support slicks."

Military argot had thoroughly infiltrated vocabularies hereabouts. A *slick* was a Bell UH-1 helicopter. Also called a *Huey*. Everyone in the lobby of the Brink had traveled in them. They could carry only seven passengers so it would take fourteen flights to evacuate just the men in the lobby. You'd have to be desperate to pin your hopes on one of them.

A hand went up. "How many Americans are still here?"

"We figure five to seven thousand."

Another hand. "Why not fixed wing aircraft? Why only choppers?"

"Have to assume the enemy will deploy SA-7s along the Tan Son Nhut flight path. That's their surface-to-air missile. Now listen up; I ain't finished with my announcement yet." Men sighed, groaned, growled.

The gentlemanly Cor Termijn sat silently to my left. He was probably wishing he'd insured his antiques better.

"So, how will y'all know that it's time to git to these assembly points? We're gonna broadcast a signal on the Armed Forces Radio. It's a weather report saying that it's a hundred and five degrees in the shade, followed by thirty seconds of Bing Crosby's 'I'm Dreaming of a White Christmas.' You hear that and you haul ass to the evacuation points. It's a coded signal that Vietnamese won't understand so they won't gum up the works the way they done in Da Nang."

He started talking about leaving portable wind socks on ten-foot poles on the thirteen rooftops to help chopper pilots land. A voice next to me mumbled, "Nobody cares." The man's casual derision amused me. I introduced myself. "Ralph White, Chase Bank."

He shook my hand. "Jackson Dunn, PA and E." That would be Pacific Architects and Engineers. He was an attractive blend of ethnicities, loosely Mediterranean. I'd met Lebanese with similar features.

I asked, "Why won't we care?"

"Because we can get out anytime we want, same as everyone in this room. There are two commercial flights daily plus a C-130 every daylight hour at Military Airlift Command. An American can get out of here any day he wants. This gentleman is speaking at cross-purposes to his audience. Let me ask you, Ralph, why are you here?"

I didn't want to admit to a total stranger that it was for the croissants and adrenaline, or to polish my Vietnamese syntax. "Trying to get my bank employees out, Vietnamese employees."

"Exactly! Everyone in this meeting wants to get their Viets out. You watch. Someone will ask him about that."

The lumberjack cowboy was saying, "Beginning tomorrow we'll be running buses out of the collection points. The drivers will make reconnoitering trips every day so we're aware of roadblocks, checkpoints, and the attitude of the people in the streets. Personal protective equipment for drivers will be distributed. Articles such as gas masks, flak jackets, smoke grenades, and first-aid kits will be stocked in the buses."

A hand went up. The speaker said, "I ain't taking questions till I'm done." He read from his notes, "The DAO has implemented Project Alamo at their compound. They're supplied with stocks of water, C-rats, and POL, plus beaucoup concertina, meaning large numbers of Americans can survive out at the airport without reliance on the local economy. BYOW."

Jackson Dunn leaned toward me and said, "Bring your own weapon. That's in case the concertina wire fails to keep the local economy out."

"Project Alamo?" I responded. "That didn't end well."

"Y'all, I got a couple announcements. Case you missed it, the Polish and Hungarian delegates to the Peace Commission have departed. Guess their work is done." That quip drew some laughs from the crowd. The Hungarians and Poles had been the communist members of the peace commission and had colluded to enable their North Vietnamese comrades to violate the treaty.

"Also yesterday the Foreign Ministry of North Vietnam announced that it would not oppose the U.S. evacuation of South Vietnam provided it is done immediately."

Someone yelled, "Guess Ambassador Martin missed that briefing!"

I said to Jackson, "My theory is that Martin's riding the tiger. Figures he'll get shot by friendlies if he dismounts. His personal predicament has got all of us mired down here." It was the first time I'd tried out my tiger-riding theory outside the bank.

Dunn answered, "Ah, yes. Very perceptive of you, though there's a special Saigon twist to the old tiger parable. I'll tell you tonight. You'll be at luau night?"

I didn't want to admit I didn't know anything about luau night. "Wouldn't miss it." I'd ask Cor later.

"Okay, gents, now I'm open for questions."

Someone said, "I need to get my staff out." Another said, "And my girlfriend's family." A dozen guys yelled, "I got kids here!" "Ten dependents." "Employees!" "Vietnamese!" "Yeah, what about Vietnamese?"

"If your dependents have valid passports and exit visas, they can process through the evac center at DAO. If they do not, then y'all got some work to do."

The mission warden's party line brought twenty versions of "That don't work!" each louder than the next. Jackson Dunn's foresight had been spot-on. Nobody cared about evac points or wind socks on ten-foot poles. It was the Vietnamese extended family that was behind all the tension. Well, that plus their fully automatic fashion accessories. Overall, aside from meeting the interesting Dunn, with his tip about luau night, it had not been a satisfactory meeting. Score one for Cor though; I'd met the mission warden. If North Vietnamese troops showed up earlier than expected and I had to abandon the bank's employees, the good old boy network would help me get out.

*   *   *

Cor needed to make a call so we stopped at the Continental Hotel. I took a table on the open-air terrace and ordered a coffee. I resisted getting a croissant because it would shatter me to abandon it if Cor wanted to leave quickly. With the possible exception of up-country rubber plantations, nothing was more French Indo-Chinese than the terrace of the Continental. Graham Greene had sipped drinks at these very tables twenty years ago. Some of the ancient cars that rumbled past on Tu Do Street had probably driven through Greene's line of sight.

It was foresighted of me not to order a croissant. A minute after Cor returned, we hailed a cab and sped off into a haze of dust and exhaust. We sat in the backseat of the tiny Fiat, and Cor pointed to a hole in the floor between the two front seats where the shift lever should have been. Three stiff wires, possibly old coat hangers, protruded through the hole, and as the driver accelerated, he shifted the gears by manipulating the wires. Downshifting required simultaneous jerks on two wires, a two-hand operation requiring the driver to temporarily steer with his knees. A cigarette dangled from his mouth and one eye was mostly closed against the stinging smoke. There was no fare meter, no seat belts, no air-conditioning. When we got to our destination Cor gave him a few moist piastre notes and we got out. I had no idea where we were, except that we must still be in the central part of the city, District 1.

We walked up the stairwell of a crumbling old French villa. Cor knocked on a door. "Bill told me he's pretty busy but that he'd make time for us."

"Sorry, Cor. Bill?"

"Sorry, it's Bill McWhirter. He's the bureau chief for *Time* magazine. Been here ten years, off and on. Probably knows more about Vietnam than any foreign service officer. Good guy. Clear thinker. Good for you to know. See what we can learn."

The man who answered the door was barefoot and bare-chested. His only garment was short pants, khaki and clean. He was in his mid-thirties and lean like a rower. He had a tousled head of hair, like a Kennedy at the beach. His face was more pugilist than journalist. "Come on in."

McWhirter offered us seats, though it appeared he intended to speak to us while he was walking around, organizing stuff, looking through books, and making notes. He was violating five or six etiquette principles while cramming in a little more work before Saigon blew its lid. I forgave him.

Looking at me McWhirter said, "You're Cor's turtle?"

I knew that expression from my year up-country. When replacement troops came into Vietnam, the veterans called them turtles, after their habit of walking hunched over. After a few months in country, they stood straight and walked like men. I said, "Cor doesn't think Ambassador Martin and Co. will give him an American's seat on an evacuation flight. I'm Ralph White. *Chao ong.*" It was as close as I could come to the standard Vietnamese greeting to a male. "I spent a year in Pleiku and Tuy Hoa with Amex Bank."

"Shame we didn't meet earlier," he said. "I'm leaving as soon as I file this story and say a few goodbyes. Don't see any point in hanging around. Risk's high and reward's low. Journalism doesn't need much bricks and mortar, but I can see how Chase would need an American here."

Cor said, "We wanted to pick your brain on the security situation. Yesterday we met the usual suspects at the embassy, Lehmann, Lowman, Ashida, LaGueux, Ellerman. Saw General Smith over at DAO. Met the mission warden today."

I noticed Cor omitted Raj from that list, his off-off Broadway foreign exchange dealer. I wondered where Bill McWhirter changed his money.

"You only went to the embassy and DAO? Not the Cercle Sportif or the Club Nautique?"

"No," I said. They sounded like just my kind of places.

"No change there, I assure you. Shangri-la never looked so good. How about the Guillaume Tell?"

Cor answered. "We're going there for lunch. Join us?"

"Say hi to Madame for me, Cor. Actually, better say bye. Don't you find it strange how normal everything is here? If you cooked for yourselves, you'd have no difficulty getting fresh vegetables and seafood. The Caravelle still has every wine on its list. You'd never know the NVA has forty thousand troops a day's march from here."

I said, "Maybe it's Buddhist serenity."

McWhirter said, "It's ostrich serenity, Ralph." He stopped shuffling papers and gave us his attention. "They know Thieu has been
lying to them about the threat of a North Vietnamese bloodbath.
They know what to expect and they've resigned themselves to it.
The communists will exchange the old dong for new dong and then
confiscate their property, including their businesses. They expect
that. It is the nature of the communist to confiscate, as surely as it
is the nature of the scorpion to sting."

Cor said, "Our employees aren't resigned to communism, Bill.
They're desperate for our help."

"Most Vietnamese have no choice but to stay. They'll find a way
to get along. They're saying to themselves, 'Whatever happens, at
least the killing will finally be over.' Only those who harbor a hope
of leaving are feeling desperate."

I asked, "How about *Time*'s staff?"

"I got them passports and visas years ago, right after the Paris
Accords. Most of them left in March. My interpreter stayed until two
days ago and I got him out on an Air America black flight. I looked
at the composition of the Peace Commission back in '73 and knew
this day would come. Frankly, the end took longer than I expected,
but here we are. I think anyone with vision could have predicted this."

Of all the people Cor had introduced me to, Bill McWhirter
was making the most sense. He was also the only one who didn't
work for the U.S. government. Well, except for Raj. He said, "Want
to know the craziest thing going on right now?"

The lunatic fringe was so well represented in Saigon that coming
up with the craziest was a challenge.

"Try this. Do you know why every Military Airlift Command
flight is a turnaround, with every single plane returning on the same
day to their home airports in Thailand, Guam, and the Philippines?
MAC does that so their military crews don't count as combatants
for treaty purposes. If just one of those MAC crews were to stay
in Vietnam overnight, America would exceed the fifty-troop limit
set by the peace treaty. It's almost comical. North Vietnam is also

permitted only fifty men, yet they currently deploy seventy thousand troops throughout South Vietnam."

As logical as McWhirter was, I doubted that turnaround flights would qualify as lunacy to any of the people we'd met at the embassy yesterday. It made me uncomfortable that the sharp cookies were bolting for the exits and the nut jobs were telling their servants to fetch their slippers and pipes. Moreover, what did it say about me that I was inbound rather than outbound, or that I was trying to evacuate Vietnamese over the objections of my host country, my home country, and for the time being, my employer?

I asked, "Going to luau night?"

"Isn't that a hoot?" said McWhirter. "Luau night! You one-upped me, Ralph. That's even crazier than the turnaround flights."

*   *   *

Back on the street, Cor asked, "Luau night?"

"I was going to ask you. The guy from Pacific Architects at the Mission Warden meeting said I shouldn't miss it."

"Dutchmen don't get invited to American embassy soirées. Call your friend from the Brink Hotel, or call Jim Ashida. As commercial attaché, he'd know."

We flagged down a taxi and Cor gave the driver our destination. "Guillaume Tell."

I checked and the gear shift hadn't yet been replaced by clothes hangers. Before I could breathe a sigh of relief, I noticed that exhaust fumes filled the taxi during stops. The longer the stop, the more smoke accumulated inside. As the driver accelerated, I listened for the telltale sound of an exhaust pipe puncture and, yup, there it was. It would be certain death to ride in this car in the monsoon season with the windows closed. In all fairness I'm not sure I'd have repaired a leaky exhaust pipe either if I expected my cab to be confiscated next week.

The Guillaume Tell restaurant felt further from the central business district than it actually was since getting there involved crossing a tributary of the Saigon River via an arched wooden bridge. Cor said, "More than once I've seen navy patrol boats towing water skiers under this bridge. The image of a U.S. Navy patrol boat with a skier off the stern and a .50-caliber machine gun in the bow is hard to dislodge."

We exited the taxi at 34 Trinh Minh The Street, our clothing and hair reeking of exhaust fumes. Cor said, "Running the best European restaurant in Vietnam has got to be a challenge for Madame Leccia. Her husband died ten years ago and she's run it completely on her own since then."

A gregarious woman wearing black glasses and a ruddy face welcomed us in French. "Bonjour, messieurs." Madame Madeleine Leccia offered us a table on the second floor.

Cor explained, "Locals believe that upper floors are less vulnerable to attack. They haven't revised that preference to account for the 122 rockets, which impact the upper floors first." To Madame, Cor said, "The ground floor would be charming, thank you."

It was too. It was a large, high-ceilinged room featuring murals of Swiss hillsides, with cattle in the foreground and snowcapped mountains in the distance. A large poster read *In vino veritas*. Another read *Carpe diem*. I counted eight air conditioners, all of them chugging loudly. The staff wore white jackets and black bow ties. We were in Switzerland. The war was distant.

Madame Leccia said, "You may take any table you like. The place is empty." It was far from empty. About half the tables were occupied. "My only concession to the present circumstances is that I now no longer accept credit cards. Please forgive me. My restaurant may be closed before I receive funds. Hell, for that matter, my bank may be closed."

It definitely would if she banked with Chase and I had anything to say about it.

Cor said, "I'm on Friday's Pan Am flight to Hong Kong. Leave with me, Madeleine. Hong Kong could use an authentic Swiss restaurant. My wife and I would host you at our apartment until you gained your footing."

With all of Cor's furniture incarcerated in a Saigon warehouse I wondered how his wife was coping in Hong Kong. I also wondered what she would think of her husband's gallant invitation. Perhaps the women would exchange Swiss and Dutch recipes. The Dutch side of that trade would have far more to gain, unless Mrs. Termijn knew how to make *rijsttafel*, the forty-course Indonesian feast which was Dutch only in name.

The menu featured everything I might expect, *Vichyssoise, duck à l'Orange, tournedos*. Missing were the classic French and Swiss wines. In their place were California wines, black-marketed from post exchanges. Cor said, "I'd order a bottle of wine, Madeleine, if you'd sit and chat with us for a few minutes." She said she would shortly, then left to welcome newly arriving customers.

When she returned, she brought a cold bottle of fendant with her. It wasn't on the menu. "I've been saving this, Cor, but you're in luck. My Chinese chef just resigned. He's been with me since we opened in '54. He'll probably be on your flight to Hong Kong. Don't see how I can stay open so we may as well drink this."

What was happening at the Guillaume Tell is what John Linker wanted me to prevent at Chase: employees evacuating before management was prepared to close the branch. The major difference was that Madame Leccia didn't appear to mind. Her chef's departure merely triggered her own. No tears. No recriminations. Time to go. The Guillaume Tell had had a twenty-one-year run. Most restaurants would sign up for that in a heartbeat, though perhaps not many banks. Madame asked Cor to uncork the bottle and we three toasted to the future, a word freighted differently for each of us.

*   *   *

Commercial attaché Jim Ashida answered his own phone and said, "Of course, I'd be happy to get you into luau night. Show up at the main gate to the embassy about six o'clock and ask the guards to direct you to the Recreation Center."

First things first. I needed to check out of the Majestic Hotel. According to Cor it was in the direct line of rocket fire from across the river. Moreover, it was also too close to the bank. I've always believed that a guy shouldn't do anything he wouldn't want printed on the front page of *The New York Times* the next morning. Even so, I saw only downside in exposing my personal life to my colleagues. After all, the more witnesses, the more likely that embarrassing call to the *Times*. Or, worse, *The Saigon Post*.

I picked up the bill for my two nights in the Majestic and went out to the newspaper stand on Tu Do Street to exchange currency with Raj. His rate was 1,000 piastres per dollar, down 5 percent from the morning. I might have haggled him lower but I didn't have the energy. I returned to the front desk and paid my bill, having saved something like $60 off of the $180 bill. In a very real sense Raj was the cashier for the Majestic. Chase had dozens of guys like him on the thirty-fifth floor in New York. They were called market-makers. I hoped Raj had other skills; the long-run outlook was unfavorable for the trade in piastres. The dong would survive though since that's what both the North and South called their currencies.

Moving from the Majestic Hotel to the Caravelle Hotel was as simple as strolling down Tu Do Street with my leather satchel in hand and depositing one pair of underwear, one pair of socks, one shirt, and one pair of pants into a drawer. I doubted I'd need a briefcase full of greenbacks or my Smith & Wesson Chief's Special at the luau party, but they were safer on me than anywhere else. I definitely wouldn't be the only armed person at that Recreation Center, though I doubted anyone would be carrying twenty-five grand. Not that it was a competition.

*   *   *

If there was a better way to get into the embassy's Recreation Center than the front gate, I didn't know about it. The Consular Section was clearly open because there was still quite a gaggle of visa applicants obstructing the gate. Or maybe they were tomorrow's applicants preparing to camp out. I shouted, "Luau!" to the guard and he eased open the gate the width of a one-hundred-sixty-six-pound American, and not a quarter inch more. The guard pointed me toward the Recreation Center. Behind me I heard the crowd chanting *luau, luau, luau*, apparently believing it was some kind of secret password. Another steel gate, another guard, and I was standing beside a very large swimming pool, surrounded by Americans wearing fragrant jasmine leis and carrying umbrella drinks. If the Defense Attaché Office was Pentagon East, the Rec Center was Waikiki East.

The pool shimmered blueness; the fruit punch pinkness. Beautiful, slender Vietnamese women wearing grass skirts and hemp-strung coconut halves for bras served drinks and hors d'oeuvres. The coconut bras had to be terribly uncomfortable. I felt bad for the women. It was probably against labor laws back home. One of the women raised her arms to put a white lei around my neck and I felt her coconuts against my chest. Another hostess fitted plastic sunglasses to my face and damned if she didn't coconut-bump me too. I willed my erection into retreat.

There was quite a crowd around the pool and, new though I was, I recognized several faces. The lumberjack who'd given the Mission Warden presentation had attracted a small following. Probably answering questions about portable wind socks on ten-foot poles to guide in the evac choppers. That type never used the word helicopter. They were always choppers, slicks, or Hueys. If they wanted to sound grown-up, they'd call them rotor-wing aircraft.

Bill McWhirter, from *Time*, was saying his last farewells. I shook his hand and wished him well. He introduced me to George McArthur, his counterpart at the *L.A. Times*. I'd heard that McArthur's wife, Kim, was Ambassador Martin's secretary, and I'd heard she was a stunning beauty. Regrettably she wasn't there.

Foreign service officers were well represented, including Conny LaGueux, Denny Ellerman, Shep Lowman. Missing was DCM Lehmann, though I heard Martin too was present. On the far side of the pool the civilian contractors clustered together, a fraternity of crew cuts, tattoos, knit shirts, and canned beer. There hadn't been much call for their services in recent months. It was probably true that the only ones who remained were just trying to evacuate their Vietnamese employees and relatives.

I asked the CIA man, LaGueux, how the battle for Xuan Loc was going. He might not be scrupulously frank with a civvie but I didn't think he'd outright lie.

He said, "The 18th is supported by the 5th RVN Air Force out of Bien Hoa, and by the ARVN 8th and 52nd Task Forces, the 3rd Armored Brigade and the 13th Armored Squadron. The ARVN 43rd and 48th Infantry Regiments are also in the vicinity of Xuan Loc. It's as strong a defense as we could hope for."

I didn't know the difference between Task Forces, Brigades, Regiments, and Divisions so I couldn't fully grasp what LaGueux was saying but it sounded like there was considerable firepower between the invading hordes and luau night. I asked, "Do we know who they're up against?"

"Yeah, mainly the PAVN 6th Infantry Division and their 95th B Infantry Regiment."

Again his terminology confused me so I asked. "PAVN must be what we used to call the North Vietnamese Army." It must mean the People's Army of Vietnam.

"Right."

He'd given me a lot of information but hadn't answered my original question. "So any news on how the battle is progressing?"

"As of now it's a stalemate."

I suspected he knew more but didn't want me to know before the secretary of defense. LaGueux was too smart to be a delusionary but too secretive to be an overt realist. I needed a new middle category to accommodate people like him, and there were a lot of them. They were people who endorsed the propagation of liberty, but who understood that JFK's *bearing any burden and paying any price* had been purely rhetorical. Maybe pilgrims would be a good term for them; not a *Mayflower* pilgrim, a *Heart of Darkness* pilgrim.

I had yet to be introduced to Graham Martin, ambassador of the United States of America to the Republic of South Vietnam, but I recognized him from behind based on his habit of tilting his head over his right shoulder as if banking into a turn.

I left LaGueux, saying I was overdue to meet our ambassador. He lifted his eyebrows in a *good luck with that* expression. I strolled along the perimeter of the pool, past contractors, diplomats, expatriates, businessmen, cocktail waitresses, and flower girls, toward Saigon's top dog. His security men intercepted before I got within fifty feet.

"May we help you, sir?"

"Just introducing myself to the ambassador."

"He knows you, Mr. White." The security guy stood inches from my chest and blocked my path.

"I assure you we haven't met. I'm—"

"You're the new manager at Chase. The ambassador's delighted you're here and delighted that the Chase Manhattan Bank plans to stay open."

"Actually Chase needs to make contingency plans to get people out. I need to talk to the ambassador about that."

"That's way premature, Mr. White, getting people out."

"Contingency planning is never premature. I want to meet the ambassador. Get out of my way! Who are you?"

"You handle the bank, Mr. White. The ambassador will handle foreign policy."

Martin still had his back to me, his head dangling laconically off to the side. I decided to back down. Our paths would eventually cross.

"Happy luau, Ralph."

"Hey, Jackson. Same to you." Jackson Dunn was a savvy operator and useful to know. "Jackson, at the Brink you said you had some insight about Ambassador Martin riding the tiger."

"Right," he said. "The usual logic doesn't apply to Martin; he's added a twist to the ancient parable. He's unafraid of the tiger because he's going to get lifted off by chopper."

Chapter Four

THURSDAY, APRIL 17, 1975

The line of desperate customers waiting for the bank to open on Thursday morning extended out to the sidewalk and curled all the way to the front of the Majestic Hotel. I suspected there must be a back entrance for employees but didn't know where it was so I waited outside for Cor to show up. The waiting customers were all Vietnamese, mostly civilian, but a few were in army fatigues, some sporting the trendy Colt M-16 rifle. I was a little surprised at the orderliness of the line. As bank runs went, it was damn civilized.

Each of our clients would face a difficult decision upon reaching the front of the line—what to do with their money. Our tellers wouldn't be much help. There were really no good options. Boarding a bus to go home or back to work with a bag jammed with piastre notes would be insane. Withdrawing a life savings equivalent to five thousand dollars would mean carrying an enormous sack of money. Moreover, those piastres had no value outside the country and they would be useless under a future communist regime.

Nor was changing their money into dollars an option, since the *P*, as Americans referred to piastres, was a noncovertible currency. Clients could legally purchase piastres with dollars or with other foreign currencies, but it was a one-way street—the purchase of foreign currency was prohibited. Even the purchase of dollar-denominated money orders, cashier's checks, or traveler's checks was prohibited.

A client could take his funds to a local bank, but eventually those accounts too would be confiscated by the communists.

If American expatriates were delusionaries, pilgrims, or realists, the Vietnamese were by now all realists. Thus the orderly line I guess. It didn't really matter if they took their savings out only to watch its value expire, or left it in Chase's custody for eventual interment in the graveyard of nonconvertible currencies.

I turned away from the anxious crowd to watch the Saigon River flow past on the far side of Ben Bach Dang, the unlovely thoroughfare bordering the river. The broad river was picturesque from a distance but up close it was muddy, filthy, and weed-clogged.

There is a parable about Buddha teaching a disciple to be patient until a dirty river runs clear enough to drink from it. It would take millennia for that to happen with the Saigon River. If I had Buddha's ear for a minute, I would suggest abandoning both his piastre-denominated nest egg and his muddy river in favor of a small handful of greenbacks and a gurgling trout stream in, say, Vermont. Though how to manage such a translocation might challenge even Buddha. If Buddha were to get in line and ask the Chase teller how she herself planned to get out, the most honest thing she could say—you can't fib to Buddha—would be that Chase had a plan, or Mr. White did anyway, and she had every reason to believe that her name was on it.

Actually, I didn't know the names of any of our tellers. The closest I had to a plan was a satchel of currency and a five-shot revolver. In my defense I might have cited obstacles imposed by the government of South Vietnam and the government of the United States of America. I'd also have to add the Chase Manhattan Bank as an obstacle, since John Linker had tasked me with business as usual for as long as I considered it possible. Buddha might have pointed out that in faithfully discharging Linker's mandate I was my own obstacle. It was a very muddy river.

Cor emerged through the crowd and beckoned me toward a small door far off to the right of the main entrance. The more I got to know Cor, the better I liked him. I liked his confident bearing, his patience, his steady gaze. He was a wise man, an impression reinforced by his owlish black-frame glasses. Stranded outside Holland for so long, even his native language must have acquired an accent. His Dutch passport was a vestige of childhood; he was more a citizen of the International Banking Archipelago than of the Netherlands.

Had Cor been an American, Chase would have been far better off keeping him at the helm in Saigon for the duration. He was a time-tested manager. He knew the nuts and bolts of commercial banking and every single moving part in the complex organism called a Chase Manhattan Bank branch. I knew accounting. I was entry-level. Turtle summed it up.

Of course Cor was right to insist on bailing out. Imagine his situation! Imagine not having a U.S. passport and having to rely on a delusionary like Deputy Chief of Mission Wolf Lehmann once the shit hit the fan. Lehmann wouldn't even cooperate with me, an unaccented, red-blooded American citizen. He took his cues from an ambassador who was immobilized with anxiety. If I were in Cor's place I'd definitely get while the getting was good. If I were Cor, I would be long gone.

He took me into the main banking platform minutes before the branch opened for business, and there was a brief lull in the background buzz as employees paused in their work to stare at us. To me Cor quietly said, "By now they all know who you are and they all believe Chase will get them out. Only the four officers know how short the short list is."

The deputy manager, Cuong, came over, already looking harried. "Settlement took an hour longer than usual yesterday. May I have your permission to close at two o'clock today?"

To his wristwatch Cor said, "Let's discuss that in a couple of hours. Now let's open up, Mr. Cuong."

In that last moment of calm, I returned the stares of the employees. It surprised me that so many of them were smiling. Given their desperate circumstances it amazed me. The tellers, all attractive young women, looked as though they were auditioning for a modeling job. Smooth skin, white teeth, tasteful eye makeup, lipstick, shiny black hair, pastel ao dai dresses.

The manager's office was spacious, about the size of my old apartment in Brooklyn Heights, though quite a bit darker since my apartment didn't have rocket-proof shutters. It had a musty, stale tobacco odor, as though the windows hadn't been opened since the French departed. Picture hooks punctured the stucco walls where Cor's artwork had once hung. He took a seat at a gray steel desk that was smaller than either the room or the man deserved. It looked like military surplus. His scuffed brown shoes protruded beneath the desk. If there had once been a carpet it was gone; the concrete floors were painted vanilla and stained chocolate. In its favor the office was extremely clean. Labor was cheap.

I remained standing, as did Bach-Mai, the credit officer, when she joined our deliberations. She was the least busy of the four officers since the branch had long ago ceased extending credit. I recalled that her husband had been stranded up-country while trying to retrieve his parents. I asked, "Any word from Cau?"

Bach-Mai was calm, mature, emotionally stable, dignified. She may have wept all night, but she wore dry eyes to work. "Nothing." She maintained eye contact. "The highways are clogged with hundreds of thousands of pedestrians, pushcarts, and bicycles. At least the NVA seems to be leaving them alone."

She didn't need to say that the North Vietnamese Army would definitely not leave Cau alone if they discovered who he was.

Bach-Mai spoke a sentence to me in Vietnamese which was too rapid to understand and she watched closely for my reaction.

I answered, "*Xin loi, Ba. Toi khong biet tieng viet.*" My delivery was monotonal and my vowels deflated but she'd get it: *Sorry, ma'am. I don't understand Vietnamese.*

"But you do. Didn't you serve here?" She reverted to English.

"I wasn't in the armed forces. I was a civilian contractor. I worked for American Express Bank and was paid by the U.S. Treasury, not the military. Why are you so interested in my résumé?"

"You mean you didn't have to be here? Nobody made you come to Vietnam?"

"I graduated from college and needed a job."

"But how about this time? Didn't Chase send you here?"

"That is also not entirely accurate. I volunteered to come and help you. I wanted to come back. There are a lot of things I like about Vietnam."

"When I look at you, I do not see a soldier, but neither do I see a Treasury contractor."

So this was about my professional identity. I knew that answer. "I'm an international banker. A Chase Manhattan banker."

She looked at Cor, who was speaking Dutch-accented French on the phone. Cor was disheveled, tired. His clothing was rumpled. The flesh covering his cheeks and neck was soft. Bach-Mai said, "Mr. Termijn is a Chase banker. You don't look like him." Bach-Mai's attitude softened. I decided she was amusing herself at my expense.

I smiled. "Not yet I don't look like him." It would be difficult to satisfy Bach-Mai on this, but I could ask for nothing more than to mature into the man Cor Termijn was.

Customers, both Vietnamese and expatriates, came to bid farewell to Cor, and I saw no profit in eavesdropping on their private conversations so I followed Bach-Mai down to the banking floor. Customers packed every space and what had earlier looked to me like pandemonium now appeared more orderly. Bach-Mai introduced me to many of the staff and they all thanked me profusely for being there. They asked her questions about me in Vietnamese.

"It's hard to explain to them exactly what you are. We no longer have the category of young gentleman in our country. The young and rich go to universities in Europe or America and they never return—in order to escape the military draft."

"I'm not so young, Bach-Mai. I'll be twenty-eight in four months. And I'm far from rich." Gentleman might also be a stretch.

The final stop on Bach-Mai's tour was the cable machine room, back up on the second floor. It was a closet-sized space housing a clunky iron contraption and a bored young operator. The machine resembled a very old-fashioned typewriter and its operator was sullen in her isolation. The technology fascinated me for its primitiveness. The contraption was receiving a cable message, and text was being printed on a spool of cheap paper at the rate of about one character every four seconds. Its slowness mesmerized me. The last five years had produced a flood of electronic technologies: the introduction of handheld electronic calculators, fax machines, the IBM Selectric typewriter, and mainframe computers. More than half of American households had color television, and some had little ovens that heated foods with electromagnetic radiation. It verged on the inconceivable that the Saigon branch of the third largest bank in America still used such a primitive device to communicate with the outside world. In an era accustomed to lightning-fast communications, Chase Saigon's cable machine was insolent in its laziness. I prayed that I never needed to send anything urgently.

Cor said he'd be returning to our Hong Kong Regional Office the next day so if there was anything he could do for me time was running short. I could have asked him to show me the civil aviation terminal in case I had to steal an airplane. I could have asked him for a tour of the deep water ports on the Saigon River in case I needed to steal a ship. Maybe he could help me purchase a used motorbike in case I needed to make my way to the South China Sea on my own. Maybe we should do what the mission warden suggested and visit the rooftop evacuation points. I will admit that part of me really wanted to see those handheld wind socks on ten-foot poles. In any event I asked Cor to take me to the antiques district. I had my heart set on a museum-quality opium pipe. A collector himself, Cor didn't need to have his arm twisted to make a last visit to the antiques district. He might have preferred locating his own household effects, but his freight forwarder wasn't answering the phone. The people who knew where his shipment was had skipped town, and the people who remained couldn't be made to care.

*   *   *

Le Cong Kieu Street sounded nothing like it is spelled, though the shops looked exactly as I hoped they would. The dense web of telephone and electrical wiring drooping from one side of the street to the other looked part of the street's architecture, like the support cables on a suspension bridge. It was a short, quiet, dusty street, cleft from the central business district by a broad, four-lane boulevard. Cor was well known there.

The storefronts were busy with blue-and-white ceramics, garden seats, stone carvings, ivory figurines, and unsurprisingly, Uma statues. Here, as she was throughout South and Southeast Asia, the Hindu fertility goddess was well represented. Fertility had multicultural allure.

Shop proprietors, most with their grandparents' Chinese names on the reverse side of their business cards, plied us with miniature cups of ultra-strong tea as they casually discussed the colorful history of the opium trade.

I was looking for a full set, meaning both the long, slender bamboo opium pipe and the accompanying silver tray for the lamp and other opium-smoking paraphernalia. I was drawn to the artistry of the carved bamboo, usually topped with a brass bowl and decorated with engraved silverwork and often inlaid with jade. I learned that the smokable form of opium, called *chanda*, had been exhausted, with all production shifted to the more profitable trade in heroin. I had antique firearms I never intended to shoot, so an antique opium pipe that I didn't intend to smoke wasn't out of character.

The tea ceremony, repeated at each shop, slowed and civilized the process. Cor jawboned with the proprietors as though they were old friends. He asked them what they intended to do after the North took over. Selling antiques to tourists generated valuable foreign exchange. It was the goose that laid the golden eggs and the North could hardly slay it. I selected one of the opium pipes and planned to return to Le Cong Kieu Street to buy it after changing money with Raj.

I had also acquired a half dozen business cards from these truly exceptional entrepreneurs. I resolved to keep the cards handy. If the city was overrun by the enemy before I could get out, I might be able to disappear for a few weeks into one of their storerooms. These guys weren't communists; for the right price they'd hide me. Then again, for the right price they'd also sell me. Hiding on Le Cong Kieu Street was an absolutely worst-case plan. Things would have to get desperate for me to shack up with stone fertility goddesses.

Cor insisted he had to get back to the bank, but I had no duties there other than the conflicting ones of keeping the branch open for reputational reasons and closing it for security reasons. Some ill-defined event was supposed to herald the end of the first era and usher in the second, but if the North's wanton violation of the Peace Accords, the rout of the South Vietnamese Army, and the siege of Saigon didn't qualify as that trigger, I'd be very hard pressed to describe what it might look like.

*   *   *

More practical reasons drew me back to the Caravelle Hotel. I'd neglected to send my socks and underwear to the laundry, and since I had only two pairs of each, I'd have to either wash yesterday's in the sink early enough for them to dry out on the air conditioner, or wear them dirty. The latter option was unappealing since they were teeming with microbial life.

I had four messages waiting for me at the hotel, one from Denny Ellerman, the U.S. embassy's minister-counsellor, economic affairs, and another from Jim Ashida, the commercial attaché, each representing the realist and pilgrim persuasions, respectively. A third was from a Lucien Kinsolving, whose note said he was a first secretary at the U.S. embassy and liaison to the International Commission of Control and Supervision, aka the peace commission. The fourth note was from the cynical but perceptive contractor Jackson Dunn from the Brink meeting and luau night. Protocol required me to respond to Ashida first. The least deserving was Jackson, whom I called first.

"Hey, Ralph, ever hear of Andy Warhol? We got a film of his, supposedly rather raunchy. Don't know your sensibilities but you're hereby invited." He gave me the location of the Pacific Architects compound and I thanked him without committing myself. I didn't know my sensibilities either. I thought of myself as a high-principled New Englander, but put a nice pair of breasts in my face and I might lose my bearing. Actually, a fairly average pair of breasts did the job equally well.

I held the remaining three notes in my hands. Curiosity overcame protocol again. I decided to call Kinsolving. The peace commission had to be a very curious place right about then. Another contact at the embassy couldn't hurt. It was so curious that I decided to visit him there rather than return his call.

*   *   *

The crowd of visa applicants outside the embassy had doubled in both size and volume since luau night. People hurled the summaries of their emigration cases at me as though our brief physical contact had somehow elevated us to companionhood. Elbowing past them I felt I was averting my eyes from some horrific disaster. The irony, apparent to every single one of us, was that while the disaster had not yet occurred, its imminence was obvious on only one side of the embassy wall.

Kinsolving turned out to be a quietly energetic man in about his mid-forties. Self-deprecating too, which is all too rare in the foreign service. He said that the initials for his organization, the ICCS, or

International Commission of Control and Supervision, actually stood for *I Can't Control Shit.* I may have unearthed another realist.

He told me that during one incoming rocket barrage he'd asked his Viet Cong colleague on the commission why he didn't just phone the VC commander and tell him to stop. The colleague had said that the commander would probably just laugh and ask him to guide the next rocket in.

Kinsolving hadn't asked to meet me to share foxhole humor. Yes, he was technically in Saigon as a delegate to the ICCS, but when that joke became stale, he'd volunteered to help with the evacuation plan. He let it slip that, despite being a foreign service officer, he considered himself an outsider at Embassy Saigon. His prior assignments had been in the Mideast and Africa, and he'd watched from outside Vietnam as the U.S. had gotten mired in someone else's civil war at an insane cost of American lives. He was vehemently against the war and blamed failed foreign policy for the current debacle.

I'd never heard a diplomat say the things he was saying. As long as we were being frank, I gave him my take on the situation. "I think that America had a legitimate role here, Mr. Kinsolving, but that that legitimacy expired."

"Please! Call me Lucien."

"Okay, Lucien then. And if critiquing foreign policy would get my employees out, I'd happily do it all day long."

"And that is not the reason I contacted you. I'm about to get to my point. Have you met Ken Moorefield, Ralph? He heads up the Evacuation Control Center out at the Defense Attaché Office compound. Ever hear of the Evacuation Control Center?"

"Neither man nor organization."

"Now there's a surprise. I heard you were buddies with the top influence peddlers in this building."

"What are they not telling me?"

"That a C-130 lands at Tan Son Nhut every couple of hours to evacuate Americans and their dependents. They also manage to get some carefully selected Vietnamese out. And everything is being coordinated out of the Defense Attaché gymnasium by an aide to Ambassador Martin named Ken Moorefield."

It didn't seem possible. "*Who* are you again?"

"Just because the ICCS is idle doesn't mean I have to be too. I've reassigned myself. I'm helping get people out of here. All I'm telling you, Ralph, is that there's an evacuation operation outside . . ."

"Independent of the delusionaries."

"Yes, and moreover, outside the chain of command. In addition to American families, the embassy is evacuating Vietnamese intelligence agents and political collaborators. Can't do that on commercial flights but we can put anyone we want on a military flight. You really need to talk to Ken Moorefield."

I was torn. It was urgent that I meet this guy Moorefield, but I had to check in with Ashida and Ellerman first or they'd think I'd ignored their messages. I navigated through the embassy's reception area on the ground floor and back up to see Ashida on the third floor.

Seeing Jim Ashida's kind face again reminded me that even a *Heart of Darkness* pilgrim could be likable. He was the ideal commercial attaché for Saigon. I also liked his being ethnically Asian. He was both *us* and *them*. On the other hand, there was a saying in the foreign service that went something like, *You have to be smart to get in, and you have to be smart to get out.* This was intended as an unsubtle jab at career FSOs who never returned to the private economy. So far, Jim Ashida had only been smart enough to get in.

It appeared that Ashida just wanted an update. Were our banking customers getting unruly? Did we have adequate liquidity to honor all withdrawals? Which commercial clients were closing their accounts?

I didn't really have all the answers but I sensed that this was just small talk so I said things were fine.

He said, "By the way, the embassy's medical officer is leaving for Thailand. His name's W. F. Shadel. I believe we're calling it a previously scheduled rotation, though there's no one coming in to replace him, so some might see it as an evacuation."

"What makes me think there's more to this story, Jim?"

"It's a funny story."

"Will I laugh?"

"It's not that kind of funny. Dr. Shadel's wife is Vietnamese."

"The plot thickens."

"Indeed. The good doctor's wife naturally insists that the embassy get her family out."

"Naturally." I anticipated the punch line but didn't want to interrupt Ashida with my guess.

"She's claiming five siblings, all with spouses. There are parents, cousins, nephews and nieces, in-laws, grandparents, and lots of kids. All tallied, Dr. Shadel has twenty dependents, a number which appears to have surprised him as much as anyone else."

I was dead certain that Ambassador Martin wasn't going to let his medical officer evacuate a score of Vietnamese. Using embassy flights to thwart Vietnam's new requirement for exit visas would be a precedent he wouldn't abide. Ashida had my attention. There was supposed to be a funny part.

"The State Department's policy is to provide transportation for an employee's immediate family, meaning spouse and children."

"And you're telling me this because . . . ?"

"Well, I'm wondering if, um, if you, um, if you might have discovered any way of getting Vietnamese out yet."

I laughed. Ashida laughed back. It was both kinds of funny. The guy who was supposed to be helping me get bank employees out was asking my help in getting embassy employees out. It would be hysterical if it weren't so tragic. Ashida had the vast resources of the United States government, and all I had was a hall pass to a moribund embassy, too many greenbacks to count, and five rounds in a .38 special. One of us, and quite possibly both, had seriously overestimated the other.

I shook Ashida's hand and was halfway out the door when I turned back. "Remind me how many Americans we think are left in Vietnam."

"We don't really know but our best guess is five thousand. Why?"

"Let's say that each of those Americans has, on average, an extended family of twenty Vietnamese, like your embassy doc. You may have none, but I have a hundred, so let's say the average is twenty dependents for each of 5,000 Americans. That's a hundred thousand people who will want out. That's the population of a small city. It helps put the scale in perspective. How long would it take to remove every single soul from, say, Fort Lauderdale? What would the logistics look like?"

His blank look said he hadn't considered it. "I don't know. I honestly don't know."

"Well, I'll tell you something for free, Jim. The longer Ambassador Martin considers evacuation planning to be seditious, the more chaotic the final days are going to be. And the longer Martin believes that leaving would be more dangerous than staying, the more of a self-fulfilling prophecy it will become."

I left Ashida's office fully aware that I hadn't passed on Kinsolving's news about the new Evacuation Control Center. That was something Ashida should be telling me, not vice versa. I concluded he hadn't caught wind of it yet.

*   *   *

Denny Ellerman headed my short list of realists at the embassy. He was a real no-nonsense guy. If he'd been the ambassador instead of Graham Martin, he'd have told, not asked, President Thieu that he was going to evacuate every American in Vietnam over the next couple of weeks and that in return for not interfering he'd give Thieu and his extended family sanctuary in Santa Barbara. Take it or leave it. Problem was, Ellerman was the minister-counsellor, economic affairs, not the ambassador.

"Hi, Ralph. You didn't have to come in."

"I was in the neighborhood."

I hadn't even taken a seat when Ellerman coughed up the pur-pose of his call. "You and Mr. Termijn are welcome to stay at my house. My family's gone so I have plenty of room for you. It's in a walled compound and I have armed guards and an electronic security system. I just want you to know that if you don't feel secure in your hotel my place is available."

I guessed that his offer violated a half dozen State Department policies. I guessed too that he wouldn't care. He was the kind of guy who preferred to ask for forgiveness afterward rather than for permission beforehand. Also, he'd been in the foreign service for only a few months and was smart enough both to get in and to get out. He wasn't going to sweat a demerit from the organi-zation's lifers.

He said, "Bank of America and First National City Bank have pulled their American staff. You're the last American banker in Saigon. I want you to know that I don't take your dedication for granted."

"Thanks, Denny, but mine isn't a lone act of bravado. I'm told David Rockefeller has become involved. Also our international department has formed a task force to back me up." I had no idea who was on the task force, where they were, or what they were doing, but it comforted me to think I was on a team. "I'd like to pocket your offer of accommodation for when civil order truly deteriorates." I didn't want to admit what I really feared—mainly that chaos, looting, and anti-American violence lay just below Sai-gon's affected calm. Realistically, five guys with guns could take over the Caravelle Hotel and ransom the American guests for a flight out. Tactically, it might take six of them since my revolver held five cartridges.

"I'm going to do something else for you too. When you decide it's time to close the bank, let me know and I'll get the American radio station to broadcast a message that the Chase Manhattan

Bank will be closed for the day. That could be the employees' signal to get to the pickup points."

Ellerman's offer was welcome but it had a couple of obvious flaws. For one thing our employees didn't listen to the American radio station. Few Americans did either. I certainly never had. But more importantly, what good would it do for our employees to get to the pickup locations if Vietnamese were prohibited from boarding American military aircraft?

Still, it was a good man's good-faith offer. "Thanks, Denny. Chase thanks you."

Denny Ellerman knew more than I did; it would be hard not to. If he'd been hinting that the exit visa code had been cracked, then getting out to the Evacuation Control Center and meeting Ken Moorefield had to be my highest priority. But it was getting late in the day and I had two more appointments: a farewell dinner with Cor and a raunchy film by a guy named Warhol.

*   *   *

Dinner found Cor and me back at the Guillaume Tell. Madame Leccia called it The Last Supper, and it was about as thinly attended as the original, and minus the celebrities. We didn't bother to order and simply accepted what Madame had left to serve. She had a German name for the dish, but I'd have called it a venison bourguignon. She produced two bottles of a fairly robust north Italian red to slosh it down and volunteered to help us with the task. She was rosy-faced to begin with and the wine deepened the hue.

Madame Leccia had abandoned the idea of starting a restaurant elsewhere in Southeast Asia in favor of retirement in Europe. We drank to her decision. We drank to Vietnam. Cor had a long string of practical advice for me and I had to borrow a pencil and paper from Madame to jot everything down. It included shredding the negotiable instruments such as traveler's checks and money orders, taking the vault combination and test keys to either the

Central Bank or the French embassy, and trying to carry away the last day's settlement. Lastly, he suggested that I book a seat each day for the next day's Pan Am flight. "You always want to be able to get yourself out."

For Cor, the minutiae of the branch's wartime defeat posed a professional challenge, like, say, disarming a land mine. For me it was emotionally draining. I couldn't have faced it without Cor's steady mentorship. That and Madame Leccia's north Italian red.

*   *   *

I was familiar with only two small parts of Saigon, the district comprising the central business district, called District 1, and the district comprising the air base and Defense Attaché Office. I didn't recognize the address Jackson Dunn had given me for the Pacific Architects and Engineers compound so I had no idea where the cabbie was taking me. I was mildly surprised when it turned out to be just outside the old DAO gate at the airport.

Jackson Dunn and his fellow engineers lived in upscale barracks designed after a minimum security prison and featuring a central, atrium-ceiling community room. The room was dark and the film was rolling when I got there. I located Jackson with difficulty. He expressed his disappointment. "It's just a fuck film. I was expecting something slightly more elevated."

It was true. The film was unalloyed pornography. I would never have imagined sex could be boring, but Warhol's film was dull. There was a snippet of conversation about the Vietnam War in between the humping and moaning, but it was mainly just sex filmed through an annoying blue filter. It was the kind of film referred to as "banned in Boston," though I doubted anyone out- side Greenwich Village would pay to see it.

When it was over, Jackson handed me a beer and explained the blue hue. "Warhol used the wrong kind of film. He'd originally intended to call the film *Fuck*, but when he saw how it came out he changed the title to *Blue Movie*. Warhol said that he'd produced the film as a protest against the Vietnam War and to show how to stop it."

"Maybe the secretary of defense should have consulted Warhol," I said. "Instead of fifty-eight thousand killed, there might have been that many born."

Chapter Five

FRIDAY, APRIL 18, 1975

I bought a *Saigon Post* at Raj's kiosk on my way to work. It was exasperating that government censors continued to blank out the tops of columns on the front page of the paper. If South Vietnam was a democracy, it wasn't much like ours. The only news about the battle for Xuan Loc was that loyalist bombers from nearby Bien Hoa airfield had stalled the North Vietnamese Army's attack. I doubted that would slow the fall of Saigon by more than a few days.

I also checked Raj's free market exchange rate. The piastre had slid further to 1,100 per dollar, a fifteen percent decline since my first purchase at 950 per dollar. The South Vietnamese government still believed it was worth 755. Raj pointed out a third indicator of trouble: the two-hundred-foot line of customers waiting to close their accounts at the Chase Manhattan Bank, which was out of sight around the intersection of Tu Do and Ben Bach Dang.

Inside the bank, Cor assembled the employees for a brief pep talk before the doors opened. "I'm very proud of you, and you should be proud of yourselves too. You are demonstrating grace under pressure and are performing a better job than most employees do under normal business conditions. Your efforts are appreciated at the highest levels of the bank, both at regional office in Hong Kong and Chase headquarters in New York. The eyes of your thirty-two thousand colleagues around the world are on you, and the example you are setting for them is inspiring. I will be leaving for Hong Kong for this three-day weekend and I wish you a happy Hung Kings Day on Monday. I shall return Tuesday. As usual, Mr. Cuong will assume the role of acting general manager. Mr. White will remain with you and maintain constant contact with the U.S. embassy."

I couldn't help noticing that Cor didn't mention that Mr. White would be booked on a Pan Am flight out of Saigon every day for the duration in case he had to abandon them. Also missing from Cor's pep talk was that our collective fate was in the hands of staunch delusionaries in the highest echelon at the embassy. What Cor called my constant contact there would more accurately be called groveling.

I was very curious about the evacuation program for Vietnamese at the Defense Attaché Office, and my challenge was to find out more about it. No wonder everyone was lying low; it was considered disloyal to discuss the evacuation of Americans and treasonous to mention evacuating Vietnamese.

When I told Cor I wanted to drive out to the airport with him, I'm sure any employees who overheard us thought we were leaving together, never to be seen again. It couldn't be helped; I wanted to find out what kind of operation Moorefield was running at the newly established Evacuation Control Center. I admitted to a prejudice, since he was apparently appointed by the ambassador, that the operative word was *control*, not evacuation, and that Moorefield was restricting evacuation rather than facilitating it. I would be thrilled if I turned out to be wrong. There was only one way to find out.

The more Cor repeated that he'd be back on Tuesday, the less I believed he would. If our positions had been reversed, I genuinely doubted that I'd come back. No one attentive to the emerging facts could doubt that Saigon's demise would be soon and violent. To me the situation resembled a jigsaw puzzle with every additional piece contributing a picture of unconditional defeat. Also like a jigsaw puzzle, the last pieces of the image fall into place much more quickly than the early ones.

*   *   *

Eight days earlier, on April 10, Congress had declined President Ford's request for $722 million in military aid. That was all any rational observer—North Vietnamese General Dung Van Tien came to mind—needed to divine Saigon's ultimate future. Guessing exactly when the city would fall would take a few more pieces of the puzzle. The collapse of the South Vietnamese Army furnished that answer, plus or minus a few weeks. Honestly, if I were Cor I'd cozy up to my wife in Hong Kong and consider myself fortunate that John Linker had stumbled into a young American in Bangkok who believed himself immortal.

This was my fifth day in Saigon, and as more of the jigsaw puzzle took shape, the more aware of my mortality I became.

Our taxi took Cong Ly Street to the airport and I paused in my musings with Cor to see what the old 3rd Field Hospital looked like these days. It had been the largest, busiest, best-equipped hospital in the country during the war. American Express had sent me there in 1971 to update my inoculations. After wandering around inside that busy war zone hospital for a day, I swore I'd never take my health for granted. After my current stint in Saigon I'd never take my life for granted.

Cor disembarked at the civil aviation terminal and I continued on to the dense military sprawl where the Defense Attaché Office was located. The guards wouldn't let the Vietnamese cab inside DAO so I had to get out at the Joint General Staff building near the main gate where Linker and Termijn and I had met General Smith on Tuesday. It seemed much longer ago than just three days.

If I were a foreign service officer like Ken Moorefield and had been tasked with evacuation control, I'd set up shop in some large building near DAO headquarters and convenient to the flight line, but well off any principal thoroughfare on the airbase. I asked for the Evacuation Control Center and the marine guard pointed me toward the base gymnasium, in a cul de sac to the east of DAO.

It was an entertaining scene. Former GIs who had stayed or returned to settle in Vietnam had filtered in from cities, towns, and villages all over the country with their Vietnamese spouses and dependents to occupy this steel-roofed holding pen. Sunlight slanted in from the open doors of the gym, leaving the closed end as gloomy as the understory of a jungle. There was no breeze and the recesses of the building were thick with cigarette smoke, body odor, and an overpowered latrine. Powdered dust billowed above the crowd. Children scampered outside, kicking brightly colored balls and shrieking. The vernacular term for these mixed-race kids was Amerasians, though my preference would have been Vietnamericans. This crop of children was one of the most ethnically diverse I'd ever seen. In a few days they'd just be Americans. Every few minutes a deuce-and-a-half, as GIs called 2.5-ton trucks, dropped off more families. They were flocking in much faster than they were being carried away.

The refugees' common cause came in the form of C-130 Hercules cargo planes operated by Military Airlift Command, Pacific. Each of the monstrous propeller-driven planes devoured a hundred people at a gulp through gaping maws under their tail sections. Enlisted men and women from the MAC flight crews, normally tasked with cargo, served as ground stewards, maintaining order, checking identification against flight manifests, and keeping lines moving.

So there definitely was such a thing as an Evacuation Control Center. By implication there must also be such a person as Ken Moorefield. Logic suggested he'd be at the administrative headquarters in the gym, though getting there looked difficult. I tried to push through but was intercepted by an airman asking if he could help me.

"I'm looking for Foreign Service Officer Ken Moorefield." I didn't know for a fact that he was an FSO, but if he was CIA he'd be posing as an FSO, so it was a safe bet.

"He ain't here, sir, and the vice consul is pretty busy."

"You don't have to call me *sir*, airman. I'm a civvie."

"I can tell you're a civilian by your hair, sir. Just being respectful."

"You say you've got a vice consul here? For what?"

"Paperwork, sir. Most of these guys was just shacking up with their Vietnamese babes. Then came kids—no surprise there. Paycheck for a retired sergeant goes pretty far out in the boonies here, sir. Party's over now though, and the consul's here to fix 'em up with papers. Marry 'em off to their babes and adopt the strays."

"Who's in charge when Moorefield's not around, airman?"

"The regs, sir." He held up a clipboard. "Regulations and the MPs."

"Suppose someone wanted to get their household staff out, or say, employees?"

"No can do, sir."

"Bodyguard, priest, doctor?"

"Nope, nope, and nope, sir."

"Undocumented family of an American?"

"I'd get court-martialed, sir. A year in the brig for every unauthorized person I let slip by. Ain't happening, sir."

"You're telling me that every Vietnamese here will be officially married or adopted before they board a flight? No exceptions?"

"Roger that, sir."

"How about Vietnamese intelligence officers? Spies? Agents? I heard there are so-called black flights."

"I don't know nothin' about that, sir, and I don't wanna know nothin'. Guarantee, they ain't coming through this facility. Maybe somewhere else but definitely ain't happening at ECC. Here everything's by the book, sir. Anybody can't get their papers squared away, we escort 'em to the perimeter and say sayonara. Say, what's this all about anyway? You lose your papers or something, sir?"

"No. I have my passport. But I'm not ready to leave."

"Not yet, you mean. Right, sir?"

"I have a little unfinished work in Saigon, airman."

"My advice, sir: don't forget to wind your watch."

I tried to shake his hand at the same time he tried to salute. It was a subtle disconnect between our two cultures. Nervous laughter reconnected us.

I walked back out into the sunshine and tried to flag down a deuce-and-a-half to take me back into District 1. They lumbered by like imperturbable elephants on the way to a watering hole. I could see the main gate to the south, and the long queue of blue and cream taxis beyond, but I couldn't summon the effort to walk that far in the sweltering heat. The strap of my satchel wore a wet stripe into my shoulder. I turned back to the gym and hailed my friend. "Excuse me! Airman!"

"Sir?"

"One more thing about your regs. Are you required to inspect baggage? Drugs, currency, firearms. You open their bags?"

"No, sir. Luggage ain't in the regs."

"Same for Americans?"

"Yes, sir. If it fits in a smallish bag and it don't leak, stink, nor squirm you can get pretty much whatever you like out of here."

There was a pallet of bottled water parked in the sun at the open end of the gym and I tore away two bottles. I downed one in quick, warm gulps. I turned for a last look at the clusters of sweaty but cheerful Vietnamese and condensed my new discovery into a compound thought: I might be able to leave via the Evacuation Control Center, but it would be my last resort since it couldn't accommodate my employees.

*   *   *

Road signs of every shape and size decorated the intersection between Air America and the DAO main building. I guessed that most of the signs pointed to long-closed air base operations. Updating the signs would be the last thing on anyone's mind. One caught my attention: *Tiger Air.* I wasn't organized enough to have a to-do list but if I were, Tiger Air would be on it. My eyes followed the direction of the arrow down the paved road to the north, toward the active runways. There was a task in my mental backlog that I wasn't quite ready to face and I could have found plenty of reasons for deferring it. Against my better judgment I turned toward Tiger Air, trying to look purposeful, rather than like the vagrant that I was.

The desolate road ended in a T intersection, with signs pointing right to *POL Storage* and left to *Tiger Air.* I figured that if there was any security this deep into the base it would be around the petroleum, oil, and lubricants field. I didn't see anyone but that didn't mean that guards weren't lurking, or sleeping, behind a fuel tank or a sand berm.

I turned away from the POL tanks and walked the short distance to Tiger and found the headquarters building easily. There was a lot of aircraft activity, with planes loading, unloading, taxiing, and sitting on the tarmac awaiting orders. The air was thick with aircraft engine exhaust. A row of ancient Douglas DC-3s, or as the armed forces called them, C-47s, was parked opposite the Tiger main building. I'd been a passenger in these long-obsolete planes and I'd always wondered what they were like to fly.

Now I knew that I could get myself out of Saigon courtesy of the Evacuation Control Center, but none of my Chase employees qualified. If the status quo didn't change, and quickly, I had to consider commandeering a plane. I wasn't going to call it stealing; I'd just relocate it, and the owner could retrieve it in Thailand. It would be safer in Thailand too, so I could claim I was doing the owner a favor. I'd need a plane that could hold a hundred people plus carry-on baggage. My pilot's license was current, but the only planes I'd ever flown were two-seat Cessnas and Pipers.

Flying machines generally have a lot in common, but stepping up from a small trainer to a twin-engine airliner with variable pitch propellers, retractable landing gear, pressurized cabin, instrument avionics, and unfamiliar flight characteristics wasn't something I would attempt absent dire necessity.

But the list of things that would need to change to make it unnecessary to steal—no, to *relocate*—an aircraft was short: General

Dung could change his mind about conquering South Vietnam and go home. The exit visa law could change. Ambassador Martin could discover his backbone. Military Airlift Command could decide to thumb its nose at the State Department and board Vietnamese civilians on its planes. Someone at the Evacuation Control Center could risk life in prison by not checking refugee paperwork. President Ford, who just took over from a disgraced Nixon nine months earlier, could start acting presidential, meaning offer his Vietnamese counterpart, President Thieu, sanctuary in U.S. in return for letting American companies escort their Vietnamese employees out. At least stealing an aircraft was something that was within my control, though landing it might be iffy.

To modern eyes the DC-3 looks like a back chapter in aviation history, not without reason since they were introduced into service in the 1930s and production ended in the 1940s. Parked quietly in formation at the edge of the airfield they also looked awkward, squatting on the tarmac with their tails down and noses angled upward. The engines looked like the bulging eyes of a prehistoric amphibian. In aviation vernacular they were gooney birds. I liked them for the reason Tiger Air owned them; they could take off and land on short runways, or in open fields, and they could carry three tons of cargo. On the other hand, I wouldn't know what my cargo would weigh and I wouldn't be able to calculate the required takeoff distance and speed even if I did.

I wandered among the nesting gooney birds, assessing each as a candidate for the greater good of the Chase Manhattan Bank. Some of the planes were configured with passenger seats, which would have limited my load to thirty passengers. I might have three times that many so I'd need one configured for cargo transport. Of these there were two, both unlocked. I climbed into the cockpit of one with Tiger Air markings and searched for the preflight checklist that all aircraft have in a side slot or compartment, or stuffed under the seat. I found both English and Vietnamese versions in a zippered bag, which also contained an ignition key. This wasn't as serendipitous as it might seem since the air base was secure, and leaving a set of keys on the plane facilitated emergency departure.

The temperature inside the plane was beyond human tolerance so I opened both cockpit side windows to get a little ventilation. I turned the control yoke left and right, watching the wing ailerons wave back at me. I pulled and pushed the yoke and saw that the elevators on the horizontal stabilizer responded. The trim tab wheel was where I expected, on the floor by the side of the seat. The heat finally tackled me so I went back outside and resumed my airworthiness check. My shirt was completely soaked with perspiration. But so far no one had taken any notice of me. I downed my second bottle of warm water.

I climbed onto the wings and opened the caps of both fuel tanks and found them topped off, just as they were supposed to be. No wasp nests in the pitot tubes, bird nests in the engine cowling, or the landing gear assembly. No visible damage to either of the propellers. I pronounced it flightworthy. Whether I could fly it was another matter. The checklist in my hand was four times longer than its counterpart for a Cessna 150. I left the rope tie-downs in place and went back up to the cockpit, pulling the retractable stairs up behind me. I clamped the door airlock closed.

I buckled myself into the pilot's seat and followed the checklist. Remarkably a lot was familiar: compass, altimeter, attitude indicator, VHF omnidirectional range. I put on the headphones. I wanted to listen to the ground controller to refamiliarize myself with the patter. I'd need to know the active runway, how to get weather updates, what air traffic was incoming and what landing pattern they were using. I was pretty sure I could turn on the electrical system and listen to the controllers without having the engines start, but wasn't sure. I clicked the key and the radio came on, and the engines did not. The instrument panel illuminated with every gauge glowing a warm orange. Fuel pressure. Oil pressure. Vacuum annunciator, whatever that was.

I listened for several minutes and the chatter was all military. It was extremely busy, and that was just the ground control frequency.

Aircraft landing and taking off would be on the tower frequency. An aeronautical chart would disclose that frequency but I didn't have one. I took a look around the cabin but couldn't find any. Pilots who flew in and out of Tan Son Nhut regularly wouldn't need one. I could keep turning the frequency dial until I chanced into it, but that would take too long.

I had a strong urge to start the engines, recalling that they were made by Pratt & Whitney, in East Hartford, Connecticut, just bicycle distance from where my grandparents lived. Damn, how I wanted to hear those beasts roar! I was a guy who struggled to resist an idea once it lodged in my mind. Whether it was buying something, doing something, going somewhere, or drinking something, I was anxious until I bought it, did it, went there, or drank it.

The checklist told me what to do with each gauge or switch to start the right engine, but not where to find the gauge or switch on the instrument panel. Flight instructors truly do earn their pay. I found the magneto, fuel boost, fuel prime; I pressed the start switch for ten seconds, as indicated, and the right engine roared to life. Mesh off, start off, mixture auto-rich, right boost off. Repeat for left engine. Smoke swept out of every pore and crevice of both engines and billowed out to an adjacent field. No one ran from the Tiger Air building. No one accosted me on the radio. Nothing. Just business as usual on this disused lot at Tan Son Nhut. I ran up the engines one at a time and watched the magneto needles hover in the green. Two things I couldn't find were the propeller pitch control, which would have to be set on full forward before takeoff, and the landing gear retractor, which would be necessary once airborne. There would be other details too like, say, navigating toward a specific destination. But I'd made some progress.

Another checklist walked me through the shut-down procedures and I was more than a little pleased with myself when I closed the windows and unclipped my seatbelt. As I was leaving, the irresistible idea came to me to abscond with the ignition key and the English preflight checklist. I also found what looked like the key to the fuselage door. My thinking was that the owner would have spares, whereas I didn't even have originals. And if the owner didn't have spares then the plane would definitely still be here if I needed it.

If I were really clever I'd pop my head into the Tiger building and say that Military Airlift Command had asked for as many aeronautical charts as Tiger could spare. That would give me both tower and ground frequencies for every airport in the region, as well as their VHF omnidirectional range headings. The downside was low compared to what I'd just risked, so I did it.

I hadn't figured on someone shouting back, "Who wants 'em?"

Well, *I* wanted them, but I couldn't very well say that so instead I said, "Couple dickhead lieutenants from U-Tapao." That would be the Thai air base where I intended to land.

"Figures."

They handed me six crisp, up-to-date copies. Back on the road to the air base's main gate I stuck out my thumb and eventually one of the two-and-a-half-ton elephants picked me up. The mahout delivered me to the doorstep of the Majestic. On my bed were my freshly laundered pair of socks and underwear. With a little soap, food, and drink I'd be a new man. I brushed the dust off the dial of my watch and decided to skip the drink. It was barely past noon.

*   *   *

My gamesmanship with the obstructionists, both the delusionary and the just-following-orders pilgrims, had led me away from human contact with my charges, the Chase employees. I hardly knew them. I only knew the four officers by name and I knew very little about them beyond their names. I worried that loss of personal rapport might result in loss of empathy and ultimately to loss of commitment. Too much was at stake to allow that to happen, yet the more time I spent with the employees, the less time I'd have to figure out how to help them.

I stopped along Tu Do Street to get a bowl of pho from a mobile vendor. It was rich with beef, onion, ginger, bean sprouts, cilantro, and garlic. I was still hungry after one bowl so I ordered a second. The vendor considered that a compliment and gave me an appreciative, if grotesque, smile with her neon red gums and black teeth. She was chewing betel nut, a stimulant more or less like nicotine. The total cost for the two bowls together was fifty cents. Well, it would have been fifty cents if I'd used piastres purchased at the official rate. But since I paid with piastres purchased from Raj it cost me thirty-seven cents. Hell of a place, Saigon. Shame it was going down the tubes.

I got to the branch at 1:00, and the line was down to about fifty feet out the door. Inside was a pretty rough scene. The ventilation was inadequate for the traffic, with the two small air conditioners unable to expel the solid clouds of cigarette smoke filling the room. My eyes burned, and blinking didn't help. It was a torturous work environment.

Cuong looked as though he'd been waiting for me to show up. Before he could say anything, I said, "Tell everyone there's no smoking in here. That goes for customers and employees. Put up signs. Open the windows. After the smoke clears out, turn the air conditioners back on. This air will kill everyone before the communists even start shooting."

Cuong was talking as I surveyed the employees, all of their eyes bloodshot. I knew before I heard Cuong's words that this was not a typical workday for the branch. "Mr. White, thank God. You cannot imagine the volume of work we had to handle this morning. It was crazy. I'm guessing over a thousand transactions. It's because of the three-day weekend. Customers are worried that we won't open on Tuesday and this could be their last chance to withdraw their money."

"I know you're worried about the settlement taking a long time. You want to close early. Does our banking license require specific closing times?"

"Yeah, our license says we must be open nine to three or face sanctions. But if we stayed open until three, we wouldn't finish the settlement bookkeeping until midnight. We don't have the electronic technology some other Chase branches have. Our calculating machines are all mechanical."

"You're the acting general manager, Mr. Cuong. Doesn't that give you the authority to close early?"

"I don't have the authority to violate the banking regulations of the Republic of Vietnam."

"I do," I said. "You can close at 1:30. Tell the finance minister I took responsibility." That was easy.

I climbed the stairs to the manager's office and the secretary informed me that Pan Am was no longer taking reservations on departing flights. I said, "I apologize for having forgotten your name."

"It's Anna, sir. Nguyen Ha Giang, but I'm called Anna."

I'd noticed that Cor Termijn typically addressed male employees by their family names and female employees by their given names. Presuming it customary, I decided to adopt Cor's convention. "Does Mr. Termijn have a round-trip booked for Tuesday? Will he be able to get out if he comes in?"

"Yes. He's all set. Paid and reconfirmed. You, on the other hand, Mr. White, appear to be stuck here with the rest of us."

"Well then, Anna, we'd better hang together or we will most assuredly hang separately." I neglected to credit Benjamin Franklin for the line.

"Something else you should know, Mr. White. It was only to be expected but our first employee has run away. It is Lan, the cable machine operator. She disappeared shortly after Mr. Termijn's inspiring speech. But do not worry because my duties will be light with Mr. Termijn gone, so I can handle cables."

I was thanking her for her initiative when I noticed the stack of papers in Termijn's inbox. "I guess Mr. Cuong has been too busy with his own job to deal with Cor's too." I had a couple hundred things I'd rather do than shuffle papers. It was too much like rearranging the deck chairs on the *Titanic*. On the other hand, that was what everyone else in the branch was doing, and it was an opportunity to spend some time with . . . my people.

I sat down at Cor's desk and I'm sure my scuffed shoes must have showed under the front panel just like Cor's had. On a typical career path, I might make general manager in another dozen years. I wasn't even sure what a GM did but by the time I got to the bottom of Cor's inbox I'd have some idea. How hard could it be? Harder than flying a twin-engine, adjustable-prop, retractable-gear, pressurized-cabin, instrument-flight-rule aircraft into another country?

My basic view was that if you thought you couldn't do something, you were probably right, whereas if you thought that you could, you stood a decent chance of pulling it off. The first form in the inbox sought waivers for letter of credit discrepancies. My secretary, Anna, said, "Mr. Termijn approves those." I initialed it and moved to the next item in the inbox.

*   *   *

Jackson Dunn said he'd meet me at the Tennessee Bar on Tu Do Street. The New York Bar was next door to it, but unlike the two states, the two bars were carbon copies of one another. Jackson said, "Didn't know when you'd show up so I already ordered my burger."

I noticed a waitress looking inquiringly at us so I held up two fingers and made a gesture like I was holding a hamburger in my hands and taking a big chomp out of it. She must have gotten the message because she laughed and nodded.

Jackson said, "Looks like you speak her language."

"Common language."

Despite its wide-open door, the Tennessee Bar was solid with cigarette smoke. It was possibly worse than the bank, but here nobody cared. Blue fairy lights conspired with the smoke to produce a gloomy ambience. A beer arrived that I hadn't ordered and a girl climbed a ladder to a platform above the bar. She turned her back to us and wriggled her firm little butt and the place erupted in howls.

Jackson said in my ear, "Hard-looking wench."

I wasn't so sure. In my experience most Vietnamese women were fairly attractive. I found no fault with the girl. I don't think I really cared. If she had been the supermodel of the month I couldn't have been distracted from my beer and burger.

The dancer took off her top and her blue-lit breasts joined the throbbing beat. Patrons let out the startled shrieks of rock climbers who'd lost their footing.

Jackson shouted over the din. "Andy Warhol would call it *Blue Saigon.*"

My eyes teared against the cigarette smoke and my vision blurred. Saigon was indeed blue. These were sad days for the city once known as the Paris of the Orient.

When we'd finished our burgers we slouched next door to the New York Bar for more beer and a faintly detectable change of scene. On Tu Do Street you didn't specify the brand of beer because they served you what they stocked. I think I recall reading that the colder beer is served the less able the customer is able to taste it, and the bars on Tu Do had the sense to serve their beer frosty.

A girl in hot pants and a tight T-shirt, not exactly the national dress, sat down next to me and without even telling me her fake English name said, "You buy me Saigon tea."

Jackson said, "It's sugar water. For one Saigon tea she'll keep you company for about fifteen minutes."

Before I could agree, which I probably would have anyway, a waitress set a demitasse of red water in front of the girl.

She said, "You no GI. Hair too long. You political."

I responded, "I'll drink to that." We clinked and took our swigs. I wondered what she'd produce next.

"Maybe not political. Hair too long. Maybe pilot."

"I am a pilot." We clinked again.

She said, "Lowan is lonely girl. Nobody keep Lowan warm at night."

It was sweltering. I didn't think warmth was what she wanted. I said, "Teach me five Vietnamese words and I'll buy you another Saigon tea."

"Word for thank you is *cam on*."

"I knew that already. That doesn't count."

"Word for kiss is *hon*—"

"I know that already too."

"How you know these words? You jerk me off."

"Trust me; I no jerk Lowan off. I want to know the Vietnamese words for radio frequency, compass heading, active runway, negative transponder, and emergency landing."

"That more than five words. You buy me Saigon tea. No money, no honey."

"What's the word for transponder?"

"I don't know."

"Were you going to admit you didn't know before or after I shelled out the dough for another Saigon tea?"

Jackson nudged me hard enough to spill my beer. "Take it easy on her, Ralph. Her parents were colonized by the French. Her grandparents were colonized by the Chinese. Her homeland is a hot potato about to change hands again. To her, America is just another colonial power on the wane."

It bugged me when anyone suggested that America had colonial designs on Vietnam. I believed we'd sacrificed heavily to set up an enduring democracy. We always believed that we'd only stay until freedom became self-sustaining. That's not the attitude of a colonial power. I practically shouted, "We're not colonists!"

This wasn't Jackson's first firefight. "Of course we aren't, but the South Vietnamese suspect we are and the North Vietnamese are convinced we are. Their perceptions are valid. It's all they've got."

The girl whined, "No money, no honey."

"Okay," I said, "you can have your goddamn tea. Do you at least know the word for runway?"

"Shit-god-damn, I no care. You no pilot. You nobody."

*   *   *

I returned to the bank to make sure the settlement was done. It wasn't. At 8:30 p.m. Cuong and his crew were still at it.

Cuong said, "This is work we normally finish at five o'clock. And we're far from done. We'll need to come in on the weekend to manually calculate the interest on savings accounts. It's a very laborious process, but necessary. We can't do it now. Our families have all eaten dinner and our kids are going to bed. We've all been here for twelve hours straight."

I thought they looked pretty chipper. "I really appreciate your dedication, and the rest of the bank will too when they hear about it." If I were them, I wouldn't find solace in those words.

One of the young women, whose name I had yet to learn, said, "Will you take us with you when this is all over, Mr. White? It's impossible that Chase Bank would not help us. During Tet in '68, the People's Army killed thousands of civilians in Hue. We don't want our dead bodies dumped into a big muddy pit like they did up there."

Before she tacked on that last sentence, I'd planned to blame the Thieu regime for blocking mass evacuation with its exit visa nonsense. But the thought of this poor woman shot and rolled into a pit was so horrifying—and she had said it so calmly—that I couldn't offer any lame excuses. What could I possibly say? That there was only a fifty-fifty chance she and her family would be slaughtered? I have absolutely no clue where I found the words I did.

"I'm not leaving without you." I still didn't know her name.

*   *   *

It was less than two hundred yards to the Caravelle, but when I got there I couldn't force myself through the front doors. My shirt reeked of smoke and my underwear, fresh only two hours ago, was already soggy. Saigon was a steam bath. I walked past the Caravelle, northwest on Tu Do. I passed by the buzzing terrace of the Continental Palace and walked deeper into the night.

The school on the left was dark and the museum on the right glowed with the eerie light of maintenance workers. I shuffled to the plaza in front of the post office and found a crowd waiting for the cool evening air. They'd still be there when the North Vietnamese Army marched up the steps and told them what to do next. I couldn't think of a better way to commune with them than buying a single cigarette from a vendor and smoking it with them on the steps under the pale yellow light of street lamps. I gagged on the first inhale but by the second I was a partisan in the crowd's collective desolation. The smoke took my breath away and the nicotine, at some statistically defined cost to my health, lifted my spirits for a minute. Like my fellows I was living by the minute. The long run was too damned depressing.

Behind me the post office clock chimed nine times. I stood up, still restless. The Basilica Cathedral of Notre Dame was directly in front of me. Spotlights lit up the white statue of the Virgin, and pedestrians wandered around the park in front of the Basilica. Old ladies in flowing ao dais glided through the doors of the church and I followed them in.

It was probably a prettier church in daytime, but at least it was cooler inside. The church was long and narrow, and I took a seat in a pew toward the front where the lighting was better and I could see the statuary and floral arrangements around the altar. The old ladies I'd followed in moved to various niches and lit candles and prayed. As small as it was, the Basilica of Notre Dame was unofficially Vietnam's national cathedral.

I tried to stay in the moment and not reprise the stresses of the previous twelve hours but it was too much to wish for. How could I have possibly promised not to leave without the Chase employees? If I couldn't get the staff and their families out would I really stay and face the communists? Suppose keeping my word meant being shot with them in the killing pits?

One of the women praying at a candle station turned to look at me. As she moved from station to station, I could tell from her movements that she was young. She swung her arms playfully and added an occasional skip in her step. When she turned her head quickly, her long hair followed in a swoosh. She did that often, like she enjoyed it, or liked putting on a bit of flair.

The girl sat down at the far end of the pew where I was sitting and briefly kneeled in prayer. Then she scooted a few feet along the pew in my direction. Her eyes were surprisingly bright in the gloomy light. She scooted closer and her face became illuminated by a bank of candles. God, what a cutie! Her impulsive movement and simple, happy expression were more like a puppy's than a girl's, a puppy freshly emerged from the awkward, stumbling stage, and just starting the attention-seeking phase. She slid closer, smiling at me, and was right next to me when she stopped.

She stifled a laugh, as though she'd thought of something absurd. She shook some daft thought from her head and her hair fell on my bare arm. She looked at it as though she was astonished at her hair's bad behavior. Then she closed the last two inches between us until our arms and legs touched. I looked around for disapproving parents but no one took any notice.

She peered up into my eyes and took a deep breath of courage. If she had barked and awakened me from a dream, I would not have been at all surprised.

What she said was, "You fuck Miss Nga, five dollars."

I'd sooner have fucked a puppy. My eyes teared up for the second time that night. She was the most pitiable thing I'd ever seen. I suppose Jackson had been right. We thought we were bringing them liberalism and they thought we'd come to fuck them. Maybe the whole war was just a decade-long misunderstanding.

The girl said, "Short time?"

In the trade that meant quick sex—not a specific length of time, but rather one sexual encounter.

I said, "How much for long time, Nga?" That would be sex all day.

"Not enough time tonight for long time. How about tomorrow?"

"How much?"

She didn't seem sure. "Maybe twenty dollars?"

Her guess was below market. I'd heard that long time was $60.

"So for sixty dollars I could have you for three days?"

Her eyes brightened, though it could have been either anxiety about what might happen to her in three days of nonstop sex, or awe at the magnitude of the reward.

"Yeah. Sixty dollars and you have Miss Nga three days." She hyperventilated while awaiting my response and looked even more like a panting puppy.

"Suppose I gave you sixty bucks to not have sex with anybody for three days? Think you could be a good girl that long?"

Now it was her eyes that glistened. "I do anything for that much, even be good girl. What does a good girl do?"

"Teach me Vietnamese words. Go to a doctor to get a checkup. Run some errands for me. Do a little translating. How about it?"

"Can do! Hey, what your name, cowboy?"

"It's Ralph. Pleased to meet you, Nga." We shook hands on our deal.

Chapter Six

SATURDAY, APRIL 19, 1975

Cuong was critical to operation of the branch in normal times, and he'd be absolutely vital in an emergency. He was a real take-charge guy, a good problem solver, and he wielded his authority without being overbearing. That was a problem in the Third World, where bosses often treated subordinates disrespectfully. I didn't know for sure but I believed the staff respected him. I did.

Cuong lived in the suburbs, though Saigon didn't have suburbs in the American sense. The outskirts of the city were marked by a looser sprawl, banana and papaya trees in front yards, chicken coops in the back, and less reliable plumbing and trash collection. The policing out there was less reliable too, so homes were generally surrounded by cinder block walls topped by broken glass. A car left outside the wall might have all four wheels stolen overnight.

Cuong and his family had only recently moved to a house in an outlying district and he had a long commute to work. By mid-April his drive was the least of his problems because, as the North Vietnamese Army raced in, the Viet Cong opened a front in Saigon's underbelly. The battle at Xuan Loc, just east of Saigon, had effectively absorbed all of the South's remaining defensive forces, leaving Saigon's western and southern districts undefended.

Chase maintained a vacant apartment in the heart of the city, District 1. Until recently it had been occupied by a young American credit analyst employed at the branch, but he had decamped in March. I asked Cuong to move his family into the vacant apartment to shorten the line of communication with him and to facilitate his evacuation when the time came. A one-bedroom apartment wasn't ideal for a family of four but neither was a house in District 10 where the embers of war were rekindling.

I gave Cuong a helping hand, moving his household effects to the apartment and learned that he too took a fatalist's view. He stood to lose everything in terms of stuff, but if things went as planned his next job would be in New York City, his next house would be in New Jersey, and his grandchildren would be born in the USA. It was heartbreaking that the likes of Ambassador Martin and Deputy Chief of Mission Lehmann were so brazenly ambivalent about the fate of the Cuongs and their countrymen. The absolute best Cuong could expect if Chase failed to get him out was four or five years in a reeducation camp, after which his kids might not even remember him. Far more likely, as an enemy collaborator, would be a bullet to the head, an image that would forever haunt the children. I watched as they carefully found spaces for their dolls and toys, as oblivious to the brewing nightmare as, well, as the American ambassador. I wished I could bring Graham Martin to that little apartment and ask him how serving up the Cuongs to the communists advanced American interests, or how helping them evacuate would damage it.

If I were Secretary of State Henry Kissinger, I'd fly to Saigon and replace Graham Martin on the spot with someone who wasn't resigned to Saigon becoming the next Little Bighorn or Alamo. I'd replace him with someone who understood that seventy thousand North Vietnamese troops against fifty American troops was an unfavorable order of battle.

Before I left the apartment, I asked Cuong to recommend a doctor. He probably thought I'd contracted a venereal disease. He recommended Dr. An, who gave employees physical exams, first aid, and inoculations. Back at the bank I called Dr. An and explained that I wanted him to check the health of a young prostitute I was considering rescuing. It was a project he strongly approved of and we set up an appointment for that afternoon.

I called the number Nga had given me, and a Vietnamese man answered. I presumed I was talking to her pimp. I asked for *Co Nga*, which I understood to mean Miss Nga. She came on the line and I told her about her appointment with the doctor. I offered to buy her lunch at the Continental Palace beforehand and she said it would make her happy to see me in daylight.

* * *

After Cuong and before Nga I fit in a little task at the British consulate. A Chase officer who worked in Hong Kong had been trying to get a visa for his Vietnamese wife. I allowed myself to wonder why she couldn't do it herself, but the bank was closed and I couldn't object to a little mission creep. I met with the British consul general, one Mr. Rouse, and tried to get the woman's visa back on track.

Unlike the U.S. embassy there was no high concrete wall out front; there was no honor guard, and its doors were wide open. The hallways and rooms were mostly vacant. There were no filing cabinets, window treatments, furniture, or carpets. Vietnamese wandered aimlessly from room to room. It looked like a museum between exhibits. The contrast with the frenzied scene at the U.S. embassy could not have been more stark. Somehow the Vietnamese didn't feel entitled to evacuation by the Brits the way they did with the Yanks.

Consul General Rouse was easy to locate. He didn't exactly have his feet up, but neither was he harried. Together we sifted through stacks of applications looking for the one for the Chase officer's family. We never found it, but he promised to keep looking and expedite it if it surfaced. As I was leaving I wondered aloud how the Brits got their Vietnamese staff out of the country.

He responded, "The usual way. We put them on aeroplanes and flew them out in broad daylight. Unlike you Yanks we did not feel obliged to ask for permission, which certainly would have been denied. Our staff is long gone. If you do not mind me saying, we British find your ambassador's obsequiousness to this regime most perplexing."

I've always marveled at the way Brits assemble their sentences. I responded like an unrepentant Yank, "I think he's got stress psychosis. He's paralyzed with fears. Physical fear, reputational fear, leadership inadequacies . . . possibly a cluster of fears that have reached critical mass. I refer to Martin and the heel-clicking idiots around him as delusionaries. It isn't until you get down to the third tier at our embassy that you find what I call the realists. There are others, I call them pilgrims, who are just going with the flow and who believe in absolutely nothing."

"My foreign secretary has asked for insights, but we're damned if we can figure out either your man or your country. If you don't mind, I'll pass your analysis upward—without attribution, naturally."

*   *   *

I had visited the inner courtyard at the Continental Palace Hotel often in my first tour of duty in Saigon with Amex. My colleagues at the time had all been, like me, fresh out of college, single, and male. We didn't have much in common other than an appetite for the road less traveled. We mostly held court on the Continental's breezy terrace, facing the Caravelle and overlooking Lam Son Square in front of the Opera House. As fondly as I recall solving the problems of the world with those characters on the Continental's terrace, my favorite place, not just at the Continental, but in all of Saigon, was the café in the inner courtyard. I was six days into my second Saigon incarnation before I reentered my old sanctuary.

It had been a cocoon of open-air civility amid the sputtering violence of war and its resonating sorrow. It was a civilized little jungle, planted with banana trees, flowering bushes, and a couple of juvenile banyan. A few tables were scattered haphazardly among the foliage. Dining there was part picnic and part salon. My only previous experience was breakfast, mainly for the croissants, French coffee, and historical ambience. The courtyard café at the Continental was one of those tempting glimpses of heaven that the memory dares not release.

I hoped that this would be Nga's first time there but I couldn't ask for fear of disappointment. It would be my first time for lunch. I perused the menu while I waited for her.

A waiter approached in white jacket and black tie. "Mr. White? A young woman named Nga cares to join you."

Cares. Sweet. "Thanks, please show her in." I carefully avoided the colonial diminutive, *garçon*, though I'm sure he was still called *boy* twenty times a day.

The waiter took it upon himself to inform me of the hotel's regulations for prostitutes. "You may already be aware, Mr. White, but before you take a woman to a room she must leave her identity card at the front desk. In case of theft, the hotel will know where to find her."

"Thanks, but Miss Nga is a friend of the family and is visiting the Continental exclusively for lunch." As he retreated I wished that I had some way of explaining about the legacy of the Pilgrims in New England, the decency of common folk there, and how Congregationalists only sleep with girls they would be willing to introduce to their mothers. I rose from my chair as the waiter escorted her in and pulled the chair out for her.

She was a sparkle of a young woman. Again, she swung her arms like a marching soldier as she walked into the courtyard, and again she threw her hair about like a model in front of a fan. She laughed from both mouth and eyes. I do not believe I'd ever seen such fresh, clear skin or gleaming white teeth. Her ao dai was pastel pink and her pants shiny white. Sunday School shoes completed the outfit. Overnight she'd also acquired a hint of a curve in her hips, though it may have been concealed by last night's darkness. Daylight suited her.

I ordered the *salade Niçoise*. She, the *entrecôte*. We agreed on sparkling water. Her French was astonishingly Parisian and made my college lit accent sound forced by contrast. She was infatuating. Nga's would be a delightful memory to add to my Continental courtyard inventory.

She ate only her vegetables and asked for a carry-bag for the untouched steak. A pang struck me that her design all along had been to take the steak back to her pimp. She couldn't know yet that my rehabilitation plan for her extended well beyond three days and wouldn't ever expire if I could help it. Nga surprised me by asking me to carry her steak in my leather briefcase. I could hardly refuse and nested it carefully between bundles of twenties, and well apart from my revolver.

*   *   *

When Cuong had referred me to Dr. An, he called him the bank's doctor, though he wasn't technically on the Chase payroll. What Cuong meant was that we had him on retainer like, say, an outside attorney or accountant. My first impression was that he was in his mid-thirties, that he was incredibly handsome, and that his demeanor was friendly and comforting. He was an internal medicine specialist and I pointed out to him that my father was too. His office was a little rundown but, hell, everything was on the left bank of the Pacific.

Dr. An's wife supervised their two cute little kids who played quietly in the waiting room. It was an endearing family. I envied them their happiness and I couldn't help being anxious for their future. I had a word on the side with Dr. An to explain my loose idea to get Nga off the streets and redirect her life. I wanted her to get a very thorough exam, more than his usual pre-employment exam. Dr. An got the idea. I'd pay for X-rays, lab tests, whatever was necessary. And I'd pay in U.S. dollars, not the local chaff that was losing gravitas by the hour.

After the exam, the An family headed out to visit grandparents, and Nga and I went to Le Cong Kieu Street to see about my antique opium pipe. The one I'd picked out was outrageously beautiful, with its amber-tinted bamboo shaft and intricate silverwork. The glass bowl had a patina of carbon from being fired with the little silver lamp. I could picture it on a shelf surrounded by leather-bound books. I'd be dining out on this very moment for decades.

Nga said, "It is not nice. It is old and ugly and smelly. How much do you pay for this junk?"

I felt the merchant's embarrassment. "Of course it's old, silly. It's an antique. And it's neither ugly nor smelly. I've always wanted one of these, and this one's perfect."

"It makes hopeless old men waste their lives."

"I'm not going to smoke it, Nga. I'm going to display it. It's not going to ruin anybody else's life. I'm taking it off the market. Why are you being like this? I brought you here to translate, not to criticize."

"I will find something wrong with it."

"No, you can't. It's a classic. What you see is what you get."

"You sit down and drink strong Chinese tea with this selling-man and I will look-look at this bad thing." Under her breath I heard, "Fucking cowboy."

The dealer was the face of hospitality but became visibly anxious when Nga asked for a magnifying glass. She examined every quarter inch of every piece, as I imagined Dr. An had just examined her. At that thought, I pictured An slowly going over her body with a magnifying glass, and I wondered what that would be like. Of course Nga's body was completely off limits. Forbidden fruit. It would at least be inappropriate and probably illegal. It reflected badly on me that I could even contemplate what was under that pink top. And, please God, do not let my imagination wander to those shiny white pants.

"Ha!"

"You didn't find anything wrong with it. You're just being dramatic. Stop!"

"It is fixed."

"Bull!"

"Come here, cowboy." She handed me the magnifying glass and held the silver tray upside down under the light. She pointed to a slightly discolored patch of silver about the size of a quarter. "This is a fix-place. The lamp fell over and oil caught fire and melted the silver. Such a fix-place makes it nothing. Sorry, cowboy."

I really didn't like being called cowboy. I'm sure herding cattle is a perfectly honorable trade, but calling a banker a cowboy was probably an insult equivalent to calling a cowboy a banker. The girl was intentionally being hurtful. On the other hand, the piece had been repaired and she'd definitely saved me money.

And how did I think I was going to get an opium pipe out of Vietnam? Neither the tray nor the pipe would fit in my briefcase, and all the little implements would be damaged if I tossed them into a bag or a box. What was I thinking? Even if I could get the paraphernalia out of Vietnam, how about getting it into the U.S.? What if David Rockefeller found out! D.R. might not necessarily assume I was acquiring it as an antique.

"Look, Nga, I'm going to thank you, but in return you're going to stop calling me cowboy."

Back out on Le Cong Kieu, under the drooping wires that made the street feel like a suspension bridge, I said to Nga, "You're on your own for the afternoon. I can meet you later tonight if you like. Have any plans?"

"Yes, Mr. White, I have plans. I cook dinner for you. Show this to a cab driver." She handed me a crumpled piece of paper with a few lines of handwritten Vietnamese. "Six o'clock, okay?"

"You could call me Ralph."

"It's hard for Vietnamese to say this name. Because so many different sounds so close together. When we try to say this name it sounds like *Raff*."

"Six o'clock would be fine, Nga. Mr. White is also okay."

*   *   *

I was confused as to what the Mission Warden's job was and I doubted I was alone. I'd asked Jackson Dunn and he said they were just a bunch of dirtbags like him who had nothing to go home to. We pooled our knowledge and found we didn't know one single thing about the wardens. Whom did they work for? Were they hired locally or dispatched from Washington? Were they foreign service, armed forces, intelligence, civil service, police, or just walk-in local hires? Who paid them and were they paid in dollars or piastres? Our best guess was that some of them were ex-military; some were walk-ins; some were spooks; and all were paid, one way or another, by the embassy. Some of them might have embassy passes but none of them were actual foreign service officers. Mission warden wasn't a career; it was a gig. I wondered if the office wasn't designed to finesse the fifty-troop limit imposed by the Paris Peace Accords. Most were street-smart hard men, with battlefield experience, communicating in an argot that was a password in itself.

From a phone in the lobby of the Caravelle I made an appointment with the deputy mission warden. This was my first full day as Chase's only American officer in Saigon and it was time I started showing some initiative, something beyond rescuing hookers. The people at the embassy who were supposed to be helping me—helping Chase—were either unable or unwilling. Attributing classifications, such as pilgrims, didn't solve the problem, except for helping me keep perspective. I needed a fatter Rolodex. Whatever the Office of the Mission Warden was, it had to be good for something more than "I'm Dreaming of a White Christmas" and wind socks on ten-foot poles.

The Mission Warden had set up shop in what was known locally as a villa. That loosely translated as a residential building dating to Vietnam's colonial era, which depending on who you asked, might still be ongoing. Villas were covered in flaking stucco, a look emulated by chic Italian restaurants in Manhattan, but in the case of the villas of Saigon the stucco was genuine, and so were the flakes. The villa's windows still had wavy colonial glass. The ceilings were very high and fans circulated air at about the same desultory pace as staffers went about their duties.

Deputy Mission Warden George White was clearly in the midst of a project, but he forced himself away from it to grant me an audience. We quickly determined that we weren't related. He grew up in New Jersey and in the 22nd Infantry, neither of which were in my family tree. I told him that one of my ancestors, George Cosper II, had fought at Gettysburg in the Alabama 44th Infantry.

He said, "Never heard of him."

His eyes darted from me to the typewriter on his desk and back to me. The body language said he had better things to do than chat, and that I wouldn't get much time to plead my case. I knew his background, but I didn't know whether the 22nd Infantry was an army or a marine regiment. There was a pair of captain's bars mounted in a little plaque on the wall behind him, so he'd served for seven or eight years. He was in his early thirties, and he still kept his hair short. Mine was a little bushy and it curled halfway down my neck. That was when it was combed. When it wasn't it was frightening.

I explained that Chase had moved me over from Bangkok to keep the branch open because our branch manager was Dutch. I dropped the names Lehmann, Lowman, LaGueux, Ashida, and saved the defense attaché, General Homer Smith, for last, hoping he'd heard of *him*.

It worked. I wasn't just another civilian off the street, placed on earth to annoy him. His twitching finger and darting eye stopped and he gave me his attention. I didn't know how long it would last, so I clipped my message down to its essence. I wanted to know what shortwave frequency the Mission Warden would be operating on in an emergency. I wanted in on that conversation, and for that I needed their frequency. It wasn't much to ask.

Nor was I asking solely for myself. I knew I could get out via the Evacuation Control Center, but I had fifty-three employees. Actually, I hadn't verified how many employees I had. Cuong owed me a list. When the branch closed, I was being tasked with evacuating them and their immediate families. That could be a hundred people. That was a guess too. Some were unmarried and some had families. Cuong owed me that list too.

I quickly explained to Warden White that Chase Bank was going to take responsibility for its staff. Immigration paperwork, relocation expenses, temporary housing, jobs. We had deep pockets. Chrissake, I had twenty-five grand in my own pocket. There was just this one tiny obstacle standing between my Viets and America's amber waves of grain, and I hoped the deputy mission warden could just, you know, nudge aside the exit visa crap. I needed someone with the authority to wave me through, cut me a little slack, you know, do the right thing. I needed to get a hundred friendlies through the gates of Tan Son Nhut and straight through to the fucking flight line. The sooner the better. If he couldn't commit to all of that right now, I'd satisfy myself with the shortwave frequency.

A Vietnamese woman came to the door and said, "Mr. White, I need to talk to you now," and she didn't mean me. I offered to leave the room, but instead Deputy Mission Warden George White followed the woman out.

I let my leather briefcase slide to the floor and I examined the room. I loved it. I admired this Captain White and his little office off civilization's grid. I envied guys like him and Cor Termijn who had found full, rich lives in the thriving backwaters of Southeast Asia. I freely admitted to having read too many *National Geographics* and too much Joseph Conrad. As a kid in my little New England village, all I had to do was close my eyes on a scorching midsummer day and I'd be ankle deep in the Mekong River, snagging coconuts off the surface to cut open for a fresh, cool drink.

Envy. I chose the word unrepentantly. Yes, it was one of the seven deadly sins, but I earnestly believed that it had its place. Originally the deadly sins were called *evil thoughts* by the Greeks, and there had been eight of them. At some point, Western civilization deleted *fornication* from the Greeks' list, thank God, leaving the modern seven. I hoped that the next time the list was edited we might discover something beneficial in envy, and mean by it an especially ardent admiration.

The window shades were down and the room was cool. Fluorescent lighting threw bright heat-free illumination into every nook. Like George White himself, his office spoke of purpose. The captain's bars, the American flag, the manual typewriter in the middle of the desk, the rifle leaning against the back wall.

Rifle? Not in a locked cabinet but propped up against the wall right behind White's chair? With a clip of ammunition protruding from the receiver? Jackson and I might have to revise our guesses about what a mission warden was. Civilian contractors weren't authorized to carry weapons. I didn't think foreign service officers were either. Nor was he a civilian in possession of an unauthorized weapon, like me. Mine was a very deep secret; his was right out there.

Something else too! A typewriter on his desk? Big-shot expatriates didn't do their own typing around here. We either dictated to secretaries or gave them handwritten drafts. Then I recalled his furtive glances at the typewriter when I'd interrupted him. There was a sheet of crisp white paper curling over the top roller but I couldn't read the upside down text from my chair so I got up and walked around to take a close look. I might not have recognized the significance of the document if it hadn't been the topic obsessing me since my first conversation with John Linker in Bangkok. It was a list of names, typed in Vietnamese, complete with diacritical marks, on a Vietnamese language typewriter. I lifted the top of the sheet to read the title of the document. In English it read *Flight Manifest*.

My breathing slowed. I stared at the names. My breathing slowed further and I finally stopped breathing altogether. I slowly returned to my chair and asked myself if there was any possible explanation for what the mission warden was doing other than the obvious. This was the subject I'd been researching for six straight days and I saw a mixed blessing in my discovery. On the bright side, I'd just met the guy who had solved the refugee enigma. Here was an embassy insider who had discovered a way of getting Vietnamese out of Vietnam. And yet there was something disquieting about the fact that the embassy hadn't shared that information with me.

George White returned and sat down. He said, "Sorry for the interruption, Ralph. I can give you that shortwave frequency now."

I made a note of it. I was a really good note taker. I thanked him. I didn't get up though. I wanted this guy to say something like, *Hey, Ralph, what a remarkable coincidence that you should visit me at this exact moment! Guess what I'm doing?* But no. He stood. We shook hands. I walked three or four strides to the door and turned to face him.

I pointed to the typewriter and said, "You're getting Mission Warden employees out?"

He looked a little sheepish. "Yeah."

I said, "Think that might be a program I could piggyback off to get Chase employees out?"

"Probably."

"You getting spouses and kids out too, or just employees?"

"Immediate family."

"Appreciate it, Mr. White. Pleasure."

*   *   *

The operator at the Caravelle put me through to the embassy. The switchboard there tried to reach the commercial attaché's office, but no one picked up. It was hard to imagine that Jim Ashida had taken the day off. In normal times he might have spent the long weekend at a touristy vacation spot like Dalat or Vung Tau, but these were not normal times, even for Vietnam. Ashida might not be at his desk, but it was inconceivable that he'd taken the day off. "May I connect you to anyone else, Mr. White?"

Who else was there? It had been Ambassador Martin himself who had assured Linker and Cor that Chase employees would get the same priority as embassy employees in any evacuation. That was the deal when I accepted the assignment. I wondered what would happen if I'd said, *Sure, operator, kindly put me through to Ambassador Martin.* But I didn't. It's tough getting through to someone riding a tiger. Instead I left a message for Jim Ashida to call me back. "Do you want me to mark that as urgent, Mr. White?"

"No thanks, operator. He'll know. Everything's urgent these days."

*   *   *

A block south of the Caravelle was Nguyen Hue Street, or as it was called in English, Flower Market Street. I didn't know if Vietnamese observed the custom of hostess gifts, but I saw little risk in error. What girl wouldn't like a nice bunch of flowers? I couldn't help wondering how often in her life Nga had been given flowers. I watched a dozen cabs roll slowly past before flagging one down that looked slightly better maintained than the others. I showed my rumpled piece of paper with Nga's address on it to the driver and he turned in his seat to examine me and my flowers very closely. A slight smile appeared on his weathered face as he depressed the clutch and nudged the gearshift forward.

As Saigon fell behind and the swarm of motorbikes became less and less dense, a layer of civilization peeled back, exposing a less civilized layer beneath it. I've always believed it possible to cultivate a sort of comfort with the unfamiliar. It wasn't adventurousness as much as simple curiosity.

As the paved road gave way to gravel, I noticed that the cab didn't have a meter. "How much are you charging me for this trip?" It was unwise to give a cabbie unchecked authority but I was literally under his power. I should have negotiated it in advance and would have if I'd known where I was going.

He said, "What do you usually pay?"

Fine. The cagey bugger wanted to volley.

It cost two thousand piastres from the airport to the hotel, and we had already gone twice that distance. On the other hand, he wouldn't be able to get a paying passenger back to central Saigon. That would generate a premium. The thought made me realize that I wouldn't be able to get a cab back either. I didn't even know if I was still within the Saigon city limits.

I said, "Wait two hours for me and take me back to the Hotel Caravelle; ten thousand dong." I didn't think the word piastre would be in common use out here. "Get yourself some pho and some beer." I hadn't checked the exchange rate today, but if it was still 1,100, that would be nine bucks.

"Twelve thousand."

We were haggling over less than two bucks. I said, "Okay." He nodded, which could have indicated comprehension, confusion, or a decision to sell my location to General Dung.

There were little fenced-off compounds all over Vietnam with clusters of temporary buildings that someone's armed forces once used for offices, barracks, warehouses, garages, and mess halls. The compound that the cabbie entered at dusk had a broken gate hanging in the open position. The guard was either off duty or dead. The cabbie again consulted the crumpled paper and deposited me at the foot of an enclosed wooden staircase which even Robert Frost might have had second thoughts about.

At the first landing, under incandescent light seeping through large knotholes, or possibly bullet holes, three women sat on the floor, mincing shrimp and pork and garlic with fearsome cleavers. I said, *"Chao ba."* They responded with *"Chao ong,"* so they at least appreciated my effort. Before I got to the top of the stairwell, I heard one of them say in Vietnamese, *"Nga's cowboy."* Another of them used the word *dep*, which meant handsome. I thought I also heard, "Needs a haircut."

I knocked. The door opened. Nga thanked me for the flowers and placed them on a table. It hadn't occurred to me that she might not have a vase, but then, why would she? She introduced me to her brother. "This is Thang." Firm grip. Eye contact. A little younger than I was. There were an aunt and an uncle, though apparently an unmatched pair. And kids. Just whose appeared immaterial.

I declined the offer of a whiskey, but when I also declined a brandy Nga became upset. What I really wanted was an ice-cold beer. "We lose face if we serve beer. Must be whiskey or brandy. Sorry, Mr. White. We have our customs and we follow them."

"I'll have a little brandy, but only if you find something to put the flowers in to keep them fresh."

Thang gave a crisp order to the eldest kid, who ran out the door where I'd just entered. I could hear him bounding down the stairs. Nga filled several tumblers with brandy and passed them out to the adults.

Nga said, "Drinking all of it at one time our custom."

I pretended not to fully understand but quickly relented. The closest thing to chugging a tumbler of cheap Vietnamese brandy is swallowing a lit book of matches.

When the kid returned, he carried a spent 155 millimeter artillery shell under his arm. The shiny brass casing was about a foot high, and it made an attractive and extremely sturdy vase. Thang handed the kid some money, but I couldn't make out the denomination or what kind of currency it was. It didn't look like piastres.

We sat down on the carpet for a communal meal and they showed me how to eat fried spring rolls, or *cha gio*. We wrapped the spring roll in a leaf and dipped it in a smelly fish sauce, *nuoc mam*. I could have made a meal of the delicious *cha gio*, but I'm glad I didn't because there were five or six courses to follow. One of the courses was a cold beef salad, obviously made with the steak Nga had brought home after our lunch at the Continental. With the possible exception of the fried sparrows, served with the heads still attached, it was a wonderfully appetizing banquet. I'd always wondered why there were so few songbirds in Vietnam.

After the feast Thang called for another round of brandy. In Vietnamese he thanked me for helping Nga. He appreciated the gesture very much. So everyone knew? If they knew what I'd done, then they knew what she did too. She may have been supporting the extended family.

Nga's brother handed me some black underwear and told me that he didn't want a guy with moldy skivvies anywhere near his sister. I was more than a little surprised that Thang was familiar with the desperate state of my underwear but there was a more important message. The black underwear Thang had handed me was the night uniform of Viet Cong commandos. In the vernacular they were *black pajamas*. Then I recalled the odd currency he'd handed the kid. Finally it clicked. Thang was part of the incoming administration, the National Liberation Front. Only then did I realize that nobody knew where I was, that is, behind enemy lines.

Thang said, "I'm going to give you some military intelligence that we want you to report back to your embassy. Want some coffee?"

Chapter Seven

SUNDAY, APRIL 20, 1975

The monsoon season was supposed to be over but a heavy rain had come overnight and it hadn't fully passed as I made my way over steamy sidewalks to the Continental for breakfast. The rain would prevent me from sitting in my favorite outdoor café, but the terrace was not a bad second choice. Croissants and coffee would be the best thing to clear my brain, settle my stomach, and reorient my priorities. At a tippy table on the plaza side, I counted the money in my briefcase. Both it and the Chief's Special were still there and still dry. My experience behind enemy lines hadn't cost me anything.

I called the embassy from the pay phone on the Continental's terrace to find that Ashida was still missing. Dammit! As commercial attaché, he was the best target for my rage. It infuriated me to be left in the dark about the Mission Warden's evacuation planning. I left another message for Ashida. Could he really be taking the weekend off? It was inconceivable.

I hesitated at the corner of Le Loi and Tu Do, and despite the rain on my face, decided on a quick detour before heading over to the embassy. I walked past the New York and Tennessee bars to Raj's newspaper kiosk outside the Majestic. I changed a little money to establish the exchange rate and I did a double take when Raj gave it to me. I'm hard to surprise when it comes to Third World currencies in the crapper. I majored in economics. I'd read about people taking wheelbarrows of cash to pay their phone bills in Juan Perón's Argentina. Raj's rate that morning was 2,000 to the dollar, versus my last transaction at 1,100, and an official rate of 755. The piastre had devalued by 80 percent in two days.

That intel was out there, available to anyone who knew a foreign currency entrepreneur like Raj. By contrast, the news Nga's brother Thang forced me to remember and made me promise to deliver to the embassy was a scoop. I had to find someone in that big white honeycomb who would listen. My first choice would be a realist, my second, a pilgrim. I wasn't going to waste my breath on a delusionary. They'd probably be playing golf anyway.

The crowd outside the consulate gate was huge, despite the rain. Many had children and some carried several days' worth of food and water. The people at the front were trying to engage the marines in conversation through the vertical bars of the high gate, and those in the back just milled about. I was flattered when a guard said, "Good morning, Mr. White. Right this way." The crowd cried out, "Mitter Why! Mitter Why!"

The receptionist awarded me my first choice, nominal pilgrim and stealth realist, Conny LaGueux. As a marine escorted me up to LaGueux's office I recalled that he'd been a commando in World War II, and that he had infiltrated enemy lines in France to support the Resistance against the Nazis. Now he was a bespectacled intelligence analyst and deputy station chief for the Central Intelligence Agency. I loved the modesty of his business card: *Conrad LaGueux, Office of the Special Assistant.*

"Regrets, Ralph, but I still can't help you with your refugees."

It was the first time I'd heard my employees called refugees. The description was premature since they hadn't embarked for anywhere yet, but I liked the word's hopeful implications.

"I'm here about something else. You might know about some of it but I doubt you'll know all of it." He gestured to a chair but I stayed on my feet. "General Dao's 18th Infantry has been completely wiped out at Xuan Loc. Artillery from the People's Army of Vietnam knocked out the airfield at Bien Hoa. That eliminated Dao's air cover, which was the only reason he was able to hold out so long. Yesterday Dao began retreating toward Saigon.

"As of last night Dao's retreat was stalled, with hundreds of military vehicles creeping bumper to bumper in pouring rain toward Saigon along Route 2. Ultimately, the 18th Infantry bought ten days for Saigon but, and I regret being the carrier of the news, the final battle of the Vietnam War has just ended. The only obstacle the North Vietnamese face now is their own logistics. As soon as they patch up their supply lines, they'll send an occupation force into the city. Realistically we've got a few days at best."

LaGueux was immobile. If Thang's intelligence surprised him, he didn't show it. He studied my face but still said nothing.

I asked, "Do you know about the daisy cutters?"

"Not enough."

"General Dao called in a tactical air strike on a concentration of PAVN fighters approaching Xuan Loc, and in response the South's Joint General Staff ordered up two massive daisy cutter bombs. Here's a couple of things you won't hear in your briefings. First, Dao didn't even know that the RVNAF had that kind of ordnance. Second, the bombs missed. The pilots knew their planes would be easy targets for PAVN surface-to-air missiles, so they dropped the bombs before they arrived at the target coordinates provided by Dao. Those bombs killed two hundred civilians." There was probably more Thang had asked me to remember but that would have to do.

LaGueux was as expressionless as a high-stakes poker player. "If this could be authenticated, it would help reduce our commitment to the Thieu regime. It's not that I doubt you, Ralph, but I would have to know your source before I pass it on."

Where would that story start—with a prostitute soliciting me at the Basilica? Whatever I came up with had to be convincing. LaGueux wasn't going to endorse my intel to CIA station chief Thomas Polgar unless my credibility was firmly established. Nor would Polgar pass it on to CIA director Colby, nor would Colby pass it on to Secretary of State Kissinger or President Ford. I'm sure LaGueux believed me, but everything Thang had told me was hearsay until proven otherwise.

I unbuckled my belt and let my pants drop to my ankles, exposing my Viet Cong night ops uniform. LaGueux would have interrogated prisoners wearing these things. I waited for some indication that black pajamas sufficed for credentials. I was relieved that LaGueux didn't insist on a closer inspection.

He said, "What about the bloodbath?"

"Not happening. They just want us to leave. They want their country back. As far as they're concerned their choices have narrowed to capitalist occupation or communist independence. This day has been inevitable since President Truman turned down Uncle Ho's pleas for help against the French." I realized I was standing there with my pants down and pulled them up.

"Keep the intel coming if you can, Ralph. Anything I can do to help?"

I buckled my belt and said, "Just one thing, Conny. If I ever disappear, here's where to start looking for me. There's a girl called Nga and a cadre called Thang." I handed him the note with Nga's address in cursive Vietnamese. "That's my only copy so I'll need it back."

He stared at it for a few seconds and handed it back. "Got it. Good luck."

Hell of a guy, LaGueux. Hell of a guy.

*   *   *

I asked the embassy receptionist for Jim Ashida again, and when she said no one knew where to find him I decided to go up the chain of command to Denny Ellerman with my startling discovery of a flight manifest with Mission Warden employees on it. Ellerman would help me if he could. After all, he'd offered to put me up in his own house if I didn't feel secure at a hotel. The receptionist said he was in and that if I knew my way I could go without a marine escort.

A few minutes later, I knocked on Ellerman's door jamb.

"Oh, hello, Mr. White. Please come in."

"Please, it's Ralph. Not to burden you, but—"

"What can I do for you?"

"I witnessed a flight manifest being prepared with the names of Mission Warden employees on it. Saw it myself yesterday. Asked Deputy Mission Warden George White if my eyes deceived me and he confirmed that he was working on getting his people out. Ambassador Martin told our senior executive for Asia, John Linker, whom you've met, that Chase employees would get the same priority as the embassy's own staff in an evacuation. I don't know how the other Mr. White is doing it, but I would very much like to get in on his program. I'd normally go to Jim Ashida on this, but he hasn't been seen for a couple of days."

"How about the Evacuation Control Center out at DAO?"

"It's just for Americans and their immediate families—wives and kids. They won't board Vietnamese employees. I checked it out pretty thoroughly on Friday. A guy named Moorefield's in charge, apparently appointed by Graham Martin, so they're following strict legal and diplomatic protocol. I don't think that's how the Mission Warden is getting people out."

"Want me to talk to Martin?"

"Thanks, but I don't think so. I believe this guy George White has discovered a channel that Martin might shut down if he found out about it. I'd rather he not know about this conversation either."

"Frankly, Ralph, if anyone discovers a channel, I think it's likely to be you."

"I think I'll take that as a compliment. But if you hear anything about an employee-specific program, I hope you'd let me know."

"Of course. You have my word on that. And you're still welcome to stay at my house."

Here was another good guy. I probably should have told him that Xuan Loc had fallen, but I didn't want to have to drop my pants again. He'd find out soon enough.

*   *   *

Leaving Ellerman's office I stood still in the third-floor hallway for a minute to test my equilibrium. If this embassy was sinking, its list wasn't yet discernible.

This particular visit to the embassy was basically mission accomplished. I'd informed key players about the intel I'd stumbled into about Xuan Loc and about the evacuation of quasi-embassy employees at the Mission Warden. John Linker would have been proud, except for maybe the Viet Cong underwear episode.

John might also be impressed that I had gained free rein of the embassy's third floor, where the top tier of foreign service officers worked, and that I had developed exactly the kind of rapport with its denizens that he'd intended. The guards at the front gate recognized me; I no longer required a marine escort to the third floor; and I was free to poke my nose into anyone's office for unscheduled meetings.

What wasn't working out quite as Linker had intended was the treatment I was getting from the delusionaries, Martin and Lehmann. Linker would have been incensed at the treatment I'd received at luau night. As if on cue, I caught sight of the ambassador's crooked figure exiting Lehmann's office and rushing into a bathroom. He was unaccompanied by a guard, so I followed him in.

I quickly saw that he wasn't there to relieve himself, unless coughing up bloody mucus conferred relief. So the rumors that he suffered from pneumonia were true. He saw me in the mirror and didn't immediately recognize me. I said, "Sounds bad, Mr. Ambassador. Anything I can do for you? Ralph White from Chase Bank. I believe you know me through some of the other guys on this floor."

Martin's head hung limply to one side and he breathed in gasps, expectorating technicolor phlegm into the sink. Strands of sticky gunk lassoed the spigot and faucets. I made sure I stayed behind him while addressing his image in the mirror. "I can't call Dr. Shadel for you, can I? He's bailed out already."

"Shadel did not *bail out*. He got a scheduled transfer to another posting."

Yeah, I wanted to say, with twenty members of his entire extended family. Martin puked blood into the sink. A bright red streak of blood trickled from one of his nostrils. I'd seen deer choke on their own blood after being shot through the lungs, but never a human. It was a desperate sight.

I said, "The bank has a Vietnamese doctor on retainer. Just let me know . . ."

"I don't need a doctor. It's just a cough. Say, what are you doing in here?"

Just a cough?

He didn't wait for me to respond. "You can't tell anyone I'm sick, either. The Vietnamese would take it for weakness and the United States can't show weakness." More coughing.

"Your secret is safe with me, Graham." Using his first name probably violated protocol but I felt us bonding. He continued coughing. I said, "If you won't let me help, at least let me ask you a question." His answer was another cough, so I continued. "With South Vietnam's last line of defense obliterated at Xuan Loc, I suppose even you will have to admit the war's over." More coughing. More blood. "So you could hardly object to Chase closing our branch here and flying our employees to New York."

He turned and coughed blood straight at me, a dragon breathing fire. I backpedaled to the far wall, wondering if I'd already contracted his disease. I prayed delusion wasn't contagious.

He barked his response. "The only reason the ARVN is losing is that Congress has been withholding financial support. Once

they grasp that fact another authorization will be forthcoming."
Cough. Spit. "Look . . ."

He seemed to be searching for my name. "Ralph," I said.

"Consider the flip side, Ralph. Why's Hanoi winning? Because Russia and China are . . . *cough* . . . are sending them massive money and matériel. Everybody, and that includes Congress, knows the ARVN just needs a few hundred million . . . *cough* . . ." He slashed at the air with red incisors as if to rip the oxygen from it. "America keeps its promises."

"Graham, let's say you're right." I had very little experience dealing with the insane, but the logic for immediate mass evacuation was simple enough for a small child to grasp. "Let's say Congress comes to its senses and approves, say, a billion in boom-boom toys for our brave ally."

His dragon eyes followed me. Whether his human consciousness did, I'd find out soon.

"Let's say the congressional committees were to reach agreement in a week and that the Speaker of the House takes another week to accumulate the votes. Then Treasury takes a week to execute the necessary documents to convey the funds to President Thieu."

Ruddy spittle streaked his lips and chin.

"So say Thieu gets his dough in three weeks. He places an urgent order for aircraft, tanks, ammo, you name it, and it takes—let's say that takes five weeks fast freight from the U.S. Total time elapsed from today is, say, two months. Problem is that the North Vietnamese are a one-day march from Saigon right now. A single day, Graham."

Ambassador Martin wheeled toward the sink and projected a half pint of bloody goop in its general direction. He clasped his heart as though bidding it farewell. He said, "B-52s from Guam could be here by four a.m." *Gasp. Wheeze.* Merely a cough.

"Graham, as of now there's not going to be a civilian slaughter. General Dung doesn't want to harm what he considers his own citizenry, and he is willing to stand off as the last Americans leave.

But if you were to call in the B-52s, Dung would hit Saigon with everything he's got. He'd blitz this exotic little place and the carnage would be nightmarish. South Vietnam is over. I need to get my goddamn staff out."

The ambassador's sharply tilted head gave the impression of trying to gain a new perspective on the accumulating disaster. He gulped air. "Whose fuckin' side are you on?" he said.

It was a question wiser than the man. I said, "My constituency is the Vietnamese staff of the Chase Manhattan Bank." He glared back at me, wheezing, drooling blood. At his level in the foreign service, civilians didn't give him lip. I said, "I'm going to get my staff out, and I'm going to do it whether I have your blessing or not."

As I spoke the words, I recognized them as rhetorical. Stealing a ship or plane might be as improbable for Ralph as calling in bombers from Guam might be for Graham. In that moment I may have flirted with delusion myself. Dear God! The two of us *had* bonded.

*   *   *

My Sunday afternoon was free until my dinner date with Nga. I was running out of energy so I made a pit stop at the Continental for a cappuccino and ended up having two. Right across Tu Do from the Continental was a tiny French bookstore where I'd bought novels in the good old days. The old days hadn't seemed so good back then, but compared to the slow-motion train wreck Saigon was undergoing now, it had been downright heavenly.

I couldn't help myself. If I couldn't have an opium pipe, I'd at least get a frivolous French novel to occupy myself if I ended up hiding out somewhere. The one I picked was about teenagers helping a log thief escape down a river with his contraband. The little book reminded me that I had overlooked the Saigon River as an escape route. In some ways, stealing a boat made more sense than stealing a plane. It is a well-known fact, for instance, that boats do not fall out of the sky. John Linker had mentioned my captain's license, but what he didn't know was that I got it to be able to take passengers on sailboat trips. I was as unqualified to helm a river barge as I was to pilot a DC-3. Still, I'd practically taught myself to fly a DC-3 two days ago. So I slipped my dime store novel in with my revolver and bribe money and headed for the river.

The so-called Port of Saigon was only a half mile downstream from the Majestic Hotel and the Chase branch, but it wasn't pedestrian friendly. It was a typical working waterfront, with a large railyard, warehouses, freight forwarders, cranes, storage tanks for fuel, and with deuce-and-a-half trucks racing around like go-carts. I thought a taxi would look conspicuous, given my clandestine purpose, so I hailed a motorbike and hopped on the back.

The gate guard stopped us and I asked about where the rice ships docked. The guard pointed toward a corrugated steel building on the quay.

It might not be quite as easy to get through that gate with my hundred refugees, though by then the guard may have taken early retirement. The motorbike driver and I got along with a few dozen words of each other's language, augmented by as many hand gestures as possible on a motorbike weaving through traffic. I instructed the driver to cruise slowly up and down the waterfront. To an attentive eye it would be obvious that we were casing the joint.

I might have expected more activity at the port, given Saigon's bleak future. Then again, a change in regime might alter this scene very little. Freight would still chug up the river and rice barges would still drift downstream irrespective of who was in charge. We dismounted in front of one of the rice ships and watched mostly naked coolies walk up a gangway with burlap bags of rice over their shoulders. The motorbike driver offered me a cigarette, which I declined, and we wandered over to the rice ship.

The vessels used in this riverine trade shared a common design with those used in the coastal trade. They were small wooden ships with long, curved hulls, and upswept bows. The wheelhouses were aft, where there were also small cabins for the crew. To my eye they looked like the hulls of the old cod schooners that plied the Grand Banks before the age of steam.

I tried to explain to my motorbike driver that I wanted to go on board the ship and look around. Our cover story was that we were considering buying a shipment of rice from them and wanted to check the sanitary conditions. My Vietnamese vocabulary didn't include the words *cover story, considering, shipment*, or *sanitary* so I wasn't sure how much of the message registered.

I walked down the gangway alongside the startled coolies and strode into the wheelhouse like the pirate I aspired to be. Based on his tattered uniform I identified the captain, who was asleep in a mosquito-netted hammock slung in the prop wash of a rattling electric fan. This guy's life wasn't going to change much under communism.

I stood at the helm and checked it for the familiar and the unfamiliar. There were single levers for transmission and throttle, so there was only one engine. There were gauges for oil pressure, engine heat, tachometer, fuel level, a Hobbs meter, a depth gauge, voltmeter, water temp, and pressure gauges. Pretty standard stuff. I'd never seen a trim gauge but it must indicate the weight distribution of the cargo. No radar, no electronic navigation of any kind. That figured.

I was checking out the marine radio when my motorbike chauffeur lit a cigarette, at which point the captain's eyes snapped open. I suppose it was my fault for not explaining to him that for my purposes a sleeping captain was better than an awakened one. But my driver was cool. He offered the captain a smoke and launched into a discussion of—I could only guess—our presumed interest in the rice business. They left to go down into the hold to, again I was guessing, evaluate the sanitary conditions.

The marine band radio had only one channel, which I was pretty sure the U.S. Navy would be monitoring. Once I had cleared the mouth of the river and pulled out into the South China Sea, I'd just ask the Seventh Fleet for a heading. If the compass was inaccurate, we'd all die of dehydration in the barren wilderness of the open ocean.

The electric panel was an ungodly mess, and all of the switch labels were in Vietnamese. I'd just have to flip them on and off to discover which ones were for the running lights and which were for the bilge pumps, presuming the ship had lights and pumps. If I had a problem with this ship it was probably going to be with batteries or the fuel filter. Navigational charts would be nice, but I could navigate visually without them, at least in daylight. I'd just follow the current to the sea. I made a mental note to procure a National Liberation Front flag to fly when we were in the river, then Stars and Stripes for the open ocean.

When my motorbike driver returned, he informed me that I owed the captain 40,000 piastres.

"For what?"

"For your twenty-kilo bag of rice."

"I bought a bag of rice?"

"Yes, mister. That is why we came to the port, yes?"

I happily paid for the rice and gave it to the driver in lieu of my fare. I will say, though, that it is unsafe to burden a 50cc Honda with a 44-pound sack of rice in addition to two adult passengers, and I cannot recommend the practice.

*   *   *

The front desk at the Caravelle had two messages for me. Jackson Dunn would be at the Tennessee Bar, around 6:00, and Nga had a military update from Thang she would exchange for a cozy French dinner at my hotel. It was nearly 6:00 so I did an about-face and headed back out.

Tu Do Street had been more or less a maiden before her arranged marriage to France. As the story went, this had been the disembarkation site of the first French colonists; it was colonial Saigon's Plymouth Rock. During Vietnam's marriage to the French, the street had taken the name *rue Catinat*, after the name of the colonizers' first ship. Widowed by the demise of the French, Catinat was renamed Tu Do, meaning independence. That must have seemed ironic to the little street since she was never more dependent than under the Americans.

Among the art for sale on Tu Do's sidewalks, my favorites were the peaceful scenes of farmers tilling palm-lined paddies with water buffalo. They were oil on black velvet and often featured formations of helicopter gunships against the sunset. No serious collector of Vietnamese art should be without one. I had several from my last trip. On a slightly more elevated plane were representations of bamboo plants against a background of black-lacquered teak, the bamboo rendered in fragments of mother-of-pearl. I had one somewhere. Tu Do also sold practical items, though, ironically, merchandise punctured or dented by bullets sold at a premium.

The Tennessee Bar was its usual self, meaning men fully dressed, women topless, and everyone bathed in the neon blue of early-onset debauchery. Jackson ordered a burger. He thought it was the safest food in Saigon until I pointed out that the lettuce was rinsed in contaminated water and that the only beef raised in Vietnam was from expired water buffalo.

He said, "We just got news from our headquarters that Pacific Architects is closing. Headquarters is worried about a Khmer Rouge situation here, a bloodbath."

"When do you have to go?"

"They're saying ASAP but I can't leave. I'm making too much money."

"Surely they'll keep paying your salary."

"Ralph, haven't you heard how much women are paying to get married to an American?"

"I'm not sure I want to know."

"The going rate is fifteen thousand dollars, payable in gold or greenbacks. For that you get them through the gate at Tan Son

Nhut, get the vice consul to marry you, and get them manifested. Then you come back to the square outside the Opera House and wait for another one."

"I hope you're pulling my leg."

"I got married five times today. Made seventy-five grand. My annual salary's only twenty. No way I can leave."

"You're a war profiteer!"

"So are you, buddy. You're just undercompensated. Follow me and I'll show you how it's done."

I followed Jackson out to the square and we hadn't been there for five minutes before a woman approached us. She'd marry either of us, she didn't care. She opened the negotiations at ten thousand and I watched in horrified amazement. She was a reasonably attractive woman in her late thirties or early forties. She was still quite youthful, with no gray in her long hair.

To watch Jackson, he might have been buying some commodity by its weight. It was strictly business. "Hit my number and you got a deal. Tomorrow the price could be higher." I wondered how desperate I'd have to be to do what that woman was doing. Was her life already a mess or was the future just unfathomably bleak? It was pitiful but Jackson made it almost entertaining. He closed the deal with, "Nice chick like you will be a big hit in America."

I told her America was a great country and that it would be even greater with Vietnam behind it. The betrothed were waving for a taxi when Nga came up to me and hooked her arm around mine. Jackson didn't say anything, but I could tell he was impressed.

*   *   *

I turned my head away when Nga left her ID card at the Caravelle's front desk. It was an obnoxious policy predating the American era and it applied to women accompanying Vietnamese men too, but it did not apply to Caucasian women accompanying either another Caucasian or a Vietnamese man. No hotel dared ask them for identification.

I knew Americans who were married to Vietnamese women. Shep Lowman, for instance, had a Vietnamese wife. I wondered what they did when they needed to stay in a hotel. Did she show her ID card or her American passport? In fairness, I also knew guys who had been robbed by Thai and Vietnamese women they'd taken to hotels, so I understood the need for some kind of security.

If the interior courtyard at the Continental Palace was my favorite place in Saigon, the elevator at the Caravelle was definitely second. It was one of those old-fashioned ones with an accordion gate instead of a door, so you could watch the progress of the elevator car as the interior wall passed by. To get off, you pulled the gate open and pushed open the hinged door behind it. To a country boy like me it was a thrill ride at the county fair. My giddiness amused Nga. She was an old hand at gated elevators.

My room faced Tu Do Street from a middle floor and it had a little balcony. Gazing down, she said, "See the policemen in their white uniforms? We call them white mice." Looking down dizzied Nga and she clung to my arm with both hands for balance. It couldn't be more natural. I wasn't sure yet what I was meant to be to her, but I wasn't going to be her customer.

Her ao dai was sky blue that evening, close to the hazy pastel sky seen though Saigon's smog. Her pants were shiny black silk. She had become a little taller too, so she must be wearing heels. She still had her excited puppy eyes and cheerful demeanor. I may have become a little grumpy from my experiences with the embassy, the mission warden, and the Evacuation Center, and I could use every bit of cheering up I could get. I suppose there was an argument to be made that we were good for each other.

Looking down from the little balcony helped my perspective too. The commonplace absurdities like the "White Christmas" alert, the wind socks, and bullet-pocked merchandise were hints that nothing was as it seemed. Speaking of absurdities, why was the commercial attaché taking the long weekend off?

Xuan Loc had been my tripwire, and with defending General Dao Le-Minh's 18th Infantry obliterated, my mission had morphed. John Linker had given me a double-barreled mandate. The first part was to keep the branch open as long as possible, which in my mind meant as long as General Dao held out. So the first part of my commission had expired. I could close the branch anytime I wanted. With the lapsing of the commercial mandate, the humanitarian one entirely replaced it.

I didn't know for sure, but I think Linker originally saw me as a facilitator. In that view it wasn't Ralph White who was keeping the branch open; the employees were. And it wasn't I who was going to get the staff out of Saigon; the embassy would do that. I shouldn't have to do much more than rub elbows with a few foreign service officers who had pledged to help us. At most I might have to place a few calls.

A couple of facts had disrupted that calculus in the last seven days. God, had I been here a week already? The North Vietnamese Army, as Americans called it, or the People's Army of Vietnam, as Nga's brother would call it, was 36 miles away, not 360. I really don't think either Cor or John fully appreciated the implications. The second was that the little hints of ill will that Linker and Termijn had sensed in their early meetings at the embassy revealed a disconnect between the U.S. government's highest representatives and—how to say it?—reality? Rot doesn't affect every apple in a barrel equally, and I wouldn't say that every FSO assigned to Saigon was bent. It was my personal observation, though, that at least some of the diplomatic corps in Saigon did not count it dishonest to lie to someone outside their fraternity.

My perception led to a redefinition of the pilgrim category. Now it would capture not only those who were merely along for the ride, but also those who drafted in the rank mendacity of others. If I'd realized this a week ago, I'd have tagged them remoras.

Nga tugged at my arm. "Stop looking so angry. You are not so good-looking when you are mad. Thang gave me more news for you but I do not like your room, except for this place."

"It's called a balcony."

"Bal-co-nee."

"I'll take you to the French restaurant on the top floor but you should order something you want to eat, not something to wrap up and take home. Take money home, not food. Aw, hell, it's none of my business. You do what you want."

Before we took our table at the restaurant we went to the bar and ordered drinks, a Bombay gin and tonic for me and a fancy French white wine for her, then we wandered over to the windows with wrap-around views to the north and west. In the early evening, from that elevation, in air-conditioning, with a gin in my hand, with twenty-five grand and a revolver over my shoulder, and a striking young woman next to me, I wondered if life could get any better. Multiple orange flashes of artillery on the horizon provided the answer.

Against every instinct we sat near the window. We would make an inviting target for a Viet Cong 122 millimeter rocket fired from any rooftop in the neighborhood. I couldn't recall having eaten anything since breakfast so I ordered a *salade Niçoise*, a *steak frites*, and a bottle of Beaujolais. I still pronounced Beaujolais with three distinct syllables, evidence I'd learned my French from books, rather than conversation. Nga said she'd have the same. It never occurred to me that the waiter would bring two of everything, including two bottles of wine but that's what we got. Sending it back might have cost Nga face, and there's really no such thing as too much wine.

I could tell by the way Nga picked up her fork that it was an unfamiliar implement for her. "Sweetheart, do you want me to show you how to use silverware or do you want to do it your own way?"

"You can show me." She replaced the fork on her napkin. "Sweet heart! It is a lovely thing to call a person. Is it just for men or do women get to say it too?"

It was too damn cute the way she pronounced sweetheart as two words. "Both can say it." I filled her glass and we clinked. "Watch this. Move your fork off the napkin and place the unfolded napkin in your lap. Hold the fork like this in your nondexterous hand."

"What is that, sweet heart?"

"It is the one opposite the one you naturally use, depending on whether you are right- or left-handed. Hold your knife like this in your dexterous hand and, pinning the lettuce to your plate with the fork, cut off a piece small enough to put in your mouth. Place the knife down on the plate and shift the fork to your dexterous hand and bring the piece of lettuce to your mouth."

"It is like work, sweet heart."

"That may be true, but it is well worth the effort to learn." Her glass was already empty so I refilled it. "Also, you mustn't drink wine as though it were water. You should sip it slowly. You will appreciate it more and it won't go to your head."

"What is that, sweet heart?"

"Going to your head means getting dizzy from the alcohol in the wine."

"I would like it more if I drank more. No, sweet heart?"

"No, just the opposite. The more you drink, the less you would appreciate it." If only I were able to practice what I preached.

"I have so much to learn, sweet heart. Maybe I should go with you to America so you can show me all the stuff a good girl needs to know. Also to say goodbye to you might make me cry."

If I were to let this sweet girl go back to her old life, I would never forgive myself. I had to keep her off the streets, but there was no way I could take her with me. "You said you had news from your brother?"

She sliced an anchovy the way I'd shown her, placed the knife on her plate, and switched her fork to her right hand. "Yes. Thang wants you to know that our side has friends who are high in the government in Saigon and we learned something from these friends today."

If a puppy could look briefly serious, that would be Nga.

"Your ambassador met with our President Thieu today and told him to resign." She brought the anchovy to her mouth and savored it. "He believes Vice President Huong Van-Tran would be more easy for the North to talk to than Thieu. Of course he is right. Any person would be more easy to talk to than Thieu." She placed her fork on her plate and took a dainty sip of wine. "But Thang says that telling Thieu to resign is a little stupid and that you know why."

If anyone was stupid it was me. She had this kind of information and I was teaching her table manners? "Yeah. I understand Thang. The reason that career foreign service officers like our ambassador never give up on diplomacy is that it is the only tool in their kit. After ten years of war our diplomats still haven't realized that guns are the only tool in the communists' kit." I sipped my wine to set a proper example, but if a young lady had not been sitting across from me, I'd have swilled it like a Viking.

Thang's information about a political shuffle was looking pretty accurate. I wondered how long it would take Thieu and his family to leave the country. I hoped Ambassador Martin wouldn't be far behind.

We alternated between table manners and foreign policy through our salads, steaks, and both bottles of wine. I learned a couple dozen Vietnamese words, and Nga was very curious about life in America. She labored to grasp what people who lived outside American cities did for a living if they were not farmers. I had a difficult time explaining how the middle class occupied itself. She decided she'd just have to go to America and observe it for herself and I encouraged her.

*   *   *

Both of us were a little wobbly when we got down to the lobby and we clung to one another for support. She asked the front desk to return her ID and the clerk replied in Vietnamese that I didn't follow.

She turned her face up to me and said, "There was a nine o'clock curfew. He says the white mice will shoot anyone out after that. I can't go home."

To the desk clerk I said, "In that case I'll need another room for the girl."

Nga said something to the guy and reached for my hand. "I change my mind about your little room. Maybe it is not so bad."

After locking the door to my room Nga asked if I had ever unhooked an ao dai and I lied that I had not. Ao dais have dozens of little hooks, very much like the hooks in the backs of bras, with which I had a glancing experience. Ao dai hooks start at the neck and snake downward in a curving line along the left collarbone to the underarm and down the woman's side, ending at the waist.

Without a trace of modesty Nga stepped out of her pants and took off her bra and panties, all the while facing me. Without clothing she looked more woman than girl. I said, "How old are you?"

"I seventeen."

"Don't lie to me. I'm going to check your ID tomorrow."

"Go check while I'm in the shower, sweet heart. I graduate from high school. I was accepted to a university that now closed. I am seventeen for sure."

"Even if I believe you, you're still ten years younger than I am."

"Ten years is nothing, sweet heart. When you forty, I thirty."

"I'm not paying you for sex."

"I know. You pay me to not have sex."

We took quick showers and toweled each other dry. We had an inebriated laughing fit as we climbed into the bed and fumbled with the bedside light. My memory blacked out with the darkness. It's conceivable that we managed a couple of kisses. Yes, I definitely recall kisses.

Chapter Eight

MONDAY, APRIL 21, 1975

When we stopped at the front desk in the morning for Nga to retrieve her ID card, the clerk asked me if I would mind settling my bill. I had accumulated only four days of room charges but a long list of restaurant, bar, phone, and laundry charges. He handed me an invoice for about 300,000 piastres. At the official rate that would be $400. Chase was paying, so no skin off my back, but the official rate was for amateurs. Nga followed me to Raj's kiosk where we bought newspapers in our respective languages. I asked Raj if his dollar rate factored in the defeat of the 18th Infantry Division at Xuan Loc.

"Oh yes, most affirmatively, my friend. Today's U.S. dollar rate is two thousand five hundred."

That rate brought my four-day hotel bill down from an official $400 to a black market $120. Raj tossed bundles of piastres into a paper bag as though they were fish and chips. He said, "I urge you to not remain in Saigon any longer than you must, my friend."

"How about you, Raj? Leaving or staying?"

"Speaking as one banker to another, my balance sheet favors flight. But Saigon is far more delightful than Gujarat, so I'm sure I'll be back. Under communism the trade in currencies is managed by the government, so I may have to join the Party."

I couldn't resist. "Under communism the news is also managed by the government. Your two-dimensional career could really take off."

"My thoughts exactly, but I am also the kind of person the Reds like to reeducate, and yet I am already quite a bit more educated than they."

*   *   *

After breakfast Nga and I walked past the Chase Manhattan Bank and I was surprised, this being Hung Kings Day, to see the lights on and people inside. Before she left, I asked Nga if she could arrange for me to borrow or rent a motorbike. Ideally she would hand it off to me in front of the Opera House around noon. Before leaving she kissed me on the lips. She did it as though it wasn't our first kiss. She remembered too.

I entered the branch from the side door to find Cuong supervising five employees operating mechanical calculating machines. Otherwise the bank was empty, quiet, dark, and still rank with tobacco smoke. These were the only employees working on the holiday. They stopped when I dragged a chair over to their conference table. Cuong tried to introduce me but ran into a predictable problem. What was I, exactly? These five were obviously junior-level, clerical employees and wouldn't even be on a long list for evacuation. My top priority was the four officers. If I could take more out it would be the officers plus six or so department heads. We had fifty-three employees in Saigon, so if I miraculously were able to get ten of them out, that meant forty-three would be left behind. The impossibility of getting all of the employees and their families out was so obvious that Linker, Termijn, and I had never once discussed it.

On my own I'd adopted a different approach. My objective would be to get them all out, meaning all the employees and all of their family members. In evaluating the DC-3, I'd imagined a hundred people sprawled out in its cargo bay. Of course if I could get only a few out, I'd know who to throw to the communist wolves. The logic for culling from the bottom was compelling; the more senior the employee was in the bank hierarchy, the more likely the communists would be to punish them for collaborating with the enemy. Lower-level clericals would theoretically get better treatment. It was all guesswork. Nobody really knew. But the downside of getting it wrong was a lifetime of blood-soaked nightmares.

Whatever story I put on the record for this little group of clerks was going to reinforce the commitment I'd given the little group doing late settlement on Friday evening. I'd told those clerks that I wasn't leaving without them. If I changed that story now, it would get transmitted to every Chase employee household by midnight.

I introduced myself in a way Cuong could not. "I'm Ralph White. Please call me Ralph. I'm a corporate finance officer assigned to Bangkok Branch. A few years ago, I worked for American Express in Pleiku, Tuy Hoa, and Saigon so I have a little Vietnamese, though my tones are not precise. In the last week I've developed a lot of contacts at the U.S. embassy and I'm trying my very best to work with them in order to get all of you out of Vietnam when the branch closes. Head Office in New York cares a lot about what happens to you. David Rockefeller wants Chase to do the right thing in Saigon." I'd exaggerated what I might do for them. In context it was deceptive. I needed to walk back those last couple of sentences, and quickly.

Before I could speak, one of the young women asked, "When is the branch going to close? Do you think Mr. Rockefeller knows about the defeat at Xuan Loc?"

"I don't know. Probably not. But President Ford knows and he has instructed the American ambassador to ask President Thieu to resign. If he does, it might be on TV tonight. Believe me, I'd like to close the branch right now, but first I have to find a way to get you out. The embassy is being helpful but not helpful enough. I wish I could be more encouraging but at least now you know as much as I know."

I left a little out of the story, but what I gave them was accurate and honest. I said, "Mr. Cuong, at your convenience, would you please provide me a complete list of all of our employees, and please include the names of all of their spouses and children."

I was way off script. If anyone had asked John Linker or Cor Termijn or anyone else all the way up to David Rockefeller what I was doing here, they'd have said I was trying to evacuate Saigon's key employees. Maybe it was just a matter of perspective. If anyone had asked Ralph White what he was up to, I'd probably have given a similar answer as Linker's or D.R.'s, except that I considered all fifty-three of them to be key employees. Conceptual as it was, it was still an epiphany. I'd get them all out if I could.

"What are you and your busy little team doing here on a national holiday, Mr. Cuong?"

"We're posting savings account interest."

"You're calculating interest with adding machines? For every single account?"

"Yes. That's how we do it here, Ralph. It's our way."

I really didn't know what to make of it. Were they incredibly brave? Were they highly disciplined? Were they just trying to make the evacuation cut? Maybe the alternative was collapsing in a heap of tears. I opted to find inspiration in what Termijn had called their grace under pressure.

*   *   *

I got to Lam Son Square well before noon so I wasn't too surprised that Nga hadn't arrived with a motorbike for me. I also wasn't surprised to find Jackson Dunn hawking matrimony. When I reached him, he was trying to dislodge some unwelcome company. A young Vietnamese army officer was offering Jackson money to get him out of the country. His collar insignia had two gold leaf clusters, so he was a first lieutenant, a *trung uy*. The guy said he was a medical doctor and could easily support himself in the U.S. Jackson had already turned down $15,000 in gold and the doctor had upped his offer to $20,000. Jackson explained that it wasn't about money. The officials at the airport wouldn't marry him to a man, so it would be impossible to get the *trung uy* out.

The next poor soul to approach Jackson was a young Buddhist monk, in full regalia with orange robes and shaved head. He said communists hated Buddhists. "They torch our temples and torture our leaders. They will kill me."

"A monk I can't help, sorry." Jackson didn't even feign empathy, and he tried to move away.

Before the monk wandered off, I asked him, "Is it a fact that Buddhist robes are dyed with saffron? Isn't saffron terribly expensive? Aren't monks supposed to display poverty?" It was something that had always perplexed me.

"We don't use saffron. We boil the wood of the jackfruit tree. It starts out yellow and gets more orange the longer it is boiled."

I'd gained some knowledge from the monk and wanted to return the favor. I said "When the American helicopters come, go to 22 Gia Long Street and get yourself to the roof." That was the Pittman Apartments, where some of the embassy's foreign service officers lived. It was one of the evacuation points.

A prostitute wandered by to see if her currency had any value. "You take me America, I blow-job you every-every day." Jackson declined the girl's gracious offer and we speculated about how prostitutes would fare under communism and gave up.

We sought refuge from the sun on the shady terrace of the Continental and as we did a beggar took up her position in the bushes between the terrace restaurant and the sidewalk. The wretched girl had been grotesquely mutilated and had to drag herself around in the dirt. Her hair looked like a tangle of rotting kelp. She was a nightmarish apparition and it turned my stomach to look at her.

Jackson said, "Hi Yen-Yen, this is my friend Mr. White."

The wretched thing smiled.

"Yen-Yen tells jokes for one hundred P. Want to hear a joke?"

I forced my eyes to look at her and assented with a nod.

The pitiable, tortured waif babbled in Vietnamese for a half minute, during which a waiter brought our coffees. I was stirring in sugar when the girl stopped her vocal rambling and Jackson laughed loudly. "Give her a hundred P, will you, Ralph?"

I edged over to the railing and dropped a coin into the dirt in front of the girl, holding my breath as I did.

She looked up gratefully and said, "Mitter Why," the way most Vietnamese pronounced my name.

I asked Jackson what her joke had been about and he said he hadn't understood a word of it.

I called the waiter over and ordered a brandy to spike my coffee. Ordinarily I would avoid drinking before noon but it was brandy or tears.

Less idly than it may have seemed to him I asked Jackson, "If you could get out anyone you wanted, who would you take? Let's assume there's no profit to be had."

"Interesting exercise. Maybe I'd take our *trung uy*, our monk, and our lady of the night. If you're letting me snap my fingers, why wouldn't I? How about you?"

"I don't know." But I did. "I suppose I'd take anyone who appreciated America, and trade them for Americans who don't."

The Continental's waiters hovered. The flourescent light created an ether the color of pale sapphire. Jackson asked, "How would we get our hypothetical refugees out? You're the expert. What would be the best way to get people out if the North Vietnamese were entering the city? I mean *exactly* how?"

If I was the expert, Saigon was in trouble. "For people with no American sponsors or authorized documentation, I'd bet on Alaska Barge. It's a lighterage contractor with a couple of vessels tied up at the Saigon docks. Someone's going to tow them out. I sincerely doubt you really are considering a humanitarian mission, but if I'm wrong, I can help you with introductions."

He said, "Don't spend a lot of time on it, buddy, but do let me know if you find anyone licensed to pilot a barge down the Saigon River."

*   *   *

Nga didn't show up until after 1:00, but she had a nice Honda 50 for me. I will say too that she looked pretty spectacular with her upright posture, her pastel pink ao dai, and her long hair streaming out behind her. "Thang say he hope you like his motorbike same you like his little sister. Bring Honda back tonight and Thang charging you only four chickens. You can take me to Flower Market Street."

Wonderful girl. I wished there was some way to keep her in my life.

*   *   *

I sometimes speculated about what the Chase Manhattan Bank brass thought I was doing all day. Cor Termijn probably thought I'd bought that opium pipe and would wake up to a communist Vietnam when my dope ran out. I'm sure John Linker thought I was sitting at Cor's desk, diligently handling his inbox and waiting for the U.S. embassy to deliver salvation. I doubt Henk Steenbergen at Bangkok branch spared me a thought. Probably the same for the seventeenth floor in New York.

How could any of them appreciate that the ambassador and his deputy chief of mission had flat out broken their promises to help us, that the defense attaché's chain of command had been breached, that the Mission Warden had gone renegade, or that the commercial attaché had gone AWOL? How could anyone outside Saigon know that the delusionaries were firmly in control, and that they were insulated by the pilgrims? Or that the quorum of realists was thinning by the day?

*   *   *

I liked motorcycles. I'd had one in college that my parents didn't know about. I learned the map of Washington, D.C., on two wheels. I had a dirt bike in Okinawa, but it rained so often I called it my mud bike. Riding a bike in Saigon made me feel fully initiated. I went up Tu Do, past the post office and the Basilica, and doglegged on Thong Nhut to Cong Ly. Near the embassy I saw an American hailing a cab and when I pulled over to offer him a lift it turned out to be the peace commissioner, Lucien Kinsolving. He accepted my offer and said he had an appointment with the Exec, his shorthand for the executive officer, the second in command at the Defense Attaché Office.

That was close to where I was headed, though I couldn't tell him I wanted to check on the gooney bird I planned to load with human contraband and fly to Thailand. On the way out to the airport, he explained that he'd been asked to *exfiltrate* (a word he especially enjoyed saying) a group of 150 *friendlies* (another favorite) who lacked proper documentation. That was precisely what I was trying to do so I asked to tag along to see what I could learn.

Kinsolving's Exec was Air Force Colonel Max Lamont, coincidentally located at Tiger Air.

The guards didn't even make me stop at the main gate but waved us through from twenty yards away. I accelerated and was about even with Pentagon East when I saw a mammoth crowd of people at the air base's gymnasium, now morphed into the Evacuation Control Center.

I stopped the bike and pointed out to Kinsolving that I'd been there on Saturday and the crowd of Vietnamese dependents had fit comfortably inside the gym. Now it had expanded to cover the entire parking lot. There were probably five times as many Vietnamese as there had been forty-eight hours ago. From a distance it was a surging, boiling pandemonium of humanity. What it was like up close I did not care to discover. I was glad our destination was Tiger Air, another four hundred yards up the road.

I accelerated and Kinsolving said, "It's the defeat at Xuan Loc, Ralph. Everyone knew that was Vietnam's last gasp."

I didn't want to start an argument with a guy who might know how to exfiltrate friendlies, so I said nothing. But if it was true that everyone understood the importance of the defeat at Xuan Loc, then Jim Ashida would have already sent me a hundred boarding passes and a bon voyage basket. Instead, the commercial attaché was missing in action. For a second I feared that Ashida had taken President Ford's order to heart and had already evacuated himself as a nonessential staffer.

I banked the bike into the left turn to Tiger Air and saw that it too had changed in the last two days. The formerly empty parking lot had several jeeps parked up against the operations shed and there was a mammoth silver cargo plane on the flight line. I didn't recognize it but it dwarfed the army's C-130 Hercules and it made my little DC-3 look like a gangly newborn. Gad, was I calling it *my* DC-3 now?

Colonel Lamont was an easygoing character with an Appalachian drawl. He was on his second war. He said he'd rehearsed for Vietnam in Korea. Nice guy. Seemed like a doer. I could see how he'd make a good adjutant to a logistics guy like General Smith.

I listened raptly as Lamont and my friend Kinsolving discussed getting his own 150 friendlies out. Kinsolving's mandate had come from his peace commission minders at the State Department, and had bypassed the embassy altogether.

Colonel Lamont said, "Yeah, we can do that, Lucien. Our C-141 Starlifters have a forty-five-ton cargo capacity so we'll take as many people as you can comfortably board."

That was it. No clipboard of regulations. No vice consuls performing marriages. No exit visas. No certificates of financial responsibility. It was a different universe from the mess a quarter mile down the taxiway run jointly by the army, CIA, and the embassy.

I asked, "What is it about your operation that makes everything so easy?" I didn't have to say easier than where.

Colonel Lamont said, "We're under PAC, the Pacific Air Command. We transport massive amounts of cargo and people every day over vast distances. It's not easy, but we try to make it look like it is. You with the peace commission? Foreign service? CIA?"

"No. I'm a civvie. I run the Chase Manhattan Bank's Saigon branch. Looking to get my employees out."

"Ahh," followed with a look of regret.

"Why do I sense that you're about to say you can't help me?"

"You'd need someone official to clear your people. I can do almost anything for a government employee but almost nothing for a civilian. Who do you know at the embassy?"

"Everyone. I know every single person on the third floor."

"So, get one of them to call me with clearance to work with you. Why not get someone at the embassy to hire your employees? Then I could get them out."

"The ambassador has refused to help me and no one under him wants to make a career-ending mistake."

"That's shitty. Not sure what to tell you. Except good luck."

"Thanks." The two of them started up a conversation, and I wandered off to take another look at my DC-3 across the lot in the tie-down lane.

I was already out the door. "Say, Ralph!" It was Lamont. "You know Bill Madison?"

"No! Should I?"

"Political officer at DAO. Bird colonel. Regular army. Brass balls. Smart. Good contact for you."

"Thanks. I'll go see him. Now, actually. Lucien, mind if I abandon you to Pacific Command?"

"Not at all. I'll get back on my own."

*   *   *

Pentagon East was lightly defended and I propped my motorbike on its kickstand just outside the main entrance. Now I was calling it *my* motorbike. Colonel William Madison wasn't hard to find, but he was a popular guy and I had to wait my turn. The title on his door read, *Commander, Political Section.* As I waited I wondered what such a job might entail and how his position differed from all the political officers at the embassy. I thought military types were supposed to stay out of politics. In fact I thought there was a law to that effect. I'd know soon enough.

Madison's uniform was army olive, in contrast to Lamont's air force blue. I didn't have a preference; I'd met sweet and sour officers in both services. If I carried a prejudice into his office it was that a direct report of Defense Attaché General Homer Smith was unlikely to help me. Nothing against Smith personally, but when four different people think you work for them you aren't really working for any of them. The general's command structure had been breached.

Colonel Madison didn't have a dominating presence. I recall short hair, a firm handshake, nondescript features, and "Please have a seat. Sorry for the wait." I doubted I'd recognize him if I saw him again. I did notice his rank insignia, a silver eagle with its wings outspread. He was a full colonel, a so-called *bird colonel.* His next promotion would be to one-star general.

I lugged my story out again. It was hard to imagine this Colonel Madison could be any help, except that he came recommended by Colonel Lamont, who came recommended by Lucien Kinsolving, someone I hardly knew but called a friend. "I'm trying to get my people out, meaning my employees at the Chase Manhattan Bank's Saigon branch. The Evacuation Control Center won't help me because they only process legal dependents of Americans. Pacific Air Command, over at Tiger Ops, won't help because my mission doesn't have the blessing of anyone in either the military or government. I know for a fact that the Mission Warden is getting its local nationals out because I saw employees' names on a flight manifest. My main guy at the embassy is commercial attaché Jim Ashida, but he's taken the three-day weekend off. As you're aware, it's Hung Kings Day. The Viets are celebrating their independence from China." I'd made my case but I hadn't clarified my desperation. "Colonel Madison, I'm going to get my people out of here if I have to steal a plane or a ship. They are as vulnerable to communist reprisal as any intelligence agent or embassy employee, and those categories have been waltzing onto black ops flights. Sorry to whine but Ambassador Martin has made me a committed adversary and I'm getting very fucking close to taking matters into my own hands."

Madison was unperturbed. I had a problem; he solved problems. "Suppose there was a way to get your people through the main gate to Tan Son Nhut? No promises about getting manifested, but suppose I could provide military buses to get your employees past the main guard post, after which you could shelter your people on the base until Evacuation Control changes its policies, as I believe it will eventually have to do."

It was almost too good to be true. "That would be a big step. Yeah, Colonel, that would help." I thought it through. If I could get my group on the base and could get them out to Tiger Air, then I'd just light up that gooney bird and fly visual flight rules to Thailand. Getting on the base solved my second biggest problem, the first was piloting an unfamiliar aircraft. "Who's my contact?" I assumed a bird colonel wasn't coordinating bus schedules.

"It's Shep Lowman, in charge of the embassy's Internal Political Affairs Unit."

"I know him very well. Why hasn't he said anything to me about this himself?"

"Shep started the program on his own to get his wife's people out. An FSO inside the embassy wouldn't typically try something like this. I'm not necessarily saying it's a rogue operation, just that Shep may not have every signature he ought to. Do me a favor, Mr. White. Lowman's got himself exposed here, so you can't blab about this program and you absolutely cannot abuse it."

"You can trust me." I shook his hand firmly. Now I would definitely recognize him if I saw him again.

*   *   *

I liked Thang's Honda a lot. I rolled it off its stand and kick-started the tiny engine. I'd worn helmets when I rode bikes in America but no one in Vietnam wore them. I wouldn't even know where to get one. At full speed, which wasn't much on a Honda 50, I could feel my hair lashing the back of my neck. I was fine with no helmet.

I passed the herd of people pushing toward Evacuation Control and was simultaneously empathetic for them and delighted that I'd discovered a way to bypass that bureaucratic abomination. My eyes stung from the wind and I slowed for the main gate.

I couldn't help marveling at the sequence of events that led to this euphoric moment. What were the chances that I'd catch the deputy mission warden typing Vietnamese names into a manifest? And then running into a disaffected peace commissioner like Lucien Kinsolving who would lead me to an air force colonel at Tiger Air, who in turn pointed me to an army colonel who knew all about an unauthorized initiative hatched by the embassy's political officer to help evacuate his own Vietnamese family. Where would I have been if any one of the links in that unlikely sequence hadn't fallen sweetly into place? I knew exactly where I'd be: still waiting for Jim Ashida to answer his goddamn phone. I'd have had nothing hopeful to report to Cor when he returned from Hong Kong tomorrow morning.

I noticed something different as I rode past the security array at the main entrance to the base. South Vietnamese Army troops had set up their own checkpoint and were stopping and checking all vehicles before allowing them to proceed to the American-staffed guard hut at the entrance to the air base. When I'd entered the base, there had been only one checkpoint. Now there were two.

If Shep Lowman's operation worked as advertised, my bus would get stopped by those same Vietnamese troops as I took my employees through those gates. If this checkpoint was going to be a problem I needed to know now. A South Vietnamese sergeant

approached me and said, *"Di-di mao!"* I knew that phrase: *Scram!*
The sergeant cuddled his M-16 rifle to his breast.

In English I said, "What's going on?"

"Di-di mao!"

I clawed through my Vietnamese vocabulary to find the words
to ask what was happening, but when the sergeant's index finger
slipped off the rifle's trigger guard and wrapped around the trigger,
my curiosity for linguistics cooled.

In front of the checkpoint an officer led a boy off of a van and
pushed him down to his knees. More quickly than I could com-
prehend, the officer unholstered his pistol and shot the kid in the
head. The shot made a pop rather than a bang, and I realized the
kid's skull had muffled the noise. The sergeant who'd been talking
to me swiveled around, and when he saw what had happened, he
pointed his rifle straight at me. I twisted the Honda's hand grips and
rode slowly past the line of vehicles waiting to pass the roadblock
and enter the base.

The rumors about our allies shooting suspected deserters were
true.

I'm not sure how I had planned to spend the rest of the day because
witnessing that murder cleared my mind of everything else. I passed
3rd Field Hospital without any notion of where I was going or what I
was doing. Passing the Basilica of Notre Dame, I recalled that I had
a sweet young friend named Nga and that I was on her brother's
motorbike. Nearing the embassy, I recalled I had adversaries there.
Even on arrival at the Caravelle I'd only half recovered from the shock.

Gradually I came back on message. Shep Lowman at the embassy
was a realist and was going to help. Yeah. He was supposed to
help get my staff on buses so I could take them to the checkpoint
at Tan Son Nhut where friendlies were executing their own boys.
Sometimes things can be perfectly clear and still make absolutely
no sense whatsoever.

*   *   *

I was supposed to pick up something before I drove out to Thang's place but it wasn't coming to me. It took a brandy-spiked coffee at the Continental to refresh me. How could I have forgotten? Four chickens, the rental fee for Thang's bike.

I'd buy them in Cholon, Saigon's Chinatown, in District 5, and on the way to Thang's lair. My mnemonic for Thang's road was *Looked In* street, since the actual name was Luc Tinh. At stops, my Caucasian features attracted attention, but in motion I was part of Saigon's atmospheric buzz.

The chickens were scrawny, about the size of wild grouse. No wonder Thang wanted four. The vendor was an old-timer whose French was better than his English. It took two minutes for me to agree on the price, produce the piastres, and watch as the vendor suspended the live chickens from my handlebars, two to a side. The old-timer produced a brown-toothed smile when I thanked him in Cantonese. *"M'goi lei."* After all, this was Chinatown. He responded in French. *"Ce n'est rien."* It was a little patch of cross-cultural civility, only a mile from the killing fields at the gates of the airport.

Chickens flapping, I followed a filthy canal westward, hoping I'd found the right filthy canal. *Looked In* Street materialized about where I expected it, as did the abandoned barracks which now housed the families of revolutionaries. Thang was relieved when he saw that I had not crashed his Honda, and he pronounced the chickens healthy, the highest compliment a Vietnamese can pay a chicken. Nga threw her arms around me and said she'd missed me like crazy. She didn't let go.

I said, "Me too." God, she was a lovely creature! It was a crime that her country could offer nothing better than, well, what it had. My own home life had had more than its share of dark moments, and their scars had disfigured me, but my life had been an idyllic romp compared to Nga's. And peace promised little relief considering the moral poverty of the new administration. I ached for Nga and for her whole damn country, and earnestly wished I had more to offer than chickens.

The dark, intermittently lit stairwell leading up the side of the old barracks to Thang's apartment brought Andy Warhol's flickerings to mind. I think his hazy message had been that sex somehow defeated war, but here the two were irretrievably intertwined. Warhol was the same visionary guru who projected McGovern to defeat Nixon. He'd never laid eyes on Vietnam. Armchair peaceniks and armchair warriors deserved one another.

The aged aunt wandered outside with an apron, the chickens, and a knife. The kids treated me like one of the family this time, and I encouraged them by pretending to understand them. They reciprocated.

A black-and-white television with a rabbit ear antenna sat on a table in a corner, the picture on but the volume off. Thang poured me a tumbler of brandy and said he had a favor to ask. He started with, "It's not for me."

"Hope I can help."

"Would it be possible to take Nga away with you?"

"I've thought about it, Thang. I don't know. It's difficult." It was worse than difficult; it was impossible.

"Excuse me, Mr. White . . ."—he pronounced my name like the beggar Yen-Yen—*Mitter Why*—"but if it is so difficult then how are thousands getting out? We see the flights. There are very few Americans here now so the planes must be carrying Vietnamese."

I said, "Thousands got out before emigration became so restrictive. Now both the U.S. government and the Vietnamese government have created obstacles. I can also tell you that neither government has treated me or my employees fairly. Both are getting out what they like to call their high-value employees, but they offer no help whatsoever for my bank's equally high-value employees. Right now my best plan is to steal an airplane and I cannot fit one more person on the one I have in mind."

"Why don't you marry her?"

It would be just too complicated to explain to her brother that Nga was too young, that I lived and worked not in America but in

Thailand, and that I'd be mortified if David Rockefeller discovered that I'd slipped a beautiful young stowaway among the legitimate refugees. If that wasn't enough, I had only just met the girl, and the totality of hours I'd spent with her didn't add up to two days. The agonizing truth was that I did want to marry her.

"Is it because she is dirty?" Thang would have used *defiled* if his English were better.

"That's not the reason."

"Would you do me a favor, Mr. White, and talk to her? Because of you she has a dream about living in America. She is a special girl. You will talk to her, please?"

"Yes. Yes, of course." He wanted me to talk a girl out of a dream?

Nga and I found a room in a disused part of the barracks with no furniture except for bunk style beds with disgusting mattresses. The only lighting came through the door from the hallway. One side of Nga's face was lit. The other had vanished.

Nga said, "I would support myself. I would work and go to university. Can you tell me one?"

I asked, "Do you know what you want to study?"

"Mat-a-matic."

"Mathematics?"

"Same what I said. What is your home state? I can go to university near your home."

"Connecticut."

"I can't say that. What's another one?"

"Massachusetts."

"I can't say that either. What state is the easiest to say?"

"Maine."

"Good. I can go to University of Maine."

"What work can you do?"

"I tutor mat-a-matic. After graduate I teach mat-a-matic."

"Maine is in the north. It is very cold. It snows all the time. You might not like it."

"I do not go for weather. I go to learn. Maybe cold is help."

Like all dreamers she simply willed away the obstacles, and they were daunting. The first of them was getting out of Vietnam. Then there was the little matter of the Pacific Ocean. Of course getting all the way to America and getting through immigration would be impossible. Applying to college without high school transcripts, paying rent, feeding herself. She couldn't even pronounce her major field of study. It would be more cruel to humor her than to discourage her.

"If mathematics is too hard to say, you can just say *math*."

"Math. Thank you. I study math."

"That's better. What happened to the university in Vietnam that you were going to attend?"

"All teachers leave. When the Khmer Rouge take over Cambodia, they kill teachers first. Then everybody with education. Thang says Saigon different, but teachers do not believe. They go to France."

Thang's silhouette came to the door. "President Thieu will give a speech on television tonight. We will eat early so we can listen. The press believes Thieu is going to resign."

I knew the main course would be chicken, but I was pleasantly surprised when shrimp and crab joined the family-style dinner. Rice got passed around and the kids listened to Thang as he explained that this was a historic day for their country. I couldn't follow all of it but Nga whispered a translation. "America made Thieu resign," she said. "He was the right puppet for war but the wrong puppet for peace." The children squealed and Nga laughed. They thought there was going to be a puppet show.

I noticed that the elderly uncle was absent. The auntie sat quietly without her companion. I asked Nga, "Where's your uncle?"

"Snake bite. He die."

I didn't understand a single word President Thieu said. Without Nga I'd have had to wait for the morning papers. But even without a translator I could tell that Thieu was rambling. It was less about his words than his presentation. He was an actor at the pinnacle of his career. Passion, tragedy, polemics, pathos. It was a master class in delivering one's own eulogy.

Nga translated in a whisper. "We defeated the communists. The war was over. They came to the peace talks in Paris with only one thing in mind: to get the Americans to leave. Of course the Americans left. They were not true friends. America stopped fighting and also stopped paying and that is same as desertion. They asked us to do the not possible thing, like filling the oceans with stones. Kissinger signed our death certificate in Paris. America was not defeated. She ran away. It was a not possible thing for us. Magic does not win war." Nga concluded her translation. "Thieu will resign. Vice President Huong is new president." The quality of the picture was so bad I couldn't tell if Thieu was weeping, on the verge of weeping, or pretending to weep.

Thang asked me why America cared which puppet occupied Vietnam's Presidential Palace.

I said, "Our ambassador believes Huong will offer compromises to the communists that Thieu could not. Martin is hoping for a partition of the country, or a phased withdrawal, or some continued American presence, or some other honorable course."

"That is foolish. No, it is a different thing from foolish. It is trying to believe things that can never be real."

"Exactly, he's delusional. It's a good word for you to know. It means believing in something that can never be real. Most of us outgrow it. Unfortunately Ambassador Martin did not, and it's going to cause a train wreck."

Nga said, "We have same train wreck in Viet language."

"That doesn't surprise me. It must be a universal expression."

Nga left to make tea, and I told Thang about witnessing a young man get removed from a bus outside the air base main gate and shot. I asked, "What's that about?"

"You have to understand the way South Vietnamese Army officers think. Any man who is military age and doesn't have papers, they consider a deserter, a draft dodger, or Viet Cong. It doesn't matter which because all are punishable by death. Killing them in front of their families makes an example of them. Are any of your employees draft age?"

"I have no idea. I don't even know who they are yet."

Thang's voice lowered to a confidential undertone. "The curfew has been moved up to eight o'clock so now it is too late for you to go back to District 1. I could have told you earlier but I have one more thing to say about Nga's American dream. It is that Vietnam's future is uncertain. That cannot surprise you, but my next words will. It would be very convenient for me to have a sister living in America in case the socialist revolution turns—"

"Bolshevik?"

"I would be much more comfortable with the revolution if I had a second plan."

"We call it a fallback plan. Looks like borrowing your Honda could eventually cost me more than four chickens."

*   *   *

The old barracks building was plumbed for running water, and as recently as three years ago would have had toilets, showers, and kitchen sinks. In fact it still did but they were inoperative. The only functioning toilet was a squatter behind the building. The shower was a barrel of rainwater and a ladle. Cooking and drinking water had to be carried up the stairs in jugs. The spiders in the outhouse looked like the huge rubber ones sold for pranks in toy stores. The stench was something no twentieth-century American would ever encounter.

Nga and I bunked in the room where she'd fantasized about continuing her education. There were no sheets or blankets on the old mattresses. The windows were open to the elements and free of screens. The insects bunking with us set up a constant whine and buzz. Nga skillfully cast a mosquito net over us or we'd have suffered. Our pillow was my leather satchel. There was no light to turn off.

"Nga?"

"Yes, my sweet heart."

"About those dreams of yours. I will try my best to help you."

"Sweet heart, my dream has many parts. What part will you help with? Leaving Vietnam, going to America, getting into university, or living until I find work?"

"I will try to help you with all of the parts of your dream."

Chapter Nine

TUESDAY, APRIL 22, 1975

Just in front of the main gate to the air base my cab veered north off Cong Ly. I shouted to the driver, "Hey, Tan Son Nhut, yes?"

"Yes, mister. Pan Am this way."

My mind must have wandered. Over the last week I'd visited the military side of the airport exclusively and had completely forgotten about the civil aviation terminal on the north side of the runways.

When Cor had departed for Regional Office in Hong Kong four days earlier, I felt as abandoned as a kid at sleepaway camp. In the interim I'd gotten by just fine without adult supervision. As much as I admired Cor, Chase Saigon was my branch now, and the employees were mine. I was an embassy regular and I'd penetrated the diplomatic, intelligence, and military bureaucracies. Off the record, I'd also stumbled onto a DC-3 and a National Front confidant.

Explaining to Cor how obstructionist the ambassador and deputy chief of mission had become might make me sound paranoid. He still thought they were on our side. I'd also developed at least two evacuation options completely independent of the embassy: an obsolete cargo plane and a decrepit rice ship. I was also solid with the guys involved in clandestine ops, namely Kinsolving, Lowman, and White at the mission warden's office. What I knew about the chaos of the Evacuation Control Center exposed it as worse than useless for Chase's purposes. It was a black hole of regulations, the first of which was that Chase employees need not apply.

If Cor would consider me paranoid for calling out the embassy's duplicity, he'd think I was certifiably insane if I told him friendly troops were taking boys off buses and executing them. Maybe he didn't need to know how depraved Saigon had become. My job was to get Cor back on a plane at his earliest inconvenience and get back to work. Working in my favor was that he wouldn't want to be here once he knew what I knew.

I began briefing Cor while we were still in the waiting line for taxis. "Cor, do you know an ex-captain at the Mission Warden named George White? Deputy warden by title."

"Don't think I know him. Dutchmen are not the Warden's constituency."

"He's getting his employees out."

"Verified?"

"Verified! How about a guy named Lucien Kinsolving? Know him? He's an American delegate to the peace commission, a senior FSO seconded from the Mideast."

"Don't know him either."

"He's getting peace commission friendlies out. That's verified too."

"Crap!"

"How about William Madison, a bird colonel at DAO? He's getting DAO's Vietnamese out. Also verified. If I gave you twenty guesses who was running all this clandestine activity at the embassy, I doubt you'd guess correctly."

"I promise to believe you, Ralph."

"It's the ever so mild-mannered, almost invisible political officer, Shep Lowman. The guy with native fluency and the Vietnamese wife. And here's the kicker. He's doing it behind the ambassador's back. Chase isn't included in Lowman's program because, if I'm right, he can't risk news of the program getting back to Martin, who would obviously shut it down."

"In that case we've got to talk to Lowman."

"I'm going to talk to Lowman. You're returning to Hong Kong. Here's your ticket. I changed your reservation. You'll be getting back on the same plane you just came in on."

"I suppose I should be grateful."

"Listen Cor, all of the stuff I just told you is hot, hot, hot. You and I may be the only American civilians who know that there's a mutiny in progress inside the embassy. I don't want anyone in Hong Kong privy to it, including John Linker, and I sure as hell don't want the seventeenth floor in on it. Just say that we're in very close coordination with the embassy. Nobody needs to know, until it's over, that we've sided with the mutineers."

Cor said, "Here's a copy of this morning's *South China Morning Post*. It's got better coverage on the situation here than you're probably getting in *The Saigon Post*. For one thing, are you aware that the new president, Huong Van-Tran, has offered the North a cease-fire?"

"No, I did not know, but did you know that Huong has less than sixty thousand troops defending the city and that the North now has one hundred thirty thousand south of the DMZ? Cease-fire? General Dung is going to laugh in Huong's face."

"Frankly, Ralph, I'm surprised you possess such knowledge."

"I have a deep undercover source, Cor. History will confirm it."

Cor had a couple of hours before he had to check in for his return flight, so he came back to the branch with me. As the taxi whizzed past Raj's newsstand, Cor asked me what the exchange rate was.

"Twenty-seven hundred piastres to the dollar. Raj thinks it's about bottomed out. How much worse could it get? He thinks that the North will just exchange their dong for our dong and be done with it. Anything else would be too complicated."

Cor summoned Cuong to his office and issued a string of instructions. Most of it was over my head. Cor included one item of mine on Cuong's list.

"Ralph needs a complete and accurate list of all employees, their ages and job titles, as well as the names of their spouses and children. No parents, grandparents, nephews, or pets. Just employees and their immediate families. This is a higher priority than anything else and I cannot stress enough how important accuracy is. You must do this before settlement because there will be no time afterward."

Cuong turned to me. "Everybody?"

I said, "I might not be able to get everybody out, but I definitely won't if I don't have their names. Mr. Cuong, their ages have to be accurate too. I know you're busy but this has to be your top priority."

"Can do, sir."

"Thanks, Mr. Cuong. Cor, I'm off to the embassy now to have a quiet chat with Mr. Lowman." We shook hands. "I'll see you on the other side of all of this."

*   *   *

I expected a massive crowd outside the embassy's main gate and I was not disappointed. The ragged edges of the throng now extended onto Thong Nhut Street, partially blocking southbound traffic. I'd forgotten how to say *excuse me* in Viet, so I just became part of the pushing and shouting. It was humbling, leveling. I joined their scrum.

Again the guard recognized me and let me slip through the partially opened gate. I registered as visiting Jim Ashida, Shep Lowman, and Lucien Kinsolving. I'd be happy to get two out of three.

I didn't bother asking Ashida how he'd enjoyed his extended Hung Kings weekend. The fact that I hadn't been able to locate him didn't necessarily mean that he'd been lying on the beach. No one could have found me either and I'd been very busy. Being honest with myself, it had worked in my favor that the commercial attaché hadn't been around. If he had, I'd have reported my findings and left the fix to him. Without him I'd been forced to scramble and had made a chain of discoveries.

Now it was me bringing Ashida up to speed instead of vice versa. And if he really didn't already know that Shep Lowman was quarterbacking the project, he wasn't going to learn it from me.

I started in the middle, with no preliminaries. "There are well-developed evacuation plans for Vietnamese staff operated by the Mission Warden, the peace commission, and the DAO. Chase staff is supposed to have the same priority as the embassy's and we're not seeing it. I'm officially reporting this as a breach of trust."

In peacetime, calling a senior government official out for a breach of trust would occasion a duel. In Saigon, in 1975, it brought, "I was afraid of that. Let me get back to you."

*   *   *

Visiting Lucien Kinsolving required exiting the embassy proper and going over to the Annex near the swimming pool. Luau night seemed like just yesterday. A nice, stiff, umbrella drink would hit the spot about now. How could I have been so censorious about luau night's figurative escapism when literal escape was all anyone thought about?

Kinsolving's plans had advanced rapidly. No surprise there; the peace commission was independent of the embassy hierarchy. The CIA had arranged for Kinsolving's 150 friendlies to be ferried out to Tiger Air in Air America buses. That seemed a lot of intelligence assets until I remembered that the embassy's medical officer's retinue included twenty family members. Applying the 20-to-1 rule to Kinsolving's 150 friendlies, there might only be eight actual CIA collaborators among them. I could hardly complain; I wanted to take a hundred with me. Maybe more. I was eager to see Cuong's list.

I was also eager to observe this quiet intellectual at work. After all, what Kinsolving was attempting—getting Vietnamese out who were unrelated to Americans—had never been done. Whether he succeeded or failed, there would be lessons for me.

I told him, "I do hope you're aware that the ARVN has their own checkpoint some fifty yards in front of the base's main gate. They're executing deserters and draft dodgers."

"I heard about that. We think we've got that problem licked. We're using two Air America buses for our operation, and we've been driving them in and out of the main gate without passengers several times a day to get the ARVN checkpoint accustomed to seeing them."

"When you go for real, I'd like to join you. Your live run could serve as a practice run for my own."

"It's this afternoon, Ralph. Two o'clock at 39 Le Quy Don Street. I'd enjoy your company."

Damn, if I'd been better prepared, I could have kept the CIA buses after Kinsolving was done with them and asked the drivers to make another round-trip to the air base with my employees. If, if, if.

*   *   *

Two down, one to go—the big one with the mutineer-in-chief. At our first meeting Shep Lowman had volunteered that he had been tasked with evacuating high-value—no, what had he called them?—*at-risk* Vietnamese. We had assumed that he meant critically important intelligence agents who might reveal vital U.S. secrets under torture. At least that's how I interpreted him. But if that had been his mandate last Tuesday it had definitely expanded, and there was no way in hell that Ambassador Martin had a clue. This Harvard Law grad was running a clandestine operation under the ambassador's nose. He'd kissed his career goodbye. He was serving a higher power. He was getting out anyone he wanted.

I had to let him know that I had discovered his subterfuge and that it was safe with me. I had to let him know that admitting Chase into his confidence would in no way imperil the secrecy of his program. It might be a hard sell. So far everyone in his program had been government-sponsored. Civilians weren't even supposed to know about it.

"Shep."

"Ralph. Have a seat."

"Well, I've now been here a week and it's been quite a learning curve. No longer fresh off the boat."

"So I hear."

"Wanted to stop by to tell you how much I admire your work."

His expression remained neutral. It was a marvel that the foreign service attracted men like him. He was earning a tenth of what he could be making in Boston. Moreover he had *five-five* Vietnamese, meaning he'd aced the State Department's language exams and could speak and write the language like a native. Talk about the right man for the job.

I crept toward my purpose. "I met you in a whirlwind of introductions on my first day in Saigon, so forgive me if I didn't fully appreciate what you did. Had I made the effort I wouldn't have been so surprised when your name surfaced recently in such a worthy context." That was sailing pretty close to the wind. This would be where he'd admit or deny it.

"Thanks, I guess."

"It must be a challenge to pursue a humanitarian initiative in a context where it is not valued or, in fact, actively discouraged."

No words. Just a nod of acknowledgment.

"I would welcome the opportunity—the Chase Manhattan Bank would welcome it—to participate discreetly in any such initiative."

Another nod.

"Our mutual friend, Lucien Kinsolving, has invited me to join him on a bus tour this afternoon with some friends of his. I'm looking forward to it."

Lowman's nod was a little slower this time, like I'd crossed a line. Kinsolving was an insider. Lowman had to be wondering how much more I knew.

"Just wanted to go on record that, if those buses were ever available, I would—Chase would—love to take our employees and their families on such a tour."

This time his nod was hardly perceptible.

"Hey, Shep, not to change the subject, but do you like old films?"

"I guess so."

"Just thought I'd mention how much I admired Fletcher Christian's courage in *Mutiny on the Bounty.*"

"Got it, Ralph. Keep in touch."

*   *   *

The Kinsolving rendezvous, 39 Le Quy Don, was a shaded, tree-lined street in a quiet, upscale residential neighborhood. Two buses idled innocently on the side of the street. At the peak of the war, Air America had run a sizable air service and it had a fleet of buses to transport pilots, mechanics, and passengers to and from its terminal at the air base. They were olive drab school buses, no different from the ones I'd seen used by the army, marines, and air force. They were clearly military issue, but they were just plain buses. Neither the license plates nor any other markings disclosed their clandestine ownership, near as I could tell.

Kinsolving was in his element organizing these Vietnamese, none of whom he knew, into disciplined rows to board the buses. In appearance he was one of them, wiry, energetic, excited. The rows formed, the buses absorbed them, the doors closed, and we were off. The excitement trailed off quickly as Kinsolving's friendlies realized they were seeing their homeland for the last time. Most were glued to the windows, pointing out places they knew: noodle shops, motorbike repair shops, pharmacies. A few made a point of staying away from the windows, presumably to avoid being seen.

Among the seventy or so on my bus there were ten or twelve young men of draft age, and the elders made them lie on the floor as the bus slowed almost to a stop for the ARVN checkpoint. I watched keenly as an officer waved us through without demanding to board. The group was so still that I could hear the transmission groan as we rolled up to the main gate. When no one boarded, a roar of cheering broke out inside the bus. From their perspective, they'd survived the most dangerous one hundred yards of an eight-thousand-mile trip.

At Tiger Ops we all disembarked and the friendlies got manifested on air force aircraft. I checked on my favorite DC-3 and was reassured that it was still tied down. Good thing too, since it was still the Chase Manhattan Bank's primary evacuation strategy. I wondered how long it had been grounded, and that led me to wonder if the aviation gas in its tanks had gone stale. There was no one I could ask without tipping my hand so I decided the fuel was fine.

It did give me pause though that the bus, which was much larger than the plane, had been overcrowded with seventy people. What made me think I could get a hundred on a DC-3? Perhaps if half of them were children. I'd double-check their ages on Cuong's list. Christ! Cuong's list! I had to get back to the branch.

On the way back to District 1, I asked Kinsolving why the bus didn't get boarded at the ARVN checkpoint. He said it was a complete crapshoot.

When we passed Lam Son Square, I saw my friend Jackson deep in conversation with a young bridal applicant. No! It was Nga. I shouted out the open window that I'd be back in a half hour.

*   *   *

Corporations, particularly large multinationals like Chase, were very fastidious about lines of reporting, and there was no org chart that had Cuong subordinate to me. I had still been studying accounting when he was promoted to deputy branch manager. He knew ten times more than I did about international banking. The only thing I had on him was a U.S. passport and unfettered access to the third floor of the embassy. These days neither of us enjoyed clear sailing. His branch was a terminal patient and the foreign service was treating me like a subversive. Despite that, Cuong and I maintained a facade of professionalism that gulled the staff into, I didn't know, trust? Complacency? As a practical matter, what were their options? Chase wasn't going to get them out if they stopped coming in to work. It was the same with Cuong. Whatever hopes he had for his family's future would be a lot brighter if he acceded to an authority I did not possess.

"Got that list for me, Mr. Cuong?"

"Here you go. Seven have left on their own, and seven have opted to stay, so we're one hundred three including dependents. We'd have more if we could bring parents and extended family members."

Cuong didn't know that I had pretty loose guidance from John Linker on this. I believed that was because he had loose guidance from Jim Bish, his New York–based senior vice president for Southeast Asia. Jim definitely had no guidance from anybody. The logic for sponsoring only employees was that Chase could easily absorb them into its head office workforce. Their dependence on Chase would be temporary. Parents and extended families could bring complications of several stripes. Also the fewer we sponsored, the less complicated the logistics. In a flat-out emergency this would matter.

"Sorry, Mr. Cuong. No parents. I know this will be difficult for people. I wouldn't abandon my parents." That was only half true.

"In that case," he said, "Here are my two lists. The first includes twenty-four employees and their dependents, for a total of fifty-four people. The second list includes fifteen lower-priority employees and their dependents, for a total of forty-nine people. The total of both lists is one hundred three. This assumes you are adamant about exceptions."

"Thanks for these lists. If you want to make a case for exceptions, you'll have the opportunity later. For now, you've got a branch to run." Cuong obviously wanted to tack more people onto the list but I wanted him to know that exceptions would be hard to come by. On the other hand, I didn't want to be a jerk. "Mr. Cuong, you may close today at any time you think necessary to complete the settlement and get it in the diplomatic pouch."

"Thanks, Mr. White." He couldn't pronounce Ralph either. "One more thing. Here is Mrs. Ho Thi Bach-Mai's home address. She did not come to work today. I suggest you try to find her and talk to her in person." He ran down the stairs, deeper into the hull of his sinking ship.

God help us! One hundred three people? The DC-3 was designed for a quarter of that number. Even with the seats removed for a cargo configuration, and even considering how skinny Vietnamese were and how doll-sized their children, it was too many. What about luggage? Ugh! And Cuong wanted to add more? Maybe a spiked coffee with friends would inspire me.

*   *   *

The Saigon Post was hopeless but I had to read it defensively since if there was anything in it of value it would be embarrassing not to know. There was always a chance that the new Huong administration had relaxed press censorship. I stopped at the news kiosk for a paper and, as long as I was there, inquired about the exchange rate. Raj was quoting 2,800, so I picked up $20 worth of piastres to cover expenses.

I hadn't quite reached Lam Son Square when a police van stopped and a couple of white mice stepped out, blocking my path. "*Chao ong,*" I said, as casually as circumstances permitted. Basically, "Hello, guys."

One of them pointed to the door of the van and said, "Please, mister."

This was trouble. When you get arrested for nothing in Southeast Asia, it's a shakedown. They take you to a small police station off the beaten track and demand money. Depending on what acting school the rodents attended, it could be harrowing, hilarious, or downright frightening. Old Asia hands knew what they were up against and settled in for the long haul. The worst thing you could do was to be in a hurry because that sent the message that you'd pay up for your freedom. The smart move was to relax, settle in, offer them smokes, and tell them how much you admire their delightful country. That had always worked for me in Malaysia, Thailand, and in the Central Highlands of Vietnam only a few years ago. The difference this time was that I happened to be carrying more money than they'd make in a lifetime. I also had a fiendishly effective five-shot antipersonnel device courtesy of Smith & Wesson.

The general rule when you're outnumbered is to start shooting before you need to. That way you can knock two or three adversaries out of the fight before they realize it's a fight. This reduces the odds against you, but it's a split-second decision right up front, and once the moment passes, it's advantage white mice.

Honestly, if it had just been me, I may well have taken the low road. But as of a few minutes ago I had acquired 103 dependents. If I went into hiding, or fled for the Evacuation Control Center on my own, my reception in Hong Kong, New York, and St. Peter's Gate would definitely suffer. And, really, what was the downside of going meekly? They'd rob me of the twenty-five grand, which wasn't mine anyway, and they'd take my revolver. Plenty of people live perfectly normal lives without concealed weapons. All the buggers probably wanted was twenty bucks apiece anyway. It might cost me a wasted hour or two.

I stepped into the van and sat down. In less than three turns I was in unfamiliar streets. In three more turns it became an unfamiliar city. The police station was an old French villa and it was rank with mildew and urine. The white mice either knew who I was already or didn't care, because they hadn't asked. In a tactic I didn't see coming they just locked me in a cell and went away. Maybe they were thinking forty bucks apiece.

I didn't really have time for this shakedown crap. I didn't have an agenda, as such, but I definitely had a task backlog. First, I needed to circle back to Jim Ashida about the embassy's duplicity. Then, I needed to track down Bach-Mai to see if she'd defected on her own or had just gone missing. If at all possible, I had to figure out a way to help Nga. I needed to find out why the ARVN were executing guys on some buses and letting other buses pass unmolested. I needed Shep Lowman and his gang of mutineers to accept me as a dues-paying member and tell me exactly how embassy employees were getting exfiltrated. Also there were several things about flying a DC-3 that I couldn't teach myself—navigation, for starters. Nothing on my list was going to get checked off while I languished in jail. I sat cross-legged on the concrete floor, my back to the plaster wall, figuring concrete would be less likely than the mattress to be infested with bedbugs, fleas, ticks, and lice.

My thoughts slowed and eventually stopped, though I don't think I'd call it sleep, and I didn't know how long it was. I was flat on my back on the concrete when a door banged open and two guys armed with rifles came in. This was pretty far outside the usual shakedown playbook, and I would be less than honest if I didn't admit to a flash of anxiety. My gun was in my bag and would take about fifteen seconds to deploy. Those rifles wouldn't take more than one second. Even if I miraculously won the gunfight, I'd still be locked in a cell. I sat upright, then stood.

I'm far from a firearms expert but I've always had a keen grasp of the obvious, and those rifles were both familiar and strange at the same time. They had wooden buttstocks and fore ends, distinctively curved magazines, and gas-return tubes above their barrels. The front sights were hooded to shield them from the abuse of jungle warfare. They were Type 56s, Chinese-made copies of the Russian AK-47 tactical rifle. These weren't just bad guys; they were the enemy. My real problem though was context. These guys weren't supposed to be in a police station in central Saigon. They were Viet Cong.

The white mouse chief came in with the keys and opened my cell. He said, "Xin loi."

I knew that phrase. He was apologizing. Then I noticed his gun was missing from his holster. The VC had disarmed him. Worked for me.

Nga was waiting for me at the door. "I saw them pick you up. These are my brother's men. You help me. I help you."

If a brandied coffee had made sense before my stint in jail, it made even more now.

*   *   *

I might not have chosen to introduce Jackson and Nga. He was too handsome and she was too needy. But now that they'd met while waiting for me at Lam Son Square, I'd have to make an omelet with the broken eggs.

Jackson volunteered some news. He'd discovered that a barge owned by Alaska Barge had been abandoned at Saigon harbor. He'd developed a plan to sell passage on the barge to people he either wasn't able to marry, say Buddhist monks and women who couldn't afford his marriage fee. "Demand is high for a discount service like this. I bet I could get a thousand passengers if I handed out flyers in the crowd outside the embassy. None of those people are going to escape on helicopters and I can get all of them out on Alaska Barge."

"You amaze me, Jackson. I had no idea you could drive a barge."

"I don't need to. There's a guy worked for USAID in Da Nang, named Bob Lanigan. He helped people evacuate on barges up there so he's got some experience. He's in Saigon now and I talked to him about it. He says he can take hundreds of people."

"Does USAID know you're charging admission? Does Lanigan know?"

"Let's just call my plan a work in progress. Lots of details yet to be ironed out. Stay tuned, as they say."

"Have you mentioned this work in progress to my friend Nga?"

"I was just about to mention that particular detail, anticipating your interest. Now, before you say anything, let me go on record that I am aware that the two of you are, in some sense involved, and I fully respect that. As such, I'd be willing to quote her a highly discounted fare. You'd need to keep it quiet, Ralph. I wouldn't want the crowd at the embassy to know about my friends and family fare."

"If Lanigan is with USAID, he isn't charging anything. Why wouldn't I just line up Nga's passage through him?"

"Right. Now let's just say that, as an ultra-special accommodation to you, I could overlook the matter of a fare in the case of your young beauty. I'm sure Mr. Lanigan has enough on his plate without having to dither with the nuts and bolts of fare schedules, et cetera, et cetera."

"And were I to run into this Mr. Lanigan, I wouldn't have to mention my young beauty? She's in your capable hands?"

"She's as good as out of here already."

"And you wouldn't accept Nga's money even if she offered?"

"Just so, buddy."

*　　*　　*

As pilgrims go, Jim Ashida was a very decent guy. But no one rises to the rank of commercial attaché in a large embassy like Saigon by demonstrating independent initiative. It's a party line job and my strong impression was that Jim was a party line guy. He was a conduit for information, not an originator. Moreover, I was an outsider and he'd tell me only what I was authorized to hear.

I rapped on his door jamb and he looked up. "Hi, Jim. Got a minute?" I wondered how many members of the U.S. business community were still here and how many of them wandered freely around the embassy the way I did. I doubted there were more than fifty of us.

"Oh, Ralph. Please come in."

Before I'd even taken a seat, he started his story. It sounded rehearsed.

"The Department of Justice has authorized the entry into the United States of one hundred thirty thousand Vietnamese nationals. Thought you'd like the sound of that."

Ashida hadn't thought it through. He was just regurgitating the contents of some diplo cable that had crossed his desk. "That's great, but did Justice give guidance on how to get even one Vietnamese out of Vietnam, let alone a hundred thirty thousand? Sort of a snafu, isn't it?" I liked the word snafu, a gentrified acronym for *situation normal, all fucked up.* "Think about it, Jim, I've gotta get 'em out before I can get 'em in."

"There's more."

I hoped *more* would include how Kinsolving, Colonel Madison, and the Mission Warden were getting their government employees out. That was what he'd promised to help me with, or had he forgotten?

"It's big, Ralph. In meetings which I myself have attended, I have become aware that the CIA is cooperating with First National City Bank to bring in a chartered plane tomorrow afternoon to evacuate their staff. My advice to you would be to get David Rockefeller to ask CIA director William Colby to authorize a similar accommodation for Chase."

He looked like a kid who'd just cribbed the answers to an exam. At the eleventh hour, disaster would be narrowly averted. There was going to be a happy ending. He knew a guy with the answers to the exam. Citibank was out front on this one, as usual.

But again Ashida hadn't thought it through. Ambassador Martin couldn't possibly have blessed such an operation. He didn't want any Vietnamese to get out. Nor would the Huong administration have approved it. The air traffic controllers at Tan Son Nhut would never permit a privately chartered flight to land. Citi didn't understand the situation on the ground because they didn't have any expatriates left in Saigon. Their local Vietnamese staff had probably phoned Citibank Hong Kong and said, "Hey, just send us a plane." It wasn't an insane idea, just painfully ill informed. If the CIA truly had been involved, which I doubted, they'd probably just said, "No harm in trying."

I wasn't going to pop Ashida's bubble. "Thanks, Jim. I'll have Rockefeller get right on it." The intent was facetious, but Ashida missed the jibe.

*   *   *

I preferred the Continental for breakfast and drinks, but I liked the Caravelle for dinner. It was home. My plan upon checking into the hotel had been to work my way through the menu, but I always ended up ordering the same thing: peppercorn steak and a bottle of Beaujolais. I tuned up my French accent with the older Vietnamese waiters.

I rarely phoned my real home back in Litchfield, Connecticut. In fact I never had. My excuse was that my day was their night. Plus, there was a fifty-fifty risk that my father might pick up the phone.

After steak and wine on Tuesday, April 22, 1975, I broke tradition and asked the front desk to place an international call for me. They said they'd contact me when it went through. They meant *if* it went through. I timed the call to catch my mother at work in New Milford.

"Hi, Mother."

"Ralph? My God! Where are you?"

"Saigon."

"Why doesn't that surprise me?"

"I'm on a temporary assignment to close Chase's branch in Saigon. Hey, Mom, I have a favor to ask. A friend of mine, a Vietnamese refugee, needs a place to live until she gets into college. Suppose you could put her up in my room? Maybe also help her with the admissions procedures? She's a mathematician but, because of the war and all, she won't have her high school transcripts, so there might be complications."

"Of course. What's her name?"

"It's Nga. You'll like her."

"Happy to help. When would she come?"

"Maybe a couple of weeks."

"Ralph, your father and I are getting divorced."

"Finally."

"Yeah."

"You'll be far better off, Mother. He's an ogre."

"Tell me about it."

"Gotta go now. I love you very much."

"I love you too, Ralph. Be safe."

Chapter Ten

WEDNESDAY, APRIL 23, 1975

Anyone stalking me in Saigon could depend on my wandering into their crosshairs at a handful of places: the U.S. embassy, the Hotel Continental, Lam Son Square, Chase's branch on Ben Bach Dang, the Caravelle Hotel's restaurant, the news kiosk outside the Majestic Hotel, or at the Defense Attaché Office at Tan Son Nhut air base. Creatures of habit are easily intercepted. Late in the day another good bet might be the Tennessee and New York bars on Tu Do Street.

My morning routine was especially predictable: newspaper and piastres at Raj's kiosk, followed by a croissant and cappuccino in the Continental's inner courtyard. If I deviated, it might be for a second croissant. I was pleasantly surprised this morning to find Nga and her brother Thang seated at one of the little round tables in the Continental's inner sanctum. They'd already ordered my breakfast. I wouldn't need my paper; Thang was better informed than *The Saigon Post*.

Nga kissed me on the cheek. I said, "*Cam on* for rescuing me from the white mice." My tones were comically flat but she and Thang would understand *thank you*.

He said, "They are little men. The big ones are worse. In capitalism every man and every woman has a price. Do you know the price we have had to pay for national liberation?"

"I probably should know but I do not."

"Three million dead, including both the North and the South. *Xin loi* if I spoiled your appetite. I only mention it to point a light on America's mere fifty-eight thousand dead."

"You're here for something else. Last time you gave me intel to pass along to the embassy. Is that it?"

"The North Vietnamese have a hundred thousand battle-hardened troops surrounding Saigon. We lost five thousand at Xuan Loc."

We meant *them*. The number didn't surprise me, though I couldn't visualize what a force of 100,000 men would look like. "Does America know that yet?"

"I don't know. But you could not know yet that Bien Hoa fell without a fight. That is just twenty miles away. Saigon is now completely undefended. The body counting is over."

"Unless Ambassador Martin instructs our marines to put up a fight."

"That would be a terrible mistake."

"Yet perfectly in character for him."

Thang said, "Where is Tulane University?"

Nothing Thang said now could surprise me. "I believe it's in New Orleans, in the state of Louisiana. It's in the South, on the Gulf of Mexico. Why?"

"President Ford gave a speech there yesterday and said that Vietnam is a war which is over as far as America is concerned." He tapped my *Saigon Post*. "That quote was not reported in your paper?"

"Afraid not, so thanks."

"You are not a military man so I must help you understand something. Our 122 millimeter howitzer's effective range is eight miles. Our 140 millimeter rocket has a range of six miles. If we met resistance of any kind it would take us an hour to obliterate the embassy, the consulate, and everything within the U.S. compound at number 4, Thong Nhut."

"It would be a shame to destroy the swimming pool."

"I will ask them to spare the swimming pool."

"As big an impression as your truck-mounted howitzers and rockets makes on me, I can assure you that Ambassador Martin does not process such facts as do other men. The circuitry required to process defeat is not present in his mind. Even retreat is alien to him."

"Then things could end very badly here." He sipped his tea thoughtfully. "You will take Nga away before Saigon dies?"

"I'm working on it, but I must rely on others." It would be cumbersome, possibly absurd, to explain river barges or Jackson Dunn. "Even getting Chase employees out is proving difficult because of the uncooperative American ambassador."

"Can you get her on Citibank's plane? It is scheduled to arrive at two o'clock."

"I forget, aviation radio is an open channel so of course you guys know about that flight. But, Thang, I think a chartered plane would not be permitted to land. It's a fantasy."

"You will not even try?"

I definitely wasn't planning on it, but I owed Thang big-time. I'd also feel pretty stupid if the Citibank plane succeeded in getting Vietnamese out while I was sitting on my hands.

*   *   *

Duty tugged me in a half dozen directions, all competing for urgency. I turned my attention to Ho Thi Bach-Mai, the head of Chase's credit department, who failed to show up at the bank yesterday. I remembered Bach-Mai well from Cor Termijn's introduction. She was the exceptionally bright woman with cover-girl features whose husband was a senior executive at Air Vietnam, the national carrier. She was also a natural leader, and as such, irreplaceable. I hoped she wasn't defecting from the Chase group.

Bach-Mai's house was in a section of Saigon called Phu Nhuan. It was a district of older, traditional, wooden houses. It had more indigenous character than the more modern, building-block-style concrete houses. She led me around the side of the house to a small back porch. I'm not sure why she didn't invite me inside. Maybe she was packing. Maybe she didn't want her mother to learn that she was leaving.

She said, "I'm so glad you came. Cau made it home and I can't decide whether to leave with Chase or with Air Vietnam. I suppose it's a good problem to have but it's a big decision for us."

I said, "I'm having trouble getting the Chase evacuation organized. The Huong regime is sticking to Thieu's policy on exit visas, and the U.S. is still respecting the host government's policies. They're making exceptions for friends of the intelligence agencies, but other than that, they're only boarding dependents of Americans."

"It's absurd. Can't David Rockefeller appeal to President Ford or Secretary Kissinger?" Even as she asked, she looked doubtful.

"Bach-Mai, please understand that Washington is taking advice from Ambassador Martin, not giving it to him. How about Air Vietnam? They're not requiring exit visas?"

"Cau can do anything he wants with any Air Vietnam plane. He's their top airframe and power plant executive. He could ground a plane by withdrawing its airworthiness certificate, then fly it out himself with anyone aboard he wants."

"Then your decision is not at all difficult. Why would you even consider waiting for me to conjure some magic?"

"I don't know. Loyalty? I want a Chase job in New York. They might not hire me if I don't leave with you. Also we might not get green cards without Chase's sponsorship."

"Bach-Mai, you can get a job with any bank in the world. Cau can get a job with any airline in the world. I've heard that the Justice Department has approved a hundred thirty thousand green cards for Vietnamese refugees. You two would top the list. If I were in your place, I'd absolutely leave with Air Vietnam. Also you could take your parents, which I couldn't do."

Her husband came out and joined us on the porch. "I only heard the last part, but I agree with you. Hi, I'm Cau."

"I'm Ralph. Hey, I have a couple of quick questions, if you don't mind. Are you certified to fly DC-3s? I'm wondering how the landing gear retracts."

"I can help you with that. You put the gear latch lever in the raised position and a red light will come on. Then you move the landing gear handle from neutral to up. If there's sufficient oil pressure the gear will retract. Then slide the handle back to the neutral position."

"What's the takeoff speed?"

"One-twenty indicated air speed."

"Propeller pitch adjustment?"

"There's a control knob for each engine on the dash. Make sure they're feathered on the run-up. Reverse pitch on landing. You planning to fly a DC-3?"

"How hard could it be?"

"Which bird?"

"I'm looking at one at Tiger, the one configured as a Skytrain."

"That one flies okay. Good luck with it. Do you know the stall speed?"

"Meant to ask."

"Just fifty-eight knots, so don't come in too hot or you could overshoot the runway. You know the tower frequency?"

"No."

"It's one eighteen point seven."

How did I ever imagine I could fly an unfamiliar plane without all of that information? Cau had just saved a hundred lives.

*   *   *

I didn't fancy another trip to the embassy, but I might have been the only American who knew about the fall of Bien Hoa. That, and the troop strengths that Thang had passed on to me, had to get into the hands of Messrs. Polgar and LaGueux at the euphemistically named Office of the Special Assistant. They wouldn't need Thang's howitzer ranges to reinforce the urgency. General Dung's range was a thousand miles.

LaGueux took the news stoically. "What took them so long?"

He knew but I answered anyway. "General Dao slowed 'em down but couldn't stop 'em."

I hadn't met everyone at the embassy, nor did I care to, but Conny LaGueux was as wise a man as America possessed in Saigon. If he'd come up through the political *cone*, as the State Department called career paths, instead of intelligence, he'd be the ambassador. There wouldn't be any delusionaries, and if there were pilgrims they'd lean toward realism. All Americans, their dependents, and definitely their commercial enterprises would already be gone; the embassy would be closed; and if a small mission remained, it would work out of a hangar at the air base, where a helicopter would constantly be running. But LaGueux wasn't political cone. He was a second-tier intelligence officer.

As I stared at his face he looked positively amused by the whole situation. He pursed his lips as though stifling a smile. His eyes winced slightly behind his thick tortoiseshell glasses, perhaps trying to divine my mind. If he were successful, he'd learn that I was glad I worked for Chase rather than the State Department, and that my resolve to see my employees to safety was getting stronger every day.

*   *   *

I couldn't leave the embassy compound without visiting Lucien Kinsolving in the ICCS office. He'd been given a new project and was bubbling with excitement.

"The commission has designated me the expert on exfiltrating political VIPs. Now I've been tasked with exfiltrating the last souls at the Australian embassy and their various undocumented Vietnamese retainers and fiancées."

I said, "Lucien, I'd pay to watch." It amazed me that this mild-mannered gentleman could twice pull off a stunt which had flummoxed everyone else. He wasn't even a savvy local diplo like Shep Lowman. Kinsolving was on temporary assignment from somewhere in Africa. How had his little team managed to solve the evacuation puzzle?

"It won't be all that hard, Ralph. We'll use embassy buses, and fly Royal Australian Air Force aircraft."

The simplicity of his solution startled me. "Eureka! Foreign-flagged aircraft! You won't be up against U.S. regulations or our ambassador's mental state."

"Not so loud. You're on embassy grounds here."

"Lucien, how many other foreign aircraft are there out at Tan Son Nhut?"

"I don't know, but the Iranian and Indonesian diplomats are leaving tomorrow. They'd probably have their own planes."

Iran and Indonesia might not be my employees' first choice of destinations, but either would be preferable to being left here. Time was getting short and even long shots were worth investigating. I got the Iranian and Indonesian diplomats' names from Lucien and would try to find them. There were only five hotels where guys like them could be staying.

Another stop beckoned before I left the embassy. Jackson Dunn had suggested getting Nga out via barge and had dropped the name Bob Lanigan. If he was in fact with USAID, and had evacuated from Da Nang, then he'd probably be somewhere inside the embassy compound, unless he was at the deep water port at the river. The embassy receptionist wasn't sure where I could find Lanigan but gave me a good description. "Square-jawed, rugged-looking guy, about thirty-five. Sunglasses, crucifix. Irish complexion."

I found a guy by that description in the embassy's map room in the basement. I said, "Wondering if I might book passage on a barge down the Saigon River for a friend of mine. I'm Ralph White, with the Chase Manhattan Bank."

"Bob Lanigan. Pleased to meet you. Sure, the more the merrier. I'll have three, maybe more, barges. I'll be on the tugboat towing them, along with a pilot named Lombardo and a Filipino engine guy. But it ain't gonna be safe. Look at this map." He pointed to a large chart hanging on the wall. "See, this is the Saigon River here, and here's the port. The channel is pretty narrow for about five miles to where the Saigon River meets the Soai Rap River. From there it's a good half mile wide but gets very shallow for about forty miles down to the South China Sea. Then it's open ocean, which is okay if the chop is light, but barges can be hard to handle in bad weather and big ocean swells."

"Plus you have to assume both riverbanks will be controlled by the Viet Cong or the North Vietnamese," I said. "Are there any bridges they could shoot from?"

"No bridges on either the Saigon or the Soai Rap river. Locals use ferryboats to get across."

"Will you have weapons?"

"No. I'm with USAID. They frown on us shooting people. I'm betting on the enemy letting us through. I look at it this way: if they wanted to kill us, they could have done it already. I think they've been camping outside Saigon to give Americans time to clear out."

"Forgot to mention, Bob, my friend's not American. She's Vietnamese. No passport, no exit visa, only an ID card. She'll have some greenbacks and an affidavit of financial responsibility from me; that's about all."

"Tell her to be at the Alaska Barge docks at the port anytime Friday because I'm leaving at dawn on Saturday. Give me her name and her phone number."

I wrote Nga's full name down on a piece of paper and handed it to him. "Can't give you a phone number. She's a member of what you might call a politically sensitive family. Please take good care of her. She's important to me." I couldn't resist another question before I left. "Hey, Bob. How do you finesse your passengers' lack of documentation? Not that I care, mind you, but you're way outside protocol."

"It's a humanitarian mission. That justifies a little rule breaking."

Here was another guy who worked for a higher authority. "With a few more well-placed humanitarians in this building I might not be in the jam I am."

"What jam is that?"

"I'm trying to get a hundred-plus Viets out. Families of Chase Bank employees. Head office expects me to work through the embassy, but they're withholding their support."

"Then come with me. Plenty of room on the barge. A few days to the ocean, then we push on through the night into international waters. Worst case, a week. Seventh Fleet's out there somewhere."

"It should work," I said. "One of my backup plans is to steal a rice ship. I imagine Alaska Barge maintains its vessels better than the average river trader. Thing is, I really don't want to wait until Saturday. Not out of the question though. When do you have to know?"

"I'll take anyone who shows up Friday."

I thanked Lanigan. Extremely decent guy. He could have departed with the military airlift but decided to stay to help people. I just wondered how long General Dung would let Saigon be. Also the shallow stretches in the river and the deep swells in the ocean were serious problems. Moreover, barges don't have toilets. I didn't want my families defecating overboard for a week. Hmm, *families*. I liked the sound of that more than refugees, employees, staff, or Cor Termijn's word for them, *people*. They were my *families*.

*   *   *

Nga had packed a small travel bag and had put her hair up. If the Citibank plane really did land, and if it really did board undocumented Vietnamese, and if it really did reach civilization, she'd look like any other precocious young traveler. My bet was that it wasn't going to happen. I'd have bet my life savings, which was considerably less than what I was carrying over my shoulder, that the Citi plane was bunkum.

She drove up on Thang's motorbike and I straddled the back-seat with her little travel bag between us. The ao dai was gone, in favor of jeans and a sleeveless blouse. I held her slender hips as we swerved through traffic. I hoped the trip was futile. I really, really didn't want Citibank to take her away.

We got waved through the ARVN checkpoint and saluted through the U.S. gate, and she asked, "Where?"

"Straight ahead. Follow the signs for Tiger Airlines."

At the parking lot I directed her toward the row of DC-3s tied down in a line near the dunes. We parked the bike behind the one I was calling mine and I unlocked the door.

She said, "This is the Citibank plane?"

"No. We're only here for the radio, to listen to air traffic control."

Again it was sweltering inside the plane as we climbed through the cargo bay to the cockpit. I took the pilot's seat on the left and she took the copilot's seat. Both of us put on headphones and I clicked the battery on. I dialed the radio to the tower frequency that Bach-Mai's husband had given me, 118.7, and American voices began crackling through the headphones. It was two o'clock.

I explained aviation radio protocol to Nga. "Each transmission starts with the sender saying who they're addressing, then he'll identify himself, using his aircraft type and registration or flight number, then the purpose of the call. I'm not sure how the Citi plane will ID itself, but it will be the only nonmilitary plane in the sky. When air traffic control responds he'll abbreviate the last three digits of the caller ID."

She said, "They talk so fast. How do they understand? What we will do if the Citi plane gets in?"

"We'd ride over to the gate where they dock and try to mix you in with the Citi employees. Now listen carefully. We don't want to miss it."

It didn't take long. "Tan Son Nhut tower, Convair 880, Victor Romeo one zero two zero niner, fifty miles east, inbound, over."

"Convair two zero niner, Tan Son Nhut tower. Negative flight plan. Negative RVN airspace. Negative permission to land. Return to your point of origin. Over."

"Tan Son Nhut tower, Convair two zero niner, understand negative flight plan, executing standard rate turn to north. Out."

We listened for a few more minutes but the action was over. Professional pilots don't argue with air traffic controllers, and they don't risk their licenses by abusing emergency procedures. The Citi plane had turned away without a murmur of resistance. I'd been vindicated, but I took no pleasure in it.

*   *   *

I once had a British friend who was fond of saying, "Time spent in reconnaissance is never wasted." I could practically hear his voice as Nga and I slowed to a stop at the gymnasium housing the Evacuation Control Center. It would have been irresponsible to pass it without checking to see if they'd softened their exclusionary policies. From the road the swarm of humanity looked like flies on carrion. We left the motorbike near the road, locking the ignition.

Nga held my hand as we walked into the crowd. I found an air force enlisted man and said, "Airman!" I couldn't distinguish air force enlisted ranks, but the first three enlisted ranks had the word *airman* in the title. "Know if Ken Moorefield's around?" I surprised myself by remembering the name of Graham Martin's aide. Possibly it was because he held the fate of my families in his hands, or would if I hadn't scrounged up some other options.

"Don't know him, sir. NCOIC's over at that table."

That had to mean the noncommissioned officer in charge. The next five ranks of air force enlisted men had the word sergeant in their titles, so when I found the NCOIC I took a chance with that. "Sergeant, I'm looking for Mr. Moorefield, from the embassy."

When these guys wore their air force blues, they looked really spiffy, but when they wore camouflage fatigues, as this guy did, they looked just as grubby as any army grunt. "Ain't here." His face wore three days of stubble and it was slimy with perspiration. He looked highly skilled in hand-to-hand combat. "We got consuls general though." He nodded toward the officials processing marriage licenses faster than the Connecticut DMV processed drivers' licenses. They were not to be bothered.

I said to the sergeant, "I'm trying to get my employees out. I'm with the Chase Manhattan Bank."

He shook his head. "Wives and kids, sir. Strictly dependents. No exceptions. I don't make the rules."

"Sergeant, between the gym and the hangar there's a thousand Vietnamese here. You're telling me—"

"They're all immediate family of an American, sir, or will be by the time they board a Hercules." The sergeant noticed Nga holding my hand. "She eighteen yet?"

"Soon."

"Don't work, sir. Gotta be eighteen." He took in the enormity of the gym with a sweep of his eyes. "This here's America, sir. Don't look like it but they . . ."—he nodded toward the consuls—"they go by U.S. law." He stared hard at Nga, probably trying to figure out if he recognized her from any of his regular bars.

"Thanks, Sarge."

Nga held my hand with both of hers. "Kind of scary in there, Mr. White."

"You might practice saying Ralph."

"Mister White! Mister White! Mister White!"

I changed my mind about one thing. I did take pleasure in the Citi plane being denied a landing. "Do you have any plans for dinner or would you care to join me at the Caravelle?"

"Ooo! I will have *coquilles*!" She licked her lips, but it made her look more silly than hungry.

*   *   *

On the other side of Ben Bach Dang from the bank, the fast current in the Saigon River carried its odiferous flotsam toward the sea. The U.S. ambassador couldn't prevent Saigon's garbage from eluding communism, only its citizens. The crowd outside the bank was furious that the bank had closed early again. I slipped in through the secret side door past men brandishing military rifles.

The buzz on the banking floor briefly subsided as I approached the stairwell leading to my second-floor office. I stopped on the third step, where I had a good perspective of the whole operation. In a sweep I took in the line of tellers, the customer service desk, the commercial accounts desk, the foreign trade department. The buzz went silent and every eye turned to me. They obviously thought I stopped on the stairs to speak to them. Maybe I should, but what to say? A progress report would be short and depressing. Every obstacle I faced when I arrived remained firmly in place. My worst-case plans—a barge, a rice boat, a rickety airplane—wouldn't be very uplifting. The impending tragedy that these decent people faced was unimaginable. There might not be mass murders, but their houses, furniture, clothing, vehicles, and all private property would be confiscated. Families would be separated and they'd be sent out into the countryside to toil in low-yield agriculture. Even if they survived, abject poverty was the best they could expect under a new regime.

Still, there had been a certain kind of progress. I had jostled at least one obstacle loose. It was conceptual more than physical. I had ceased being their hostage and was now their guardian. If it was too subtle a change for them, it definitely wasn't for me. They stood quietly attentive.

I didn't plan the words that came. "You're my family. You're the only family I've got." That would have to do. I didn't really have anything else. I turned and walked slowly up the stairs and the buzz below quickly resumed.

Getting through on telephones had become a problem in Saigon so I asked Cor's secretary to make calls for me. "Anna, please try reaching Shep Lowman at the embassy. Also would you try finding out where the Iranian and Indonesian diplomats are staying. I also need a guy at Pacific Architects named Jackson Dunn."

Jackson was easiest for her to find. I said, "I ran into Bob Lanigan, the guy with the barge. He's expecting Nga so all you have to do is make sure she gets to the port Friday or very early Saturday. Don't leave Saigon without her."

"You can depend on me, buddy."

"How many times did you get married today, Jackson?"

"Only once. The lines are so long out at the airport it takes a couple of hours."

"What's the standard dowry up to?"

"Twenty grand. It's a good day's work. My barge business is picking up too."

Anna found Lowman next. "Hi, Shep. Just checking to see if there's any official change in the embassy's emigration policies for under-documented Viets."

"No change. But Chase will be my first call if things were to loosen up."

"Any openings on the Pitcairn Island cruise? I have about a hundred passengers who'd love to make that trip."

"You would be the first to know, Ralph."

Anna also found one Mr. Jafari, a senior Iranian diplomat. Not all that surprisingly, given the few class A hotels in Saigon, he was staying at my hotel. He wasn't available, but Anna left a message for him to contact me.

I'd given a lot of thought to what should go in an affidavit of financial responsibility so it didn't take me long to draft one. I asked Anna to type one for each person on Cuong's lists, both priority and nonpriority. My thinking was that even if I could only get half of them out before the fall, Chase should still be on the hook for the others' support if they subsequently escaped by themselves. Basically the letter said that Chase promised to reimburse any expenses incurred in aiding employees bearing the affidavit.

Cuong came in as I was signing the last of these letters and I asked him to distribute them to the employees. Instead of taking the stack of envelopes and leaving, he sat down and said he had a few things to discuss.

"There are some other names that belong on our list. They're going to need affidavits too."

Cuong apparently harbored a fantasy that putting names on a list would somehow make a difference. In some ways adding names was simple. I definitely had the authority. I had no oversight. There were no rules, no controls, no policy. I was closing the branch and that was that. There had been some mention of priority employees, but that had always been an ill-defined category. Cuong had watched and learned. If it was so easy, well hell, why not just add a few more? Until I found a way to get people out it was nothing more than ink on paper.

Cuong said, "My wife's brother is in the States on business. His wife and child are staying with my family. If we leave them here, the family would be separated. If we take them, my brother-in-law would support them. They will not be a burden to Chase Bank. There are just the two, my sister-in-law and her child."

I couldn't claim to know Cuong well, but I figured this as a test balloon. If I accepted his relatives under my wing, there would be more. If I said no to them, he wouldn't bother trying any others.

Fully aware of the risk, I said, "Okay, Mr. Cuong, put them on our list and have Anna prepare another affidavit, but instead of the letter saying say that Chase will take financial responsibility, say that they will be Ralph White's responsibility."

Cuong clearly feared his wife's wrath if his gambit had failed, and he beamed with relief. Cuong might have had second thoughts if he knew how thin my personal finances were and how little security my financial umbrella offered.

"We should also take the bank's doctor. I believe you've met Dr. An. He says he examined a friend of yours. He is confident of passing the medical boards in the States and working there as a medical doctor."

"Dependents?"

"Wife and two kids."

I could see scenarios in which having a medical doctor with us would be very useful. Illness would be predictable if we ended up spending a week on a barge. How about if someone got shot from the shore or wounded by shrapnel? "Okay, let's invite Dr. An's family, with me on the hook for them too." I didn't explain to Cuong that every additional name on the list made it less likely that any of us would get out.

"There's also a Chase officer at Head Office named Kevin Garvey."

"Wonderful! If he's in New York we won't have to evacuate him."

"Not so fast, Mr. White." Cuong was enjoying this far too much. "Garvey's wife is Vietnamese and he wants us to bring out her family. There are ten of them."

Ten people! Just like that. Ten more. If I didn't say no now, when would I? Did this Mr. Kevin Garvey even want his wife's ten relatives to join his household? Maybe he'd said, *Sure, sweetie, if they can get out I'd be happy to provide them with bed and board forever and ever*, safe in the knowledge that the odds were a million-to-one that it would happen.

I smiled at the absolute absurdity. Cuong smiled in sympathy with my smile. Then, as clearly as though it was happening in front of me, I imagined Mrs. Kevin Garvey showing up at JFK arrivals, eagerly watching for her parents and sisters to disembark, and being told that I was the beast who signed their death warrants. "Okay, Mr. Cuong. Ten Garveys, also on me."

I revised my mental spreadsheet and, assuming Bach-Mai and her husband defected, my extended family now numbered 117. That would take two round-trips in the DC-3. I'd have to file a flight plan in U-Tapao to return to Tan Son Nhut in the midst of anarchic collapse. I'd be fortunate if they committed me to an asylum for the deranged before I taxied to the active runway.

Unaware that he was in the presence of an unhinged lunatic, Cuong thanked me profusely, conveyed my freshened instructions to the secretary, and left to distribute the affidavits. After he'd left, I asked Anna if she would be kind enough to prepare yet another affidavit, and I gave her the name Nguyen Thi Nga. She was my family too.

I skipped down the stairs and asked if I could help settle the bank's accounts for the day. Cuong said that with or without my assistance the settlement wouldn't be done until 6:00. I asked for a calculator and he gave me an adding machine. I must have helped because we'd wrapped it up by 5:30.

Before we closed the branch, I decided to tell the employees about the coded radio message for Americans to assemble at the helicopter rescue sites. These were not people who listened to the American station unless they needed a little rock 'n' roll therapy, so I had to tell them the AM frequency. I said to listen for a weather report of 105 in the shade, followed by "I'm Dreaming of a White Christmas," sung by Bing Crosby.

Cuong said, "None of us knows that song, Mr. White."

Of course they didn't. The Mission Warden had, by design, picked a song that no denizen of the tropics could ever have heard. If I'd made a list of the hundred things I'd like to do most at that minute, singing "I'm Dreaming of a White Christmas" would not have made the list. But there was a chance, some small probability, that being familiar with the melody might save one or two members of my Chase family. Only badly misplaced modesty would lead me to refuse.

Moreover, it was something I could do fairly handily. I'd sung baritone with the University of Maryland Madrigal Singers. I read sheet music. I'd sung madrigals at the White House twice, once for a Paraguayan thug whom President Johnson hosted to a state dinner, and once for Nixon's White House Press Corps.

Once again, I mounted the third stair and, with no pitch pipe to prime my voice, just belted out the lyrics. It would be impossible to divine what they collectively made of my performance. Forced to guess, I'd bet they would recall my abiding immodesty long after they'd forgotten the tune. There was no applause.

*   *   *

When I arrived back at the Caravelle, Nga and the mutilated beggar girl were chatting on the front steps. Nga said, "The manager of the hotel offered Yen-Yen a thousand P if she would go away and she refused. She said she had the right to wait for her friend. Did you know you were her friend?"

I said, "Here's three thousand P, Yen-Yen. Good night." As she picked the coins out of my palm, her flesh touched mine. It didn't kill me.

Yen-Yen said, "Tank you, Mitter Why," then she headed across Lam Son Square toward the Continental, propelling herself with her one arm and her one leg, and sweeping the length of the square with her long hair.

Inside at the Caravelle's rooftop bar, a white-jacketed waiter said, "Calvados, Mr. White?"

I gave a slight nod. I was as much a creature of habit at the close of the day as at its opening. They stocked three brands of calvados at three different price points. Unless compelled to do so by National Front cadres like Nga's brother, I rarely drank hard spirits, but I made an exception for this golden apple cognac from France. On my first night at the Caravelle I'd ordered a flight of their three offerings and had correctly placed them on the quality spectrum. With the piastre flirting with 3,000 per dollar, even the pricey one was essentially free.

Nga and I stood side by side at the northwest-facing windows and watched attentively for the pyrotechnics of war. The horizon remained dark as I sipped my calvados and Nga did the same with her freshly squeezed orange juice. A hundred thousand NVA regulars were advancing toward us, not marching, just ambling toward Saigon from the north and the east along paved highways. Trucks full of food and ammunition would follow, though the ammo would be unnecessary.

We took our vulnerable table by the window and the waiter brought menus we'd already memorized. Steak for *monsieur*;

coquilles for *mademoiselle*. Beaujolais for *monsieur*; Sancerre for *mademoiselle*. Nga affected womanhood, but her giddy excitement about her *coquilles* revealed the girl. I'm sure boys have a counterpart phase, but it occurs so poetically in girls.

A man dressed in a dark suit materialized beside our table and introduced himself. "I understand you have been asking about me, Mr. White. Well, here I am."

It was an accent I was certain I had never heard before. "Sorry. I do not recognize you, sir."

"Oh, I am Jafari, representing the Imperial State of Iran."

I stood and shook his hand. "I'm so pleased to make your acquaintance." To Nga I said, "Please excuse me for a minute." The diplomat and I drifted over to the bar. I said, "I was wondering how and when you are planning to leave Saigon. I'm asking because I'd like to get my young friend"—I gestured toward Nga—"out of the country on a non-U.S. aircraft. If that were possible, I would be willing to cover her airfare." I saw no reason to go into detail about how critical a foreign-flagged carrier was to avoiding the U.S. embassy's punctiliousness about papers. It was the clever little trick Lucien Kinsolving had inadvertently discovered in getting his Australian friendlies out.

"Ah. Yes, I see." He looked appreciatively toward Nga. "I hope I may be of assistance."

I said, "I'm going to need to get back to my guest before our dinners arrive so forgive me for being so direct, Mr. Jafari. What kind of aircraft will you be using and how much would her fare be?"

"I suppose it will be Iranian military transport. That's what they flew us in on. And as for cost, why don't we just round it off to a thousand, U.S., in cash? Oh, our departure is tomorrow morning."

Getting Nga out would be worth a thousand, but I could not get myself comfortable with the man. Call it a prejudice but there were too many slippery souk merchants where Jafari came from.

"I'll talk it over with my friend. If she decides to join you, we'll meet you at the front desk in the morning with the cash."

"Excellent, Mr. White. See you in the morning, Allah willing."

After dinner Nga and I stood closely together in the little gated elevator as it descended from the restaurant to my floor. I asked, "Are you leaving or spending the night?"

She pouted, smiled, and slapped my butt. "I will stay with my sweet heart."

In the room she said, "I would ask you to help me unfasten the hooks on my ao dai but you are too slow." She was right. In twenty seconds, her outfit was draped over an armchair.

When she came out of the shower, I asked her to put on a bathrobe and sit down. I had something to say. "I've arranged two possible ways for you to get out. One is on an Iranian aircraft and the other is on a river barge, with Jackson Dunn." I handed her a wad of twenties "Here's enough money to get you to New York. Here's my mother's phone number. She'll come and pick you up and take you to the house in Connecticut where I grew up. She'll help you with your application to college and she'll drive you up there to see how you like it. I'm going to pay for your education. I'll visit you on my home leaves as long as I'm working overseas with Chase. I know you'll be a great student and you'll get a good job after school."

She was tipsy from the Sancerre and rosy from the hot shower. She was a damn cute girl and would make a seriously beautiful woman. She said, "I do not know what to say. Thank you is too little. It is very exciting, this way to see my life. It is above a dream."

"Do you accept?"

"Yes, sweet heart. I do accept."

"Then let's try to get some sleep, okay? Our next few days will be very busy."

She came to bed and I turned out the light. We hugged and her skin was still moist from the shower.

She said, "What's this?"

"You leave that alone."

"But it likes me."

"I was not planning on having that kind of relationship with you."

"What kind, then?"

"More like a little sister."

"We are not same-same brother-sister."

"We were more like brother-sister when you had your clothes on and the lights were on and you were a goofy little puppy dog."

"You like puppies? Okay, watch." In the flickering blue neon from the window on Tu Do Street she straddled me on her hands and knees, licked my cheek, and barked, "Arf, arf, arf." Then she lay down beside me and whimpered, exactly like a forlorn, abandoned puppy.

Chapter Eleven

THURSDAY, APRIL 24, 1975

The Caravelle's reception desk was hardly long enough for a clerk and a cashier. The lobby was dingy and cheaply furnished, like a low-budget French country inn. The bulky window treatments were impregnated with decades of Gauloises cigarette smoke with a recent infusion of Marlboro. It had likely changed very little since Tu Do Street had been called *rue Catinat* and since the Opera House actually had operas. It wasn't as though I didn't have choices. The Rex and the Ambassador were chic and slick, with girlie bars and marijuana dealers on their open roofs. The Majestic was perfectly named and was far closer to the bank. The Continental was one of the *grande dame* hotels of Southeast Asia, a destination in itself. So why the Caravelle?

In a word, *character.* Staying there made it more likely that the opera would make a comeback, that the side street would somehow revert to *rue Catinat,* that people under forty would blossom into francophones. Its tiny, gated elevator was both its crown jewel and a time capsule through Saigon's punctured soul. A stay at the Caravelle lured the traveler into Saigon's serpentine history. A Caravelleiste became a Saigon insider, inked into the city's graffiti-scrawled legend.

The Iranian diplomat was checking out and making quite a commotion about it. "I do not carry cash. You must bill the Iranian embassy."

The clerk said, "But Mr. Jafari, your embassy has closed. What do you expect us to do, send an invoice to Tehran? To whom, then? The Shah?"

"Believe me, Mr.—ah—Tran, my bill will be the least of your problems in the coming days."

Jafari's driver called from the front door. "Sir, make haste. Today is Pan Am's last flight. We dare not miss it."

I bid Jafari good morning and added, "We? You are evacuating your driver too? How democratic of you!"

"Ah, Mr. White. No, I'm afraid that stinky wretch must remain here. But, and I am sure you will understand, I avoid paying him severance by hinting that I might fly him to freedom then abandoning him at the airport."

"Most clever of you. And do I also understand, sir, that you are booked on Pan American World Airways? If so, that implies you are not flying on an Iranian-flagged aircraft, and would have been unable to evacuate my little Vietnamese friend."

"Change of plans. Yes, that's it. Change of plans."

Today's Pan Am had sold out a week ago. "So you would have returned my thousand dollars if I had paid it out to you last night?"

"But of course. Now I must take my leave. Promise to look me up if you ever discover yourself in Tehran. We will trade stories about this outhouse of a hotel."

*   *   *

I tried to not look too despondent as I traversed the lobby of the bank toward the steps to my office. My office. My families. When Cor spoke of them he called them *people*. I wondered if the Dutch word for people carried more human empathy than the English word did. I pushed the inbox into a corner of the desk and tried to determine which of a dozen calls I'd make first.

I said to Anna, "Call HMS *Bounty*. I need to speak with Fletcher Christian. Wait, cancel that. Let's call Shep Lowman."

Before she could dial, Cuong bounded up the stairs. "Call Regional. Get them to approve a noon closing. Klimm said we could but we need Linker."

Juergen Klimm, another of the Nationale Handelsbank Dutchmen, was the senior operations executive at Hong Kong Regional Office. He wielded considerable authority, but Cuong was right: no Handelsbanker was going to make this kind of decision. We needed John Linker at the least, and that was not a call that Cuong was going to make as long as there was an expatriate to do it.

To Anna I said, "Get me Mr. Termijn in Hong Kong. Linker's secretary will know how to reach him."

In five minutes, Cor's husky voice came on the line. There were no formalities. "What's going on there?"

"Bach-Mai has left. The cable operator left. Otherwise everyone's still here. Xuan Loc and Bien Hoa have fallen, so Saigon is entirely defenseless. There are a hundred thousand NVA within a day's march. The embassy's set up an Evacuation Control Center at DAO but only for Americans and their relatives. Shep Lowman, as I think I mentioned to you, is running an evacuation program for the embassy's own undocumented Viets, but it's effectively a mutiny and he's worried that, were he to include Chase employees, word of his insubordination might somehow get back to Ambassador Martin. I've lined up some barges that will be taking people down the river, and a small cargo plane I would be comfortable piloting myself, and they're viable options. I distributed affidavits of financial support and have provided the employees the evacuation points. The priority list is now sixty-eight, and the second list is forty-nine. That includes Dr. An's family and Mr. Cuong's sister-in-law. It also includes a family said to be that of a Chase officer named Garvey. The grand total, if we took everybody, is one hundred seventeen. Hey, Cor . . . ?"

"I'm listening."

"The ARVN have set up a checkpoint just in front of the Tan Son Nhut main gate. They're boarding buses and removing young men they suspect of being draft dodgers and deserters and they're executing them in front of their families. This is not a rumor."

"The main gate is the only way in? The base is completely surrounded by a fence?"

"The civil aviation side is still accessible but Pan Am is suspending service to Saigon as of today. So getting through on the civil side would be pointless. Our entire group would have to walk across two active runways."

"Ralph, I want you to know that the seventeenth floor is calling two and three times a day asking what's happening in Saigon."

The seventeenth floor. David Rockefeller.

Cor asked, "Do you want Rockefeller to call Ambassador Martin?"

"Martin isn't listening to either Henry Kissinger or President Ford so I doubt D.R. would have any better luck. Shep Lowman's mutiny is our best hope, but he'd freak out if D.R. knew about it. There's another viable strategy: foreign-flagged aircraft. The Aussies and Brits got their friendlies out on their own planes and didn't bother with exit visas."

"Cathay Pacific is a Chase client. I'll try to get them to divert a flight."

"Might work but probably not. Air traffic control turned Citibank's charter plane away." Then I recalled the original purpose of my call. "Listen, Cor. I'm closing the branch at noon today. I'm not seeking permission because Linker already delegated that authority to me."

In a rational world—which might exclude 1975 Saigon—my authority would rely on the notion of my being the head of household to 117 souls. If that was a fantasy, I'd have much to answer for on the seventeenth floor.

*   *   *

The verb *close* carries a range of meanings. Commonly, it's a temporary act, as in closing a book or a switch. In that application, the word does not foreclose the possibility that the book or switch may be reopened at some future time. This same word, however, can also refer to something permanent and irreversible, as in a closed invitation list or a closing out sale.

When Cuong sought permission to close at noon in order to complete the settlement within a reasonable time, he almost certainly intended the quotidian definition. After all, the branch had closed every afternoon since its grand opening in the sixties. When I acceded to his closure request, I meant the more conclusive meaning. We needed to chat.

Bach-Mai's departure left three local officers. In addition to Cuong Vu-Huy there was Nguyen Hong-Lien and Tran My-Nga. I called them up to my office, knowing that I couldn't keep them from their duties for long on such a godforsaken day. There weren't enough chairs in the office for us all to sit, so we all stood.

"What I'm going to tell you is highly confidential. It would be very unfortunate if employees on the nonpriority list should hear about this. Chase Saigon will close permanently at noon today. My evacuation plan is still a work in progress, but no rational purpose is served by keeping the branch open any longer."

They were still and stoic, prisoners receiving their sentences. "If you can do it without alarming the others, start shredding negotiable instruments, such as money orders, travelers' checks, and cashier's checks. Keep good records of what you're shredding. Cuong, Hong-Lien, and I will deliver credit files, legal documents, correspondence, accounting ledgers, and combinations to the French embassy, which I understand will remain open. We must somehow make that transfer appear to be a normal business activity. We will not inform the National Bank that the branch has closed its doors until our work is a fait accompli. In fact, we'll leave it to the U.S. embassy to inform the National Bank. And the embassy isn't going to know until I tell them. Our landlord doesn't need to know either."

Cuong said, "Our landlord evacuated to Singapore last month."

"Make sure you destroy the test keys used in international remittances. That's the first thing Regional will ask us about. Retain enough local currency to pay out accrued wages and termination bonuses to employees who elect to stay, but obviously do not pay them out until the closing becomes common knowledge."

"How are we getting out, Mr. White?"

My-Nga's question was perfectly reasonable but an honest answer would necessarily be laden with contingencies, unresolved issues, educated guesses, and a prayer or two. There were also truthful answers that would be misleading. A thoroughly truthful answer could be very short, as in *I really don't know*, or it might track my pinball odyssey over the last ten days.

I chose to say, "The American embassy has a way of getting us out, but the diplomat in charge hasn't clued me in on it yet. If he doesn't come through for us soon enough, we have two other options, one by air and the other by river. After settlement is completed, we'll make sure all employees on the priority list know to stand by. I haven't given up on getting everybody out."

Hong-Lien asked, "Will it be dangerous? We have families."

"The embassy option would be the safest. The river option is fairly safe too, though uncomfortable, unsanitary, and weather-dependent. The air option involves a higher order of risk."

This would be the time, if ever, to mention the executions. "Now, I'm going to ask all three of you an important question and your answer has to be one hundred percent accurate. Is there any employee or family member on either of our lists who the South Vietnamese Army might consider a draft dodger or deserter?"

"No."

"No."

"No."

*   *   *

We returned from the French embassy and closed out the settlement by 4:30, and were switching off the air conditioners when the phone rang. Anna had already left, so I picked it up. "Chase Bank. Ralph White."

"Hi, Ralph. Jim Ashida here."

I had mixed feelings about Ashida. Instinctively I liked him, but the last time I'd spoken to him, after he'd disappeared during the Hung Kings holiday, was when he solemnly alerted me to the nonsensical Citibank charter plane.

"What's up, Jim?"

"Good news. I've got seventy seats earmarked for Chase on an embassy bus tonight. That will get you onto the air base."

I knew exactly the circuitous route that this offer had traveled. It had to have originated with Shep Lowman, who handled political affairs at the embassy, and was being executed by Colonel William Madison, who handled political affairs for the Defense Attaché. Ashida was, as they say, just the messenger.

"I'll take it. Thanks, Jim."

"Great! The bus will pick your group up at number 39, Le Quy Don, at six-thirty. Your contact there will be a USAID guy named Mel Chatman. He evacuated friendlies at Da Nang and speaks fluent Vietnamese. Should be easy to find."

"Thirty-nine, Le Quy Don, two hours from now, Mel Chatman. Thanks Jim." It was the same pickup location the Kinsolving group had used.

Our priority list had seventy names. But that included Bach-Mai and her husband, Cau, so it was down to sixty-eight. Should I try to shoehorn two more onto this Noah's ark of a bus to fill Ashida's seventy spots? Not with two hours left. I assembled the three officers and gave them the news. They had questions. I had very few answers. I gave them the job of splitting up the phone list of priority employees and calling each of them, swearing them to secrecy, and giving them the rendezvous point.

The crowd outside the bank looked dangerous. It wasn't loud like the one outside the embassy, but these folks were extremely angry. The embassy didn't owe its crowd anything but we owed these people their money. Many of the men had M-16 rifles slung over their shoulders. A grenade launcher would blow the doors off the bank, though I didn't see any of them. Even using the side door, I wished I had a hat to pull down over my American face. On the way out, I dipped in and out of the nearly adjacent Majestic lobby, hoping the crowd would take me for a guest.

*   *   *

Two hours. I had a lot less to pack into those 120 minutes than the others. One thing I did have to do was square up with the Caravelle. But first I walked to the far side of Ben Dach Dong, an irresponsible one hundred feet out of my way, to take a final stroll along the bank of the Saigon River. I was watching the current, when a massive swarm of pastel yellow butterflies filled the air. They flew at about head height over the ground, with the edges of the swarm out over the river. The yellow cloud flowed from north to south, in the direction of the river's flow, and stretched as far as I could see in both directions. The migration immobilized me and I tried to estimate their numbers. Easily a million. Maybe three million. It was one of the most astonishing sights I'd ever seen in nature. Hell of a country! No end of surprises. The love-hate cycle came to rest at love.

*   *   *

"Raj, I'll need your best wholesale rate today. Paying my hotel bill."

"For you, my friend, I'll make it an even three thousand. My fortune-teller told me this would be a very good day for dollars." He exaggerated the *very good* in a parody of his own Indian accent.

Chase employees at the Guillaume Tell restaurant
Left to right (Vietnamese name order): Cuong Vu Huy, Cornelis Termijn, Tran My Nga, Nguyen Hong Lien, John Linker. This photo taken April 1, 1975, five days before Linker recruited the author for the Saigon assignment. At this point the bank had no plan to rescue Vietnamese. (*Bach Mai Ho*)

Ambassador Graham Martin at his Senate confirmation hearing
On paper, Martin was perfect for the assignment as U.S. Ambassador to the Republic of South Vietnam. However, during the fall of Saigon, he created a foreign-policy disaster out of what could and should have been an orderly withdrawal of Americans and vulnerable Vietnamese. (*Getty Images*)

The Saigon branch of the Chase Manhattan Bank
The vehicle in the foreground is a cyclo, a pedaled taxi used for short-distance transport.
(*JPMorgan Chase Corporate History Collection*)

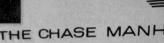

Armed Vietnamese soldiers in the teller line at Chase's Saigon branch
It was quite common for both American and Vietnamese soldiers to carry rifles and pistols while doing business at Chase Saigon.
(*JPMorgan Chase Corporate History Collection*)

U.S. embassy, Saigon, Republic of Vietnam
Note the helipad on the roof. The offices of senior foreign service officers, including the ambassador, were on the third floor, deemed safe from ground attacks from below and rocket attacks from above. Photo from about 1967. (*Getty Images*)

Shepard Lowman in his 1953 Harvard Law School yearbook
This photo was taken twenty-two years before "Shep" set up a clandestine refugee evacuation program in Saigon under the nose of the U.S. ambassador. He was revered as saintly by a generation of Vietnamese refugees. (*Harvard Law School Yearbook, 1953*)

U.S. Army Captain Kenneth Moorefield, here with his Vietnamese counterpart, Captain Ngan
A few years later, in his role as a foreign service officer, Ken Moorefield ran the Evacuation Control Center at Tan Son Nhut Air Base in Saigon, saving thousands of Vietnamese civilians by applying "flexible" eligibility standards. (*Ken Moorefield*)

DC-3 Skytrain, aka C-47
Made by Douglas Aircraft, the DC-3 was popular throughout Southeast Asia for its ability to take off and land on short, unimproved airstrips. The newest of them were thirty years old by the fall of Saigon. It was also affectionately known as the Gooney Bird. (*Courtesy National Archives*)

Lam Son Square
In the center of Saigon's District 1, Lam Son Square was the heartbeat of the old city, hosting weddings, executions, demonstrations, and rallies. This view is facing west from the rooftop restaurant of the Caravelle Hotel. The Continental Palace hotel is in the center, the National Assembly on the right, and the French bookstore on the left corner. The steeples of the Basilica of Notre Dame of Saigon are visible in the distance. (*Getty Images*)

Waiting line for visas outside the gate of the U.S. consulate
Based on the orderliness this is probably late March or early April 1975. If it were mid-April this crowd would have been tense and panicky. The vehicular gate is to the left. The roof of main entrance is visible in the distance. (*Getty Images*)

Tent City at Orote Point, Guam
Designated "Operation New Life," Tent City was one square mile and could shelter and feed 30,000 refugees. 111,000 refugees were eventually processed here. (*Getty Images*)

A family of Vietnamese boarding a C-141 Starlifter at Tan Son Nhut, Saigon
There were no seats; about three hundred refugees sprawled out on the metal floor in the huge cargo bay with their meager luggage. It was two and a half hours to Clark Air Base in the Philippines, and everyone wept. (*Getty Images*)

Refugees from Chase's Saigon Branch with David Rockefeller
Grateful refugees from Chase's Saigon Branch present a plaque to Rockefeller in gratitude for underwriting their rescue, emigration, job placement, and resettlement in America. *Left to right*: Yen Suong Le, Bach Mai Ho, Van Nguyen, My Nga Tran, David Rockefeller. (*JPMorgan Chase Corporate History Collection*)

Chase Manhattan Bank Senior Vice President Tony Terracciano and the Vietnam Task Force in New York, May 1975
Left to right: Tony Terracciano, Joyce Holwell, Mel Anderson, John Mitchell, Paul Didier, Ralph White. (*JPMorgan Chase Corporate History Collection*)

Reunion of author with former refugees
A group of former Chase Saigon refugees who have settled in New Jersey celebrates Tet, the Vietnamese lunar new year, in 2022. *From left to right (using the Americanized order of their names)*: Nga Dang, Kim Borja, Mai Huynh, Liem Nguyen, Ralph White, Chan Ho, Phuong Hoang Nguyen, My Nga Tran, Sinh Tran. This was the first time in forty-seven years that the author had seen any of them. (*Dr. Cuong Kim Lam*)

"Need any help getting out, Raj? I have a friend who's boarding all comers on a barge. A barge might work for you, assuming you'll have bulk currency and gold."

"Might be good for me. Where, when?"

"He says he's leaving Saturday morning, but I'd board tomorrow if I were you in case he has to leave earlier. He'll be at the Alaska Barge wharf. Ask for Jackson Dunn or Bob Lanigan. It may help if you said I sent you."

"But, my friend, I have forgotten your name."

My name might not mean much to Lanigan. "Just tell them you have a friend at Chase Manhattan."

*   *   *

Checking out of a hotel is easy when your worldly possessions fit in a shoulder satchel. One glitch was that one of my three pairs of underpants was in the laundry, so I left with only two. Regrettably the pair I left behind was the black pajamas of a Viet Cong sapper. Counting out bundles of piastres for the cashier soaked up valuable minutes.

The cab wasn't able to get anywhere close to number 39 Le Quy Don. There were throngs of people in the street and clustered in the shade along this cool oasis in District 1. A line of olive drab buses, five of them, was parked to the side, and an American with a bullhorn shouted instructions to the crowd.

Mel Chatman stood out. He looked like a welterweight boxer, tanned and handsome, if a little banged up, and he was dead fluent in Vietnamese. I couldn't see him as a USAID consultant; he was more infantry sergeant. There were hundreds of Vietnamese and Americans shuffling about in the shade of the trees, but there was clearly one man in charge. It was hard not to envy him. He was mesmerizing, but the longer I watched, the more my admiration waned. What on Earth was this guy going to do for a living next month?

I approached him and waited for the bullhorn to fall away from his face.

He said, ". . . can I do for ya?"

"Ralph White. Chase Manhattan Bank. Sixty-eight Viets without exit visas. Referred to you by commercial attaché Jim Ashida."

Damn if he didn't pull a clipboard out from nowhere and begin to flip pages. "Last bus in the line. Should be number 22. If it ain't, let me know. Confirm when you got everyone on board."

Before I could thank him, he was loading his bullhorn with the comingled vowels, glottal-stopped consonants, and punchy tones of vernacular Vietnamese. Here was another guy who should be higher in the pecking order than he appeared to be. There certainly were many who should be lower, starting with the ambassador.

The first bank officer to show up was Hong-Lien. I asked her to put her family on the last bus, then come back and help check off employees for me, since I wouldn't recognize them. We had the bus half loaded before My-Nga showed up with her family. Her English was excellent, so I asked her to relieve Hong Lien and come back to help me after getting her family on board.

I crossed out each name as the person got on the bus until there were only six names unchecked, Cuong, his wife and kids, and his sister-in-law and her kid. One bus departed for the air base. Another. Then another. Eventually ours was the only bus left.

Chatman came over and said, "You understood you were supposed to confirm when you were full, right?"

"We have six no-shows. He's our deputy general manager."

"Get in, dammit. We're leaving right now. Get on that fuckin' bus!"

I turned to My-Nga. "Yeah. We gotta go." It was 7:30. Cuong was an hour late. The sidewalks were deserted. The shadows of the tree canopy over Le Quy Don made it look like dusk.

On the bus I asked My-Nga to make an announcement in Vietnamese. All men between the ages of sixteen and twenty should move to the back of the bus and sit with Mr. White. I placed five young men in the seats near me and the bus pulled out of the delightful shade of Le Quy Don into the garish sunshine of Cong Ly.

I put my leather satchel on my lap and reorganized the contents, moving clothes to the bottom and bundles of greenbacks to the top. I took the Chief's Special out of the interior side pocket and flipped open the cylinder to inspect the five cartridges. That model of revolver has a double-action hammer, meaning that it can be fired either with the hammer down or cocked back. When it is cocked it takes only a light touch on the trigger to fire it. Cocking it improves accuracy, but it also increases the risk of unintentional discharge. It was a trade-off nobody should have to make on a crowded bus. I decided to cock it.

Instantly, I realized that that was premature. The threat was not immediate. In fact the threat was merely latent, just an impending checkpoint. But uncocking a loaded, double action revolver is dicey. It's easy enough on a shooting range or out in the woods, in fact I'd practiced doing it with one hand and never had an unintentional discharge. I didn't recommend it, but it could be done.

The smart way to uncock a loaded revolver on a crowded bus, if there is one, is to open the cylinder and slide out the live cartridges, but if I were that smart I wouldn't be in such a pickle. So I put my left hand in the satchel and grasped the stubby, two-inch barrel. Then, holding the hammer back with my right thumb, pulled the trigger, and with my finger still depressing the trigger, let the hammer slowly down. Bingo, an uncocked Chief's Special, a far safer weapon.

*   *   *

The queue of embassy buses was just rumbling through the South Vietnamese Army checkpoint as we arrived, and to my enormous relief we got waved through with them. I can only guess at why it was so easy. There may have been some brass from the embassy or the Defense Attaché in the first bus to throw the fear of God into them. Maybe they'd already killed enough innocent young men to meet their daily quota. I honestly can't say. I wasn't the only one relieved. Some of the parents clasped their hands and bowed their heads in prayer. Some of the boys seated around me patted me on the shoulder and said, *cam on*.

The buses in front of us proceeded to the Evacuation Control Center flight line. I asked our driver to stop on the main road while I took a look. In an area where a hundred people would have constituted a crowd, there were a thousand. It was a goddamn madhouse. It would be impossible to keep my family together while I figured out how to board a military aircraft illegally. It infuriated me that all of this would have been avoided if someone had strapped Ambassador Martin into a straitjacket a week ago. Kissinger could have recalled him for consultations. No, that would have left Deputy Chief of Mission Wolfgang Lehmann in charge and he'd been bitten by the same snake as Martin. How many delusionaries would Kissinger have had to recall before a realist like Shep Lowman or Denny Ellerman or Conrad LaGueux would be calling the shots at Embassy Saigon? Possibly Washington didn't care. What had President Ford said at Tulane? *Vietnam is a war that was over as far as America is concerned.* Well, guess what, Mr. President, it was a long way from over for the couple of thousand Americans still here, or for their tens of thousands of Vietnamerican dependents.

To the bus driver I said, "Let's continue on to Tiger Airlines." I reached in my satchel and grasped the keys to my DC-3. U-Tapao air base in Thailand was only five hundred miles away. The DC-3 cruises at two hundred miles per hour. We'd be safe two and a half hours after takeoff. I was reasonably sure I could get it into the air. A practice flight would have been great but that wasn't in the cards. The tower was going to go apoplectic with my unauthorized takeoff. If I did make a second flight it would be to return to Saigon to pick up the rest of my Chase family. Bach-Mai's husband, Cau, had tutored me in the half dozen things I hadn't been able to figure out on my own. What could go wrong?

I got the answer to that question painfully soon. The bus turned into the parking lot at Tiger and my plane had vanished. The other DC-3s were all configured with passenger seats and not for cargo, and couldn't possibly hold sixty-eight persons plus baggage. Sixty-nine including me.

My plan was blown totally to hell.

I couldn't have the driver and my passengers think we'd come to Tiger just to circle the parking lot, so I disembarked and entered Tiger's ops building. It was longer than a long shot but I asked the duty officer if he had any planes that could get sixty-eight undocumented Vietnamese out today. If it was the craziest thing he'd ever heard, he didn't reveal it. He didn't even look up to see who was speaking to him. A clipped *No* was all I got.

Back on the bus I said, "Looks like we'll have to go back to the Evacuation Control Center." On the one-minute ride I decided to park my refugees somewhere they wouldn't get separated. I'd go alone into the gymnasium and claw my way to the front of the crowd and find someone willing to overlook the exit visa requirement in exchange for a cool two grand. Four grand. Six. I never met a vice consul I couldn't bribe. Actually, I'd never met a vice consul.

On military bases most buildings have signs above their front doors to indicate their purpose in the affairs of humans. The signs assist newcomers in finding their way around, while also reducing the disadvantage of being beastly dumb. Adjacent to the evacuation center was a building signposted *Bowling Alley*. I thought it unlikely that a bowling alley would be busy at this juncture in history, and it was not.

The bowling alley had the singular disadvantage of being hellishly hot, with absolutely no ventilation, but I preferred to leave my family indoors, and didn't think it would take me long to find the crack in some vice consul's integrity. What I was trying to do shouldn't even have been illegal, and wouldn't have been if—Damn! I had to stop blaming the embassy's delusionaries for everything and just play the cards I'd been dealt. No more what-ifs for Ralph.

Expecting borderline anarchy back at the Evacuation Control Center, I was surprised to find a modicum of organization. Airmen blocked me from cutting in front of people and they asked me my business. "I need to know what I've got to do to get locals out without papers." This time I didn't say they were Chase Manhattan Bank employees who were vulnerable to communist reprisal. That line hadn't gotten me far so I abandoned it.

"Follow the yellow line, sir." The airman pointed to a stripe on the wooden floor. "We're processing people pretty fast."

Fast is relative, depending on how many family members you've got in a slow-cooker of a bowling alley. I will admit to being pretty nervous. I bummed a smoke from the guy in front of me in an effort to settle my nerves. The yellow line ended at a row of five conference tables, each labeled *Vice Consul*. Oh boy, oh boy, oh boy. My scrotum itched like the dickens and I forced myself not to scratch it.

"Next!"

I approached the vacated table.

"Passport." All business, this vice consul.

I withdrew my passport from my multipurpose satchel and handed it to him.

"What can I do for you, Mr. White?"

"Well, I suppose you could help me put some Vietnamese on a plane."

"Wife and kids?"

My answer would be truthful in some vague semantic sense. There *were* wives in my group. There *were* kids. "Affirmative."

"Are you willing to take financial responsibility for them?"

He'd clearly asked the question hundreds of times a day for many days. I repeated, "Affirmative."

"You'll need to fill out this form for each individual." He held up a single sheet of paper. "How many do you need?"

I toyed with the idea of asking for seven, then getting back in line ten more times, and hope they didn't recognize me. Then I thought of how terribly my colleagues and their families must be suffering in the stifling bowling alley. I took a breath and said, "Sixty-eight." If he said *no* I'd quickly determine how much *yes* would cost. I unlatched my satchel of cash, underwear, and revolver, prepared for pretty much anything.

The consul looked up at me and said, "Did you say sixty-eight, sir?"

"Affirmative."

"I seriously doubt you can support sixty-eight wards. How old are you?"

He was performing his duty as a sworn consular officer. "I'm twenty-seven, but I have very deep pockets."

"What's your relationship to these individuals?"

"They are my family." I maintained eye contact, just as I would in any honest, sincere, serious conversation. If I considered them family then they were family, and that was all there was to it.

The guy paused, truly undecided. He was a government official, but he was also human.

I leaned over and said, "You can do a lot of harm or a lot of good."

He snatched up a bundle of forms without counting them. "Should be enough here." He stood and offered a firm handshake. "God bless you, Mr. White. Make sure you bring the forms back to this table when you're done."

I found a jeep parked outside the gym in the sun and tried filling out the forms on a fender but it was as hot as a radiator. I tried laying my leather satchel on the fender and using it as a writing surface but became anxious that the heat might set off the cartridges in my revolver. Sweat dripped from my face as I opened the satchel and slipped the gun into my pants pocket. Each form took me a minute, so it took an hour in the full sun to finish the job. My face was slick; my clothes were moist. I was woozy with thirst. How did humans survive in such a climate?

Back inside the gym it was a few degrees cooler but still sweltering. I had to get back in the yellow stripe queue again and wait my turn, then wait still longer for my conspiratorial consul. He said, "You'll want all your wards on one flight, but I only have twenty more places on this one, so just stand by until I start a new manifest, okay?"

My answer was to move around to his side of the table. I asked, "What do you do for water here?" He called out to an airman who disappeared for ten minutes before returning with a couple of quarts of water. I returned to the front of the table when he started a new manifest. I watched carefully as he entered every name. I had to correct him a couple of times. Vietnamese names can be tricky.

When he finished, he said, "Listen very carefully to the public address system. Your group is on manifest 85. It'll take a few hours before you're called. You'll be going to Guam, courtesy of Military Airlift Command, Pacific."

"Thank you very much. Say, if it's not too much trouble, think you might get sixty quarts of drinking water delivered to the bowling alley? It's right next door. My wards and I are holed up there and there's zero ventilation." I walked away, realizing that I'd never asked his name. His signature on the forms was illegible.

*   *   *

Military installations in Vietnam had two kinds of outhouse. One type was just a white PVC tube slanting out of the bare ground. They were called *piss tubes*. Presumably there was a small leaching field at the underground end of the tube. I hoped it didn't go through to the other end of the globe, because that was where my hometown was located. There were no walls around these piss tubes. Modesty was achieved by people who were offended looking in the other direction. Conversely, people who were entertained by such a spectacle were welcome to watch.

The second type functioned as feces incinerators and they were often paired with showers where the water was heated with burning excrement and kerosene. A shower sounded pretty good about then so I looked for the distinctive plume of dark smoke indicating the location of such a facility. In the shower I found a sliver of Ivory soap about the size of my little finger, and proceeded to scrub myself all over until the soap dissolved into the netherworld. When I put my gamy clothes back on, the bacteria lodged there cheered the return of fresh meat.

On the way out I passed a familiar face, and as often happens when someone appears out of context, there was an embarrassing delay until his name came to me. "James Ashida, commercial attaché extraordinaire!"

"Hi, Ralph. Wait here for me, will you? I've got some news for you."

A few minutes later he exited the outhouse and said, "I can get another bus for you tomorrow. Seventy more seats."

I pulled up my mental spreadsheet, which said I had forty-nine on the nonpriority list. Fifty-five if the Cuongs showed up, plus myself. "I'll take it. Thanks, Jim."

"This time we'll send a bus wherever you want us to pick you up."

We couldn't use Le Quy Don; it would be too conspicuous after today. The ARVN and white mice would have heard about the pandemonium. The Viet Cong would too, probably before anyone else. I said, "One eighteen, Phan Din Phung." It was Cor Termijn's house. "Say, noon?"

"You got it." Then as if to make amends for having been so unhelpful until this very moment he said, "Let me take you back to the city in my limo."

Exactly to where, I wasn't sure. I'd checked out of the Caravelle. Ashida told me where his car was parked and I said I'd meet him there in an hour.

When I finally got back to the bowling alley it was deserted, the heat inside unbearable. A female employee I didn't recognize was waiting for me to return, and led me to a dirt parking lot between buildings where my group was strung out along a strip of shade. It was a pitiable sight, but when they saw me their faces brightened. There were even a few smiles. Each one of them clutched a gallon bottle of water.

I had a final conversation with the two officers, My-Nga and Hong-Lien. "I'm going back to get the rest of the employees and I'll be taking them out tomorrow. I'm putting My-Nga in charge of this group. Here's a copy of the list of everyone's names. Listen carefully to the loudspeakers for an announcement saying that manifest number 85 is boarding. I think they're on 62 now. Then go to the flight line and tell them who you are. They'll check off each name on the list and you'll all be able to get on the same plane together. They tell me you'll be flying to Guam. It's an American possession so your families will be safe there. A task force from Chase's head office will eventually find you and provide accommodations and food. Don't ask me how they're going to find you or how long it will take them because I don't know. I'm sorry to leave you like this but I am sure you'll be treated well. Don't forget: listen for the announcement that manifest 85 is boarding. Miss that and you're in deep trouble."

*   *   *

James Ashida's brand-new 1974 Lincoln Town Car was a marvel to behold. It was big, black, and beautiful; slab-sided and imposing. The uniformed driver was a handsome young blond guy in his early twenties. I clearly recalled that on the Friday of the Hung Kings weekend, days before Xuan Loc had been decided, President Ford had ordered the evacuation of all nonessential embassy staff. Who knew the commercial attaché's chauffeur was such an essential cog in the American wheel of state?

The insides of the car were, if possible, even more imposing than the exterior. The shiny black leather seats were broad enough for sumo wrestlers. There was burled wood trim and chrome accents. Nearly invisible switches opened and closed the tinted windows electrically. I'd heard of electric car windows but had never seen them. To a New Englander they were decidedly effete. Someone who worked for a living shouldn't object to cranking his own car windows up and down.

Ashida's limo also had air-conditioning! Holy cow! I wondered how many cars in Vietnam were air-conditioned. And here I was, Ralph White, Litchfield High School class of 1965, riding in the backseat of a Lincoln Town Car with the commercial attaché to the Republic of South Vietnam. I was glad now that I hadn't chewed him out for disappearing over that long weekend. I might be hitch-hiking about now.

Gliding down Cong Ly Street in the princely splendor of a beautiful new Lincoln was transformative. Yeah, it was a sweeter ride than a cramped, smoke-filled, cream-and-blue local taxi with coat hanger wire in place of a shift stick. The difference was orders of magnitude. The swarms of motorbikes didn't make as much noise. They didn't spew as much exhaust. The aroma of garlic from the noodle stalls was missing. And that dust? What dust? Even the scraggly coconut palms along Cong Ly became charming. This car insulated its passengers from Saigon. It deprived them of its experience. I wondered if the embassy's cluelessness could be traced to the Lincoln Town Car and to its equivalent in posh helicopters.

A creature of habit still, I asked Ashida to drop me off at the Caravelle, and I stood and watched as he and his grand car departed. That car was going to make some North Vietnamese general very happy.

Cuong was in a deep funk in one of the smelly armchairs in the lobby. Failing to show up at the bus rendezvous in time to save him from execution and his family from starvation had been a tragedy of nightmarish proportions. When I walked up to him, he blinked twice to make sure I wasn't the incarnate spirit of recrimination. To his credit he was dry-eyed and sober. I doubted I would be if I were him.

"Mr. Cuong, I suggest you take your family out for a nice dinner tonight and get to bed early. Please show up ready to rock and roll at the bank tomorrow because I will need you."

"I . . . I, you . . ."

"I know, Mr. Cuong. Now I'm kind of busy, if you don't mind." I resolved to never ask Cuong what had delayed him that day. It would force him to relive an experience that must be extremely painful. "Good night."

*   *   *

The Caravelle put me back in my old room, which I paid for in advance to reduce checkout time. I opened the balcony door to let in Southeast Asia. I thought I couldn't be happier, and then the laundry people delivered my black underwear. I forayed into the city for a few travel supplies and a farewell stroll down Tu Do Street.

The New York Bar was immersed in the cool blue light of an underwater photograph, with bikini-clad girls gliding by in place of angelfish. I ordered a beer and would make myself happy with any brand they served. I'd do the same with the girls. Whichever one sat down with me first would be my language tutor for the evening.

A chubby young woman said, *"Chao, ong Bach."*

God, she knew me! I didn't think I'd been there so often that I'd even be recognized, let alone known by name. I'd learned the word *white* from a brand of facial tissues called *Bach Tuyet*, or White Snow. I suppose I should have been flattered, but instead my anonymity had been breached. I told her I'd buy her a Saigon tea if she would teach me a few new words.

She was quick. "I teach *ong Bach* how Viet say, *no money, no honey.*"

Chapter Twelve

FRIDAY, APRIL 25, 1975

The Saigon docklands came to life early so I did too. Sunrise was 5:37 and I wasn't far behind. Even so there was already someone aboard the Alaska Barge tugboat when I arrived. Bob Lanigan, the co-hero of the Danang evacuation, along with Mel Chatman, was cooking bacon and eggs in a blackened skillet over a charcoal grill.

Lanigan greeted me from the deck of the tugboat. "Want some? This cruise is on modified American plan. I've got enough rations for a company of men for a week."

I had no idea when my next meal would be so I gladly accepted his offer. I slung a red duffel onto the deck and dropped down into a Vietnamese squat like Lanigan's. It's a tough position for a Westerner to acquire and tougher to maintain. With feet flat on the ground, or the deck in our case, the person sinks downward until his knees are cupped into his armpits. I learned the squat in the Central Highlands, around a cauldron of potent rice wine with large, winged insects floating in it. The key to the squat is to angle the ankles forward so that the center of gravity is over the balls of the feet. The key to Central Highlands rice wine is to spit out the insects.

Lanigan pointed to some barges moored near the channel. "Each of them can hold a thousand people. There's already a couple hundred refugees on each of them. They'll be full by the time we shove off."

I said, "Three thousand people and no toilets?"

"I'm guessing closer to five thousand. And they didn't have toilets where they came from."

Nga arrived an hour later with Thang, surrounded by the squad of Viet Cong that had sprung me from the jail on Tuesday. God, was that already two days ago? Suspiciously, the VC carried duffels too. Nga was as excited to see me as, well, a puppy. Her squirming and hugging and squealing were thoroughly undignified and embarrassing, and it took a couple of minutes to settle her down so I could explain everything.

"A rogue faction at the U.S. embassy finally did the right thing. They secretly bused half of my employees to Tan Son Nhut yesterday, and when they offered to help with the other half today, I elected to stay another day and leave with them."

Lanigan offered Thang and his nationalists some breakfast and they accepted. It was the bacon alone that sealed the deal. If Kissinger had served up some thick, fragrant, slab bacon to Le Duc Tho at the Paris Peace Talks . . . But I'd said, no more what-ifs.

Thang said, "The Hawaii office of your Federal Aviation Administration has announced that all commercial flights to Vietnam are suspended."

"That alert won't have much effect since Pan Am was the only commercial carrier and their last flight was yesterday. Oh, I forgot; there's Air Vietnam. I guess their planes can still take off, but now they can't return."

Thang said, "Foreign embassies were using commercial aircraft to extract their diplomats and ICCS people. Now it all has to be military."

"Any foreigners still here are asking for trouble."

"You're still here, Mitter Why."

As we chatted, more Vietnamese refugees rowed out to the barges and began to settle in. There was no one from the embassy or DAO to check papers. Bob Lanigan's operation welcomed Vietnam's huddled masses yearning to be free. He was decidedly not ambassadorial material.

It was looking as though Thang wasn't going to volunteer why he had showed up, so I asked, "Have you decided to defect to the capitalists? I took you for a committed revolutionary."

"My men will remain with Nga as far as Vung Tau. They will provide security down the river and get off just before the tug heads out to sea. The delta is not secure." He issued an order in Vietnamese to his men and they removed their rifles from their duffels.

Lanigan immediately noticed the distinctive banana-shaped magazines of their Type 56 tactical rifles. He said, "Aw, shit!"

"Not to worry, Bob," I said. "It's the incoming administration. They're here to protect your most valuable passenger." I pointed to Nga. "She's their commander's little sister. She's also my ward."

"I am your *ward*? This means what?"

I took the completed immigration form from my satchel and gave it to her. "Show this to the officers on the American ship and they will help you. It makes me your guardian and you my ward."

"Does it mean we are married?"

"It means I am legally responsible for you, more like a father than a husband. The American authorities will not have to worry what will happen if they admit you into America because I am required to support and protect you. Since I won't be there, my mother will become, well, your mother."

"Then you will be my brother, not my father."

Lanigan said, "If they're disembarking at Vung Tau she and her guards can stay on the tug with me and the river pilot."

A delivery van came to a stop on the wharf and Jackson Dunn leaped from the rear doors. At first I assumed that he had so much gold to transport from his commercial marriage business that he needed a van. He proved me wrong by rolling a wheelchair down a ramp, with what looked like a cadaver in the seat. He pushed the wheelchair across the wharf and up the ramp onto the tug and stood there, apparently waiting to be welcomed.

None of us knew Dunn well, so we couldn't know if taking cadavers on river cruises was in or out of character for him. I said, "Hi, Jackson. I see you found someone to pay your evacuation fee."

The eyes on the body in Dunn's chair slowly opened and cautiously studied their surroundings. Its head was shaved and it perched upright on its slender stalk of a neck. The facial features were well proportioned, like those of a mannequin awaiting a change of wardrobe. When the passenger smiled, Nga recognized her.

"Yen-Yen! It's Yen-Yen! Look Mr. White, Jackson is taking Yen-Yen."

Jackson finally spoke up. "All she needs is some prosthetics. No reason she couldn't live a productive life if she had four limbs. They're making them out of composites now, with cool new electromechanical features to make them more functional. The human body is kind of like an engine; you replace the parts that aren't working and it's up and running. She says she wants to come back to Saigon someday and be a stand-up comic, and for that she'll have to stand up."

Thang said, "I'm leaving now, Mr. White, but I have something I need to tell you. We learned that a top man from the Bank of Vietnam, the National Bank, has plans to leave and that he is taking his entire family. Where can we discuss it?"

"I'll be at the Chase branch for the next couple of hours."

"Then I will return and meet you outside. Goodbye. Thanks for helping Nga."

I said, "No, let's meet at the Majestic. The crowd outside the bank is going to be out of control. And if you can wait a second, I'll hitch a ride on your bike."

I hugged my sweet Nga and promised to visit her on my home leave. I wanted badly for this to be a painless separation. I presented her with the red duffel I'd brought with me and I quickly left with Thang before she unzipped it. Inside she would find fresh water, toilet paper, a life preserver, a papaya, a sun hat, a camera, American suntan lotion, seasick pills, a bottle of *nuoc mam* food seasoning, and sticky rice with sweet coconut wrapped in a banana leaf. She might think it a strange bon voyage package, but it was all I could come up with in two dusty hours of found time.

I would be less than honest if I didn't admit to loving every little thing about her. I'd often thought about making a life with her, though I also had to admit they were more fantasies than actual plans. One fantasy did stand out and it governed my emotions as we parted. The gist of it was that I would wait for her to complete her education, then check in to see if her youthful infatuation with Mr. White had survived. Some long-distance romances defy the odds, but considering the difference in our ages, the odds were heavily against us. Also being honest, just as I didn't want her to think she had to sleep with me, I also didn't want her to think she had to marry me. Finally, keeping things in perspective, she wasn't the only one who had some growing up to do.

As Thang and I were passing through the gate to the dockyards I saw my foreign exchange dealer, Raj, driving in. I was glad he had decided to leave Vietnam. Lanigan's tug was ideal for him. And for his gold.

*   *   *

I'd been right about the angry crowd outside the bank and was glad I'd asked Thang to drop me off at the Majestic. It was a few minutes past 9:00 and the bank's clients had just learned that Chase had closed in the sense that the Republic of South Vietnam was closing. It was easy to sympathize with them. In contrast to the clients, the closing opened up a hopeful future for my families and for their descendants in perpetuity. For our clients the locking of the bank's doors was the first stage in Saigon's implosion.

Although the side door was only about fifty feet from the bank's main entrance it looked like an entrance to an entirely different enterprise. I breezily let myself in and quickly closed the door behind me.

The employees inside were only slightly less angry than the crowd outside, though less well armed. They'd observed that none of the bank's officers or department heads had shown up. They knew Saigon branch had closed. They knew they'd been left behind. And they knew why, because their lives mattered less. Again, I empathized. Fortunately they'd only had a few minutes to stew in their anxieties before I presented myself. I could see the wheels spinning: if Mr. White was still here then all was not lost.

Cuong came in behind me. He had obviously been watching outside so that the employees would confront me first. I was very pleased he did show up. I couldn't have blamed him if he had just gone to the pickup point that evening with his family. His presence made the closing far more orderly. He was able to personally interview all the employees and determine who wanted to stay and how much their termination pay would be. Having him there also made it easier to explain that I defined family as spouse and children. I wasn't evacuating parents or siblings. I also wasn't transporting anyone's suspiciously heavy suitcases.

There was another difficult conversation I couldn't have had on my own. One of the employees had been raising her sister's child. How that situation came to be was obscured by her anguish, but her own children considered the cousin to be their sibling. I'd been so adamant about who Chase would and would not support that she'd become fearful I'd rip her family apart. I'd taken that hard stance because, having lived in Vietnam three years earlier, I knew well how fluid the concept of family was there. Entirely unrelated women called one another sister. Anyone over forty could be called aunt or uncle, in fact those titles were widely used as simple honorifics. The guy who replaced the water barrel in our cooler in Pleiku was Uncle Tran. North Vietnam's patron saint was Uncle Ho.

I wanted the employees to understand that exceptions to Mr. White's definition of family were going to be next to impossible. In fact I welcomed the brief drama involving the employee's appeal. Extremely reluctantly, and only after Cuong strongly vouched for the child in question, did the grumpy Mr. White relent. It must have been the right thing to do because the whole group cheered.

Cuong began releasing employees in ones and twos out of the side door, coaching them to engage one another in casual banter as they passed the increasingly hostile crowd of depositors outside. I mounted the stairs to the manager's office to take stock.

The phone on my desk was ringing but I was reluctant to pick it up. What if it was an irate client? I wouldn't want any of them to know I was inside the building. But what if it was Hong Kong or New York? I picked it up.

Instead of *hello*, I said, "Ralph White."

"Hi, Ralph. This is Denny Ellerman at the embassy. I'm getting reports that Chase is closing."

I had a slight pang of remorse. I should have told him earlier. "Actually, Denny, we closed yesterday at noon. Our officers and department heads are already in Guam."

"I'll need all the details. What redress do depositors have? Whom should they contact, and where? How about your files and records?"

I gave him everything he wanted. Twice he called back with questions from the Vietnamese minister of finance. It became a nuisance, and I had to remind myself that these were not the questions of Denny Ellerman, card-carrying realist, but of a finance minister about to lose his job, his country, and very possibly his life.

My last words with Denny Ellerman went something like this. "Ralph, they want to know on whose authority the Chase Manhattan Bank closed its Saigon branch."

"Feel free to give them my name, Denny."

* * *

I heard whirring and tapping in the cable machine closet and went in to see who was trying to raise us. The message came in agonizingly slowly. I sat in the operator's chair and watched each character materialize on the roll of coarse paper.

```
THIS IS CHASE REGIONAL OFFICE CLG CHASE SAIGON IS
ANYONE THERE
```

The machine was solid, bulky, and gray, like a typewriter designed to withstand a thermonuclear fireball. The only thing familiar about it was the QWERTY keyboard. I rested my fingertips on it and typed,

```
YES MR WHITE
```

I was a lightning-fast touch typist but it took about forty-five seconds for those three words to appear on the paper. I swiveled in the chair, waiting. I looked for a shift key to produce upper and lowercase letters but found none. Nor was punctuation possible.

```
WHAT ARE YOU DOING THERE AND WHY DID YOU NOT LEAVE
TERMIJN
```

```
WHO IS THERE NOW
```

That was a kind of a long story, and one that would be hard to tell on this slow-paced machine given the time available.

```
THIS IS WHITE STOP SAIGON IS STILL FAIRLY QUIET AND
SECURE AND ADDIONALLY
```

I was looking for the backspace key to fix my misspelling when Cor came back at me.

```
ARE ANY OTHER PEOPLE STILL THERE
```

People. He calls my family people. I adopted his quirk.

```
YES MANY PEOPLE ARE HERE STOP
```

HOW MANY HAVE LEFT

He deserved a fuller story, notwithstanding the ponderous technology. I tapped away.

SIXTY-TWO SIR AND HAVE FIFTY SIX FOR TODAY STOP ALL
OTHERS HAVE ELECTED TO STAY STOP THERE SEEMS TO BE
NO PROBLEM IN THIS REGARD STOP ELLERMAN EXTREMELY
CONCERNED ABOUT HOW DEPOSITORS WILL GET THEIR
FUNDS STOP HE DOES NOT WANT CUSTOMERS PENALIZED
FOR HAVING DONE BUSINESS WITH AMERICAN BANK STOP
RIGHT NOW RECORDS AND KEYS ARE AT FRENCH EMBASSY PER
YOUR INSTRUCTIONS STOP WOULD YOU LIKE ME TO GO TO
GOVERNOR OF NATIONAL BANK WITH ELLERMAN AND TRY TO
TRANSFER ACCOUNTS TO OTHER BANKS STOP I BELIEVE THAT
I HAVE THE TIME TO DO SO WITHOUT JEOPARDIZING THE
OTHER OBJECTIVE

My message was several minutes going out. The tone of Cor's incoming startled me.

PLS STOP THIS NONSENSE AND YOU ARE HEREBY
INSTRUCTED TO LEAVE VIETNAM TOGETHER WITH THE OTHER
GROUP TODAY STOP HEAD OFFICE WILL INSTRUCT NATIONAL
BANK WHAT TO DO STOP I REPEAT GET OUT OF THERE
TERMIJN

YESSIR MY PLEASURE STOP IS THAT ALL

MESSAGE FROM MR KLIMM TO MR WHITE

It was the second time I'd heard Juergen Klimm's name in two days. The Dutchman running the back office at Regional must be going nuts with no settlement data from Saigon.

```
PLS MAKE SURE TESTKEY DESTROYED AND ALL AVAILABLE
MICROFILMS WOULD BE HAND CARRIED BY YOURSELF TONIGHT
STOP
```

Of course I'd already destroyed the test keys. I was a turtle, not a dodo. Microfilm was a different matter. That was part of the daily settlement. I thought Cuong had been sending that in, though now I wondered how.

```
MAY I SEND MICROFILM AND LAST DAYS WORK THROUGH
DIPLOMATIC POUCH
```

I thought I might get Ashida or Ellerman to drop our settlement into the embassy's communications package.

```
ONLY IF YOU CAN NOT CARRY YOURSELF NONE OF THE PRIOR
POUCHES HAVE REACHED US YET STOP
```

That was disastrous news. Unless the daily bookkeeping settlement got through, all our efforts in keeping the branch open these final days were wasted.

```
OK WILL CARRY STOP ANY MORE
```

```
TKS AND PLS TELEPHONE OR TELEX ADVISE US FROM YOUR
ARRIVAL POINT STOP OVER BYE BYE
```

```
BYE BYE CAM ON
```

Chase Saigon's last words were Vietnamese. *Thank you.*

*   *   *

I met Thang at a window seat in the lobby of the Majestic Hotel. I found it astonishing that everyone here was going about their business as though life as they knew it would continue forever.

Thang asked, "Do you know a senior official at the National Bank of Vietnam named Long Pham Truong?"

"I do not. Should I?"

"You might be interested to know that he has been issued some of the exit visas that you have been looking for so hard. Even more interesting is that he also has U.S. entry visas for himself and his family. We know this because members of his family are proudly telling many people—"

"Bragging. We call that bragging."

"They are bragging that they are getting everybody in their family out."

"Hmm. Do we know where the Long family is going? All the other senior guys in the government and military have ended up in the U.S., mostly California."

"This information will also interest you. The Long family is going to Washington, D.C., and on a U.S. military flight, not Air Vietnam."

"That's fishy." It didn't sound like something that Shep Lowman would get involved in. A central bank governor wouldn't fit his selection criteria. His program was for American dependents and Vietnamese who were at risk for having collaborating with Americans.

"Sorry? Fishy?"

"In this context fishy just means suspicious." I wished I could find out what Mr. Long of the National Bank of Vietnam was up to, but I couldn't even start thinking how to go about it. It definitely tickled my curiosity.

*   *   *

With little to occupy me until the embassy bus found us at 7:00, I wandered around District 1, curious about what happens when a city is gradually removed from life support. The buildings were not going anywhere. The Basilica of Notre Dame would always be there. The post office, the Opera House, the three hotels in my life: the Majestic, Continental, and Caravelle. The French colonial villas would continue to crack and crumble, just as the French themselves would become forgotten and their language unrecalled. The blue flame of carnal desire at the Tennessee and New York bars would struggle to produce honey on far less money. The Presidential Palace would be rebranded, and some of the streets would acquire the names of North Vietnamese generals, or as is oft the communist custom, revolutionary slogans. The botanical garden should survive communism, but there would be no defending the captive animals at the zoo from a starving populace. The Chase Manhattan Bank, being close to the port, might make a good import-export office. Tan Son Nhut, with its ultra-long runways and massive infrastructure, would make a world-class airport. The U.S. embassy would inevitably be demolished. The victors might try to rename the city itself, but it had been called *Sai Gòn*, meaning kapok forest, for two and a half centuries, and that might prove too hard a habit to break.

Once the idea visited me to pay my last respects at the terrace café at the Continental Hotel, I was powerless to do otherwise. Somerset Maugham had been charmed to the same location for its merry ambience at what he called *the hour of the aperitif*. A decade before I was born, Maugham took particular care to describe the Continental's open-air terrace, with its bearded, gesticulating Frenchmen and their sweet beverages. Maugham—I bless him and wonder—called Saigon *a blithe and smiling little place*. If any part of that Saigon were to survive the coming onslaught, it would be on that very terrace. But if the spirit hovering there were butchered along with the animals of the zoo, then the next most likely survivors would be the blue-hued demons on Tu Do Street.

Where Maugham discovered bearded, gesticulating Frenchmen, I found the U.S. embassy's minister-counsellor, economic affairs observing the hour of the aperitif in contemplative solitude. "Hi, Denny, may I join you?"

Ellerman looked pleased to see me. "Hi, Ralph."

The metal chair screeched against the ceramic tile floor as I pulled it away from the table and a waiter ambled over. I described the drink I'd invented around Henk Steenbergen's swimming pool on the day John Linker recruited me for Saigon. "Freshly squeezed lime juice, raw sugar, and cheap whiskey, in any proportion convenient to the barman." Above the waiter's head, slowly rotating ceiling fans whisked galaxies of insects into spiral clouds.

With my preoccupation about employee evacuation more or less sated, Denny Ellerman and I no longer had a professional tether and I took it upon myself to weave in a new thread. "You believe that the consensus view of Ambassador Martin is off the mark."

He sipped his beer and said, "That's right. I believe Martin became the fall guy for a specific failure of foreign policy. Once the American public had washed its hands of Vietnam, and our government initiated a policy that the Vietnamese had to defend themselves—"

"Vietnamization."

"Precisely. When legislative appropriations to support that policy were defeated it became convenient to tag Martin with the failure of the policy. There were a dozen officials in our government more deserving of blame, but Hollywood casting could not have come up with a better character than Martin for the part and he played it well. The media took the bait and ran with it, depicting him as detached—or worse."

My drink arrived and the sweet, tarty lime gave me a tingle. I was in a position to be a lot more charitable about Ambassador Martin now that I'd figured out how to circumvent him. "Even if I were to agree with you, I'd still believe his inaction contributed to the looming humanitarian disaster."

Ellerman said, "Only a few people outside the embassy know this, but evacuation planning started discreetly after the fall of Da

Nang. We've actually gotten a lot of people out, Ralph, both Americans and Vietnamese. From outside the embassy, you see evacuation as a glass half empty, but from the inside, we see it half full."

"Denny, both of our glasses are completely empty."

"Then I suppose we both ought to get back to work."

*   *   *

118 Phan Din Phung, Cor Termijn's house, was in Tan Dinh, a quiet, upscale neighborhood, as was fitting for an executive who was expected to entertain clients. It was a far cry from the elegant home of Chase's country manager in Thailand, with its Palm Beach ambience, but it was pretty much what I expected when I designated it as the pickup point for my second installment of refugees. It was a small, pale yellow, two-story residence separated by narrow lawns from similar homes. It wouldn't have looked out of place in any mid-priced suburb in America except that in lieu of a fastidious picket fence it was secured by a thick concrete wall. Cor's house also had the advantage of being just one circuitous mile from the main gate at Tan Son Nhut. A couple of Cor's servants admitted me when I introduced myself.

I apprised Cor's staff of what was afoot and invited them to join the rest of Chase's employees on the Ark of Salvation, but they said in effect that the communists would be no more unwelcome than a rainy day. I passed on pointing out the difference between a drizzle and a deluge. Thanks anyway, they said, but they would be staying.

Cuong arrived next with the Garvey family. He gave the servants their exit interviews and issued their termination pay in a currency that had lost most of its value in the last two weeks and whose prospects were bleak. The servants didn't feel shorted; it wasn't about money. The war was over. How could things not get better?

As the embassy bus pulled up outside the wall, one of the bank employees became seized by grief and began wailing in Vietnamese and clawing at her neck, tracing lines of blood. I grabbed her hands and insisted she stop hurting herself. I tried to communicate with her. "What's wrong? Please tell me. Stop!" She must have understood English in order to have a job at Chase, but she wouldn't talk to me. "What is it? Are you okay?" She wasn't okay; she was having an uncontrollable emotional meltdown.

One of the refugees kneeled in front of the woman's chair and spoke quietly to her in Vietnamese. Whatever he said calmed her and she began weeping words. I asked the guy who he was and he introduced himself as Trinh Van Chu. I said, "Tell her I just need to know if she wants to go or stay. I'm sorry she's so upset, but I need to know right now because the bus is outside."

Trinh spoke to the distraught woman gently and tried to coax a decision from her. Her mother, it turned out, was alone and incapable of supporting herself. The employee dreamed of a new life in America but the trade-off would be intense suffering for her mother. She blurted her story out between sobs. Trinh was patient. The woman inconsolable. Everyone in the room encircled us, their collective anxiety distilled to this one woman's outpouring.

The woman's bloodshot eyes found mine and she said, "I could never forgive myself. She is so alone. Please, Mr. White, let me take my mother. The bus could pick her up. One more person could make no difference. It would save her. One more person. Please."

I willed myself not to imagine the mother of this wretched woman, but my will faltered. I tried not to see her surviving off begged rice and begged charcoal to cook it. I tried not to see her hygiene deteriorate, as hot water and soap became luxuries. I saw the old woman lying on a dirt floor and for an instant she had my mother's pretty face and auburn hair.

"I believe you had better not leave your mother. If she needs you so badly you must stay here and care for her." The idea evolved. "Why don't you go get your mother and bring her here? The two of you can live with Mr. Termijn's . . ."—I almost said *servants*—". . . his domestic staff, until the communists arrive."

I didn't witness her decision, but subsequent headcounts show she remained in Vietnam. I thanked Trinh for his intervention and asked Cuong to start boarding the bus.

With that one defection and four no-shows it made fifty-one refugees who boarded the bus at Phan Din Phung, plus a young New England lad, now somewhat less callow than he'd been on his arrival eleven days earlier. As evidence of my transformation, I offered my admission of non-Chase refugees entirely on my own responsibility. I wouldn't have done that two weeks ago. I'd also underwritten the emigration and education of a recently reformed teenage prostitute, a girl for whom I'd developed an incredibly ambiguous affection. I was no longer the guy on my passport.

*   *   *

I wondered if Cor Termijn's telephone was still connected, so I picked it up. There was indeed a dial tone. Next to Cor's telephone was a list of emergency numbers and one of them was U.S. ambassador Graham Martin. I dialed it. His secretary picked up. It was an American woman's remarkably calm voice. I tried to imitate a Dutchman in a tizzy.

Recalling that Martin's secretary was the wife of George McArthur of the *L.A. Times*, I said, "Oh, good afternoon, Mrs. McArthur. Oh my! Cor Termijn here. May I speak to Mr. Martin urgently for just two minutes?"

"Of course, Mr. Termijn."

Ten seconds later, "Martin here."

"Graham, this is Ralph White at the bank. How's that little cough?"

"You!"

"Hey, Graham. Why's Long Pham Truong, at the National Bank of Vietnam, flying his family to Washington, D.C.? How'd he get exit visas for his whole clan when I can't get any of my Chase Bank employees out? What the hell's that all about?"

"Well, Mr. White, if your employees were escorting eight tons of gold out of the country, they might have gotten exit visas too."

"Eight tons, eh? Sounds like the National Bank's gold reserves. Mr. Long got his American visa on Tuesday, Graham. You were still telling me on Tuesday that victory was possible. I'm not exactly claiming that I've caught you in a lie, but I do think you owe me an explanation."

"Oh, Mr. White, poor Mr. White. Let me be frank with you. I simply informed Henry Kissinger that I considered Vietnam's gold to be a higher priority than the Chase Manhattan Bank's employees. And now I'm a little busy here so is there anything else I *can't* do for you?"

"Thanks, but no, Graham, and I absolutely appreciate your candor."

*   *   *

The bus was olive drab. All that meant was that Uncle Sam had painted it. It could have belonged to the army or the marines, to the embassy or the Central Intelligence Agency, or possibly the Defense Attaché Office. It would probably take a master sergeant in the motor pool to tell for sure where it came from, and by now that guy was probably mowing his lawn in Davenport, Iowa.

As I waited at the end of the line to board the bus, I realized my terminal impressions of Vietnam were forming—the first of which was that the black cloud of diesel exhaust emitted by the bus resembled the black ink that squid eject as they flee predators.

The driver was an American in civilian attire. I guessed he was with the Mission Warden's amateur security force. He wore a flak jacket and helmet, but I could not see a rifle and I do not believe he had one. I would have loved to listen to him speak a few sentences and try to guess his nesting grounds based on his accent, but that was a game for more placid times—and for a more callow Ralph.

In choosing an aisle seat in the back third of the bus, on the left side, I consciously put the forward section of the aisle within my pistol's field of fire. Being blind in my right eye, I had to shoot rifles and shotguns left-handed, but I handled pistols in my more dexterous right hand. With me in the back were the four or five young men of my group who were draft age. Handsome, skinny kids, their fidgeting showed they'd heard about the executions at the South Vietnamese Army's roadblock.

The windows were half open, admitting hot air and barely visible fine dust to billow freely inside, depositing tan frost on every surface, including passengers. This bus spoke the same dialect as the one I'd taken yesterday; the timbre of its engine and whine of its transmission were identical.

We merged with Cong Ly Street within sight of the roadblock and I wondered how our driver would handle it. Some drivers made a rolling stop, as though at a rural intersection. Others added a split-second full stop, as though they were handing a coin to a toll booth attendant. I'd seen some drivers rumble through slowly, watching the gendarmerie for any gesture of disapproval. The rules of engagement were unwritten. The fog of war had mostly dissipated but the human mind remained disoriented. Our driver came to a full and complete stop. Someone knocked hard on the door and our driver swung the lever to open it.

Without taking my good eye off the front of the bus, I raised my satchel from the floor to my lap and slipped my right hand inside. The Chief's Special rose up to my hand like a spaniel starved for attention. In one motion I cocked it and lifted it out of its side pocket, though not entirely free of the leather. I was set. I owned the moral high ground; I had surprise; I was unconflicted. The muscles in my neck and shoulders went soft and my breathing became studied.

I started hunting at age fourteen, when my parents bought a house in Litchfield, Connecticut. The house came with eight acres of forest, and that land was a gateway to three square miles of hunting and fishing. I landed trout and bagged deer from as far away as I could haul them back. No one else in my family hunted, so I was entirely self-taught. After a high school friend of mine showed me how to field dress, skin, and butcher a deer, I began thinking of myself as a woodsman. Firearms were tools of our trade.

Deer stands are little platforms built ten to fifteen feet up in trees. The hunter hikes into the woods in the predawn hours and climbs up to the stand to become one with his tree for an hour or so before the nuthatches and chipmunks begin to amuse themselves. Deer mobilize in the early hours after dawn in search of food and sex. The treed hunter continuously scans the forest for movement.

The first movement I saw this time was a military cap emerging up the stairwell of the bus. A head followed, then shoulders bearing the insignia of a South Vietnamese officer. My left eye had 20-15 acuity, one step better than 20-20. From twelve or fifteen feet away, I could make out the insignia on his collar, the three brass clusters of a *dai uy*, the third officer level: a captain.

When a deer wanders into a hunter's range, the instant decision is whether to risk a shot immediately or wait for a closer presentation of the target.

The captain reached the top of the steps of the bus and faced us refugees. I didn't know what he saw. I was up in my tree. Immobile. Unthreatening. Breathing. He was foraging through the Berkshire forest. My forest.

He took a step down the narrow aisle between the seats of the bus. Another step. Another. He scanned our anxious faces very much the way a deer scans the static features of the forest before placing its next step.

With growing certainty, I realized that I wanted to kill the captain. I saw his vengeance and mine as opposing forces. He took a step into the middle of the bus and eyed my boys.

In the field, you pick your shot and you take it. You've invested far too much to watch seventy pounds of meat walk out of range.

I lined up the captain for a kill. He was the size of a young deer. The Chief's Special prefers its targets within five feet. But a coolly aimed shot or two into the captain's chest would get my new family through the U.S. gate and onto what amounted to American soil, Tan Son Nhut Air Base.

But I couldn't kill this guy for merely boarding my bus. Until he barked an order in Vietnamese to take one of my boys off, I had to allow him to live. But point at one of my boys and demand he stand up and the captain's life would end. Neck and shoulders relaxed. Regular breathing. Eyes on his heart and lungs.

As the sole American on the bus, other than the driver, I must have been fairly conspicuous. It was too late for me to stop. I'd already made the decision to kill him. Right here, Captain. Come back here and check somebody's ID. We could settle this whole foreign policy misunderstanding right now, or the little piece of it that concerns the two of us.

I couldn't say how closely he examined me since my eyes were locked on his chest, not his eyes. I couldn't know if he saw my hand in the satchel. He did not exhibit the anxiety of a man facing imminent death. I do not believe I intimidated him into turning around and walking away. I do believe that my presence may have deterred him from harassing Chase's refugees. He likely saw me as a chaperone rather than the bodyguard I'd momentarily become. I do not claim that I saved those boys' lives. I will say that, for reasons of his own, the *dai uy* saved his own life by doing the right thing. I will also say one more thing. There is something about focusing on a man's thorax at the exact moment he expects you to meet his eyes that signals a readiness to kill. If I had been that *dai uy* and had seen my hand in that satchel and my eyes on his chest, I would not have liked it one little bit.

*   *   *

If possible, the pandemonium at the DAO gym had trebled in the twenty-four hours since I'd left. The crowd had swollen all the way around the outside of the gymnasium, completely engulfing it. The bus had to discharge us in the PX parking lot. I knew that good order was maintained at the business end of the crowd, but the periphery was a study in hysteria. There were no pallets of fresh water and there were no portable toilets. There was no shelter and no policing. An accidentally discharged weapon or even a shrill scream could provide the tinder to set off a full-scale riot. If that had happened the vice consuls would have closed up shop, flight manifests would no longer be filled out, and the idling aircraft would have left empty. After that, the options would be stark: helicopters from roofs, or leaky boats.

I recalled Cor Termijn's cabled words this morning: *You are hereby instructed to leave Vietnam.* Without his wisdom I might be sitting at the National Bank at that moment trying to transfer customer accounts to other banks. That would have made luau night look sane.

I couldn't ask my families to endure the ordeal of the crowd. It was inconceivable that we could even remain together for very long in that melee. Moreover, they didn't need to. Based on yesterday's experience, all I needed was a list of the personnel I wanted to adopt. It must have appeared that I knew my way around when I led them to the vacant space between two buildings where yesterday's group had cloistered, with its precious patches of grass and shade.

As I marched off toward the ruckus at Evacuation Control, I discovered that I had acquired a friend. The soft-spoken gent who had calmed the crying woman at Cor's house followed me. I tried to get him to return to our group, but he said, "I help more on my feet than on my ass."

"Remind me your name."

"Trinh Van Chu. I'm the bank's facilities manager."

He didn't look like any facilities guy I'd ever known. He was powerfully built and compact, like a commando or a running back. He also had the quick eyes found in those trades. When we arrived at the back of the crowd, he got in front of me and politely, though more stridently than I would have on my own, forged a path through the sea of humanity. He rarely had to push people out of his way. His voice was calmly insistent and they yielded.

I didn't keep track of how long it took to gain the front of the crowd and bring the consuls into view, but it was well after 5:00 p.m. when we got there. I drew a different consul this time and couldn't decide if that was beneficial or disadvantageous. The other one had been warm to my humanitarianism, but even he might consider my adopting another fifty-one wards to be an abuse of the embassy's hospitality.

I had to laugh at myself. Two weeks ago, Chase's Asia Pacific brass insisted that our employees were entitled to the embassy's assistance in Saigon's final days. Fast forward, and there I was fretting that asking for help might be an imposition. It wasn't so much that Chase's position had deteriorated, but rather that the embassy's schizoid nature had revealed itself. The United States' top two diplomats, Graham Martin and Wolf Lehmann, had functionally defected to their client, leaving the foreign service middle class to represent U.S. interests.

It wasn't an academic issue. If the consul I approached was a Wolfgang Lehmann loyalist, Chase's refugees might be damned. If he turned out to be a Shep Lowman loyalist, escape was possible.

The consul asked, "Marrying, adopting, or both?"

"Adopting."

"How many?"

"Fifty-one."

"Sorry, was that five? It's kind of loud in here."

I spoke up. "Fifty-one."

He pointed to a stack of forms. "Take as many as you need. Sounds like a hell of a story."

"Guess you could say that. Still working on the ending."

He waved me away, but I didn't retreat very far.

Trinh said, "You can write on my back," and he anchored one knee to the dusty floor and presented his brawny back as a writing desk. I began transferring personnel data from my list to the immigration forms and the swarm of refugees parted around us. From overhead we must have looked like a boulder in a slowly flowing river.

The consul smiled and shook his head at the stack of forms I presented, and then transferred the names to a flight manifest. When he gave me a carbon copy of the manifest, I learned that we were on flight 1127. The public address system was boarding flight 1117. It was 6:00 p.m.

Before leaving I asked the consul, "Where can I get some water and grub for my family?"

"We're all out, Mr. White. Sorry."

"Where does the American staff get its provisions?"

"At the DAO mess across the street."

A half hour later Trinh and I were dragging two large duffels of water bottles and C-rations back from DAO supplies toward the grassy clearing between barracks where we'd left the others. Trinh made sure he got the heavier of the two duffels. We'd also managed to scrounge some cold milk for the children. Overall, a successful raid.

The loudspeakers called up flight 1118 and then announced that no more aircraft were departing that day. I didn't go back to the consuls to ask where we could bivouac because I already knew the answer. Instead of telling everyone that we'd be homeless that night, I showed them. I was as much a refugee as they were, so I found the most inhospitable, dustiest patch of ground, completely barren of grass, and lay down, fully clothed, on my back. I used my leather satchel for a pillow. I may have made an exaggerated display of stretching, yawning, and generally settling in for the night, but I did not need to feign instantaneous, profound sleep.

Chapter Thirteen

SATURDAY, APRIL 26, 1975

The sun, the loudspeakers, the insects, the ache in my back—I couldn't say what finally woke me up. Soon after came an echo of Cor's orders: *You are hereby instructed to leave Vietnam together with the other group today.* That had been yesterday. I was already insubordinate.

Sleeping on the bare ground tortured my back. When I was about five years old, I'd wanted to show my mother how strong I was so I put my arms around her legs and lifted her off the ground. My back was never the same. Whenever I felt that twinge in my lumbar spine I couldn't help recalling that childhood incident. But along with the pain came a little pride. It had thrilled my mother.

Along with a sore back and filthy clothes, I noticed something else. I wasn't on bare ground anymore. There were large sheets of cardboard beneath me. I was a sound sleeper, but it was inconceivable that anyone could have slid cardboard under me while I slept. Less enigmatic was who was responsible. Three of Saigon branch's pretty young tellers stood off at a respectable distance, amused by my puzzlement. I walked stiffly toward them.

"Please let me know your names so that I can thank you."

"I am Anh."

"My name is Linh."

"And I'm Mai."

I almost could have guessed. They were three of the most common girl's names. "I don't know how you did it, but that was extremely clever and incredibly thoughtful. I thank you from my heart. *Cam on.*" I also noticed that they all wore Western clothes. As had been the case with my Nga, the ao dai was part of a past they were leaving behind.

The loudspeakers called up flight 1119. The morning sun inched higher and began its relentless search-and-destroy mission against all traces of shade. I fished a toothbrush out of my pack and headed for the latrine. I was not surprised to find Trinh alongside me.

"Good morning, Mitter Why. Want me to go over to the DAO mess and bring back some breakfast?"

It was hard to imagine that a Vietnamese could get into the Defense Attaché Office Annex alone but there was no harm in his trying. I wanted to get over to the flight line to get an estimate of our departure time. "Sure, Trinh. Go ahead and give it a shot."

Despite being a fully evolved New England human, I had the hair of a lower primate. It was comically coarse, bristly, and unruly. Even when I've slept in a real bed, the initial reflection in a bathroom mirror was shocking. Add a little facial stubble and sunstruck eyes and I was an animal control officer's worst nightmare. Trinh kept an eye on me as we stood side by side brushing our teeth, probably worried my spatter might carry rabies. Running fingers through my wetted hair went a long way toward restoring my self-esteem and my rightful place on the genetic hierarchy.

The air base looked like Max Yasgur's pasture on the third day of Woodstock. The ground was littered with debris and people, and the two were largely indistinguishable. The air was ripe with garbage, aircraft exhaust, and incinerated feces. There were long lines for water. There was no respite whatsoever from the sun. Small children made new friends and played together, oblivious to the engulfing pathos. All of this, every bit of it, could have been prevented if only— *Can it, Ralph!* Time to start acting like a head of household.

I found an air force staff sergeant willing to give me some time. It looked as though he had plenty to spare since there was essentially nothing happening.

"What's the delay, Sergeant? Seems like a half dozen flights could have already left since daybreak."

"We got 'em incoming, sir."

"From where?"

"MAC-PAC, sir."

"That would be . . . ?"

"Military Airlift Command, Pacific, in Honolulu, sir. They're dispatching planes from Guam, the Philippines, Thailand, Okinawa, wherever."

"What kind of planes?"

"One-thirties, one-twenty-threes, some Caribous."

"So, back to my original question, Sergeant. If we have all those resources, what's the delay?"

He gave me a look like the conversation was approaching the end of its natural life. "It's a big ocean, sir. And even bigger sky."

I had a few questions for the consuls, but the crush of refugees was too thick for me to get close to them without Trinh running interference. I might be just another refugee, but the logistics didn't add up. There were thousands of people standing, sitting, squatting, lying, and shuffling about. And that was only those that I could see. There were probably many more thousands inside buildings, under hangars, and generally out of sight.

Suppose, conservatively, that there were five thousand refugees queued up on this doomed air base. Suppose a C-130 could carry a hundred passengers. Suppose a C-123 could carry half that, and a C-7 half that. Suppose most were C-130s, so that the average load was, say, eighty. It would take more than sixty flights to evacuate the refugees already occupying the base, and more were pouring in by the busload. If the air force could turn around twenty flights a day, it would take four days to clear us all out. Saigon didn't have four days. And the air force was nowhere near one flight an hour. It was closer to one every two hours. The conclusion was inescapable. Only about a quarter of the refugees already on the base were going to get out. Manifest numbers were being handed out as pacifiers.

That was one way to look at it. Another was that this was an incredibly massive operation to be happening surreptitiously, without the American ambassador becoming aware of its scale. It was also a precarious one, since the ambassador would shut it down if he knew about it.

I imagined a scene in which Martin turns to an aide and says, "Okay, now that we've got South Vietnam's gold secure on American soil, we can start evacuating those Chase Manhattan Bank employees." And his aide, fully aware that said employees were by then cavorting around Rockefeller's compound in Pocantico, says, "I'm on it, sir."

I had some work to do before that scene could become a reality. I headed back over to the gymnasium to see what I could learn.

Vietnamese civilians and their American sponsors had formed disciplined queues leading to whichever officials they'd been assigned upon entering the gym. In some cases the vice consuls simply stamped the applications. In others, the officials signaled to the manager of the Evacuation Control Center to step up and make a decision. I approached the decision-making guy at the back of the gym. He wore civilian clothes but had an army haircut, buzzed down to the skin on the sides. He wore metal-framed glasses, like the safety glasses used for shooting. I walked up beside him and opened with, "What are the different lines about?"

He didn't take his eyes off the crowd. "Basically the easy cases and the more difficult ones."

I couldn't help asking. "Were you here when I came through? What line was I in?"

"You? You were put in the difficult line. Your relationship to your evacuees was not of a customary nature. Your case was atypical. We call them difficult."

"It didn't seem so difficult."

"Yeah, we've kinda got it figured out now. If you'd come through a couple of days ago, things might not have gone as smoothly for your group."

The guy surveyed the crowd as he responded to my questions. It was strange, carrying on a conversation with someone so seriously distracted. "Looking for somebody?"

"ARVN agents, mainly. They've warned us that they would close us down if they caught us evacuating Vietnamese officers or intelligence agents."

I said, "Those category people wouldn't come through here. They'd use clandestine flights, the so-called black flights on Air America, Tiger Air, or foreign-flagged aircraft, and most likely in the dark of the night."

"You're remarkably well informed, and up on protocol," he replied.

He meant that most guys who knew what I knew got their haircuts courtesy of the U.S. government, and I was pretty shaggy. He still wasn't impressed enough to look at me.

"I don't know if I'm well informed or just single-minded. It took a lot of legwork but it looks as though I'm going to get all of my employees and their families out. Probably violating a dozen regulations."

That brought a smile, a cynical one, but a smile nonetheless. "There aren't any formal regulations. The Secretary of State has given us guidance, which we administer flexibly to deal with the reality of the situation we are facing."

He was a guy who chose his words judiciously and he'd clearly said that *we* chose flexibility. It made me wonder who *we* were. He was just one guy. "Are Graham and Wolf on board with your initiative?"

"In a generalized sense, yeah. As to the difficult ones, the exceptions, that's never come up in our conversations."

"Then it's a win-win. You get flexibility. They get deniability."

"You said it, not me. I believe that if they had wanted someone to rigidly adhere to a formalized set of regulations they would have found someone else to do the job."

"So who did they find to do the job?"

The guy took his eyes off the crowd and casually took my measure. He extended his hand. "Ken Moorefield, second secretary and consular officer, Embassy Saigon. You?"

"Ralph White, assistant treasurer, Chase Manhattan Bank, Bangkok."

I'd heard about Moorefield in the course of my sleuthing. He'd gone to West Point and had been a captain in Vietnam when he'd been badly wounded in action. He'd joined the U.S. Foreign Service and had eventually become a close confidant of Ambassador Martin, so close that Martin had entrusted the Evacuation Control Center to him. One thing for certain, Martin didn't know Moorefield was boarding the *difficult* cases. Here was another guy, like Shep Lowman at the embassy and Bob Lanigan on his tugboat, who served a higher power.

Moorefield's gaze had returned to the crowd, looking for the friendlies who'd turned homicidally unfriendly. I hoped my refugees and I were in the air before he found what he was looking for.

*   *   *

I hardly recognized the little patch of turf where my Chase families were sequestered. Parachute cloth strung between the buildings on either side turned it into a shady retreat. They all had water. Some were eating. There were books, decks of cards, and someone was playing a traditional Vietnamese mouth harp.

"Trinh?"

"You didn't think I could get in there, did you?"

"Looks like you got out too."

"There's a lot more in there to scrounge."

"Let's try to avoid attracting too much attention while everyone around us is suffering so badly."

"Want a beer? It won't stay cold much longer."

It was awfully early for a beer, not yet noon. "A cold beer would be very nice, thank you, Mr. Trinh."

The loudspeakers called for flight 1120. Ours was 1127.

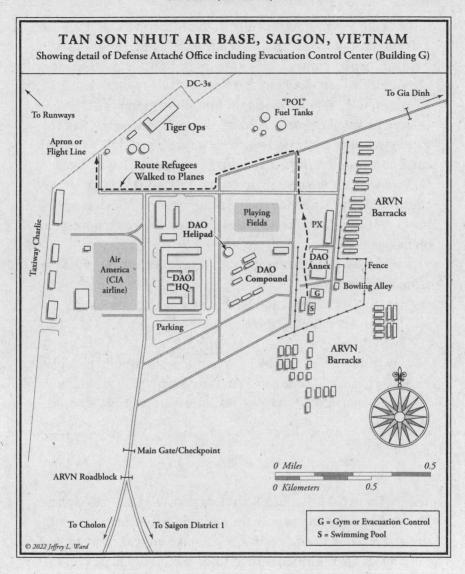

TAN SON NHUT AIR BASE, SAIGON, VIETNAM
Showing detail of Defense Attaché Office including Evacuation Control Center (Building G)

DC-3s

To Gia Dinh

To Runways

"POL"
Fuel Tanks

Tiger Ops

Apron or
Flight Line

Route Refugees
Walked to Planes

ARVN
Barracks

Playing
Fields

PX

DAO
Helipad

Taxiway Charlie

Air
America
(CIA
airline)

DAO
Annex

Fence

DAO
Compound

DAO
HQ

Bowling Alley

G

S

Parking

ARVN
Barracks

Main Gate/Checkpoint

0 Miles   0.5

ARVN Roadblock

0 Kilometers   0.5

To Cholon   To Saigon District 1

G = Gym or Evacuation Control
S = Swimming Pool

© 2022 Jeffrey L. Ward

*   *   *

It was about 5:00 p.m. when we got the call for our flight and broke camp. An airman with a clipboard checked our names and put us in a line that disappeared between buildings in the general direction of the runways. Our initial elation evaporated when the line didn't move at all. We all stood silently in the withering heat. Even the kids among us lost their cheer. We advanced a little. A little more. I have watched columns of army ants on the Kon Tum plateau move more quickly than we did in that line.

We rounded a building and the line ahead disappeared behind a dense hedge, then past a field of rubble, a parking lot, a corrugated steel shed, a latrine, for which we were grateful. Six o'clock came and passed. Army ants could have lapped us twice. We were told we were on the next flight but that it hadn't landed yet. My shirt was damp. My balls itched. The air was so hot that it hurt to breathe. If I'd known it would be this bad, I'd have put everyone on Lanigan's barge.

We heard a plane arrive and shut down its engines. I asked an airman, "That us?"

"Yes, sir. Got to refuel and let the crew out for a smoke."

"Tell 'em not to smoke too close to the fuel."

"Everything's going to be okay, sir."

"Say, airman, I can tell by its accent that that's not a Hercules. That's a jet, and a big one too. What are you putting us on?"

"Good ears, sir. That's a big ol' Starlifter. Eats Hercules for breakfast."

*   *   *

The Lockheed C-141 Starlifter is an elegant, shapely, plus-sized plane. The loading ramp lowers from the rear, under the canopy of a massive stabilizer and tail assembly. It can take off with forty tons of cargo in its hold. Airmen loaded three hundred refugees on that flight, including our group, and I reckon that was one of the lightest payloads that aircraft had ever transported. The cargo bay resembled Carlsbad Caverns so much that I scanned the roof for bats.

As big as a C-141 is, I can attest that three hundred people sprawled out on its cargo deck left zero personal space. On top of that, baggage littered the floor around us since MAC-PAC wasn't contracted to load it separately, nor, thankfully, had anyone checked for contraband like, say, handguns.

Time had crept so slowly since we'd entered the gates of Tan Son Nhut the day before that when things began progressing at a normal pace, everything felt rushed. It surprised us when the loading ramp actually closed, the engines actually started, and the plane actually bounded toward the runway. It was beginning to look like we really were going to escape Saigon.

I sat roughly in the center of the cargo bay and was able to watch the airmen at their duties. I could not have been more dumbfounded when, as we were still taxiing, a helmeted airman removed the window from one of the doors and mounted a .50 caliber machine gun in the gaping hole in the fuselage. He then attached a long belt of awe-inspiring ammunition to the gun. We were about to take off in a four-engine jet with a hole in the side. It's not the way I'd have done it, but nobody consulted me.

The noise level inside the cargo bay when that plane took off was impossible to describe. The jet engines alone poured out a hellish scream, and that was before we even got airborne. We all pressed our palms to our ears, but the noise penetrated through our hands unabated to our eardrums. Once the aircraft became airborne, wind turbulence boomed around inside the bay like continuous thunder.

Mostly the passengers in a C-141 are inanimate objects such as jeeps, artillery, and pallets of ordnance, and they are tolerant of this kind of aural torture. The decibel level to which we refugees were subject on that takeoff was well beyond most human experience. It damaged my hearing and I never since have been able to detect sound in the frequency of my tinnitus. Again, a leisurely weeklong voyage on a barge down the Saigon River might have been preferable, even if it meant defecating overboard.

Somewhere below ten thousand feet, the altitude above which air gets too thin to breathe, the airman latched the glass panel back into the door, and the screaming and thunder ceased. I shook my head in utter disbelief and, ears ringing, looked around to see how the others had weathered the experience. What I found was a sea of wet faces, as all of the refugees were weeping—for their families, their country—they had a multitude of reasons. For their hearts to hurt more than their ears, the pain must have been excruciating.

I checked my watch. It was 7:30 p.m., Saigon time. Only then did I realize that no one had informed us of our destination. We had no idea what country we'd be in when we woke up. That doesn't happen often. Then again, the last two weeks had been a rapid sequence of nonrecurring events. Not knowing where I'd wake up was easily the least remarkable of them.

Chapter Fourteen

THE PHILIPPINES AND GUAM

Sunday, April 27

It was midnight when we were herded down the Starlifter's ramp to terra firma. Airmen directed us to a pair of blue air force buses, their engines idling. If there was a terminal, we never saw it. I asked the airman driving the bus, "What country is this, airman?"

"The P.I., sir. Philippine Islands. This here's Clark Air Force Base. If you don't mind me saying, sir, you don't much look Vietnamese."

"Good catch, airman. I was on a business trip when Saigon tanked. I'm a banker."

He shrugged, smiled, and looked away. "Don't look much like one of them neither."

I reached up and discovered that my hair had reverted to gorilla mode. I was also wearing the extremely dirty shirt and dusty bell bottoms that I'd worn two days straight and slept in two nights.

The Chase group was allocated one disused barracks for its exclusive use, but that might not have been a conscious decision on the part of the air force as much as a consequence of our having arrived as a discrete busload. Inside, bright neon lights illuminated a very long, very narrow space with bunk beds extending from both sides. The obvious quandary was that we were not the single gender group typically housed there. There was also only one shower room.

I threw my leather satchel on the second bed on the left and gave instructions for the women and girls to have access to the showers and bathrooms for an hour, after which the men could take over. Trinh quickly commandeered the first bed on the left and the three pretty tellers took the three nearest bunks on the other side of me. In minutes everyone had claimed a place to sleep.

I went outside hoping to find an air force duty officer to report Chase's successful escape from Saigon, but the base was too large, too dark, too quiet, and our location on the base too remote. I couldn't find anyone in authority other than the crickets. When I planted my face in a spiderweb the size of a lacrosse goal I decided to wait until morning to complete my walkabout.

The hot shower was a gift from God. I would have liked to have sent my clothes out to the cleaners. Clark Air Base was the size of a small American city. The map on the wall indicated facilities like *Theater*, *Teen Center*, and *Hair Salon*. Tomorrow I'd try to find the laundry. Then I realized it was already tomorrow. I needed to find my bed and close my eyes for a few hours. The barrack was extremely dark and I had to wait for my eyes to adjust. I knew I'd found my bunk when Trinh, some four feet away, whispered, "Good night." I hadn't had a roommate since my freshman year in college, and now, if my count was right, I had fifty-one of them.

The bunk was comfortable and the pillow was stuffed with feathers instead of currency. Simple pleasures. Crickets. Safety. Soap. No crazy ambassador, mutiny, incoming rockets, armed customers, or friendlies executing boys on the roadside. I'd miss Maugham's Vietnam, but I wouldn't miss Uncle Ho's Vietnam. We still had nine thousand miles to go, but our chances of surviving it were looking up.

*   *   *

In a dream, a woman's hand delicately lifted my flimsy blanket and a cypress-slender figure slipped into bed with me. She entwined me in the center of the narrow bunk and held a finger against my lips. Her hair fell across my face. Hold on! This wasn't a dream. I tried pushing her away, but all four of her limbs constricted and immobilized me. Her lips found my ear. *Shhh.*

Before I could recover from the shock, she began kissing me. Not sweet little kisses either—no, no—but long, wet, ravishing kisses. I turned away to see if Trinh had noticed yet, but he was facing away, breathing heavily. The girl pulled my face back to hers and got back to exploring my tonsils. I listened for squeaks in the bedsprings but they were mercifully quiet.

It had to be one of the three tellers. If Trinh didn't wake up and if the two other women were co-conspirators, then the closest person who might hear us would be four bunks away. I supposed my ravisher must have felt me surrender because she took my hand and placed it on her breast.

What were their names? Linh. Mai. Who was the third? Anh. Right. I tried to picture them. This one had long hair, slim hips, and small breasts. But that described all three of them. I tried touching the woman's face to discern some distinctive feature that might reveal her identity. She knew exactly what I was doing and pulled my hand away.

It was just a matter of time, in fact I'm surprised it took as long as it did, but I began to respond to her provocation just as my Creator had drawn things up. In my defense, I do not believe that even a New England gentleman is expected to resist such primeval temptation. It would make it easier though if I knew her name. Call me cloistered, but I'd never been intimate with a woman without knowing her name.

She squirmed to the top position. I tried again to look over at Trinh, but she snapped my head back to the main event. That may have been the moment I fully joined the conspiracy. After all, resistance was futile, or at least counterproductive. She knew I wasn't going to shout, *Hey, whoever you are, stop making love to me, dammit.* The path of least resistance was acquiescence.

The teller who started off as a dream, then morphed to flesh and blood, returned to dream for her Garden of Eden cameo. In the physical world things are never quite as perfect as they are in dreams. Love rarely lives up to its promise. Certainly, obviously, the simple fact of its perfection betrayed this seduction as an illusion. Abstinence will do that. Distant ports will too. The combination is volatile. She kissed me one last time and slipped away. I quickly tumbled back to dreamland, or had I been there all along?

Monday, April 28

Everyone was already awake by the time I opened my eyes. I pulled my pants on under the blanket and tried to get my hair to look semicivilized by tamping it down. When I stood up, the rest of them did me the favor of not staring, with one exception. Trinh came over to explain how the showers and bathroom had been allocated that morning to women and men. I was strapping on my watch when I noticed a spent condom on the floor next to my bunk. I put my foot over it before Trinh noticed.

I would liked to have put a shirt on, but my foot was anchored to the spot and my shirt was in a rumpled pile at the far end of the bunk. Trinh showed no inclination to leave, so I was forced to stand bare-chested while we spoke. My solution was to give Trinh an assignment.

"Do something for me, would you, Trinh? Go around and find out if our colleagues have any problems I should know about. Find some paper. Make a list."

"Yes, sir. Right away."

"Oh, Mr. Trinh?"

"Yes?"

"I do hope you slept well. I know these are difficult times."

"I slept okay, I think."

"The crickets weren't too loud for you?"

"The crickets in Vietnam are every bit as loud, Mitter Why. I am used to them."

As soon as Trinh left, I picked up the condom and threw it in the trash. Actually I stuffed it well toward the bottom.

As I walked past the three tellers, I examined them carefully to see if I could discern which of them had had her way with me. They all looked equally guilty. As amazed as I had been that they could have slipped cardboard sheets beneath me while I slept on the ground, it was more incredible that one of them had managed to apply a condom without my realizing it. A trick so clever had to be an acquired skill, leading to the conclusion that at least one of them was not nearly as innocent as she appeared.

In New England the gentleman is obliged to call the lady on the following day and tell her how wonderful the evening had been, how much he had enjoyed her company, and how sincerely he was looking forward to renewing her acquaintance. This ancient protocol becomes problematic when the gentleman doesn't know exactly which lady is owed the courtesy.

*   *   *

The diagram on the wall showing the layout of the base included a key indicating *Building 2100* as *Base Headquarters* and *Building 2093* as *International Tel Centers*. They were as good a place to start as any. The barrack to which we had been assigned didn't warrant a building number so it took me a while to determine where I was on the map.

Eventually I found base headquarters and reported in. They gave me some notifications about Saigon and I sat down to read them carefully since I'd have to pass on the information verbally to the others. There were a few highlights. President Huong had resigned and had been replaced by Big Minh, whom I'd never heard of. Three NVA rockets had hit Saigon, one a direct hit on the Majestic Hotel, destroying the top two floors and tumbling the Polish ambassador out of bed. Thirty thousand South Vietnamese troops were cowering in Saigon, leaderless. Looting was widespread. It might seem a slow news day unless your universe was the kapok forest.

The room where John Linker had stayed on April 15 and 16 was in the part of the Majestic Hotel that had been obliterated by a rocket. With the removal of the two floors above it, my cheap room on the third floor was now the penthouse.

*   *   *

Would Clark Air Base Headquarters be willing to put a quick call through to Chase Hong Kong Regional Headquarters? *Sorry, sir. You need the overseas call center for that.* How about a domestic call? *Yeah* (grudgingly), *we might do that.* Could you look up the number for the Chase Manhattan Bank's office in Manila and put me through? *You mean look it up in the local phone book?* Yeah, I guess that's what I'm thinking. *The bank on base is American Express; would that do?* Sorry, airman, I'm thinking Rockefeller's bank. *So I should call Mr. Rockefeller?* No, just his man in Manila. *You got a number, sir?* In fact I did. 63 2 575 1199. *Do I got to dial the country code, sir?* I don't think so, airman. *Say they call back after you leave, where I'm going to reach you, sir?* Just tell anyone you are able to contact that the employees of Chase's Saigon branch are all safe and here at Clark. They'll take it from there.

Back at the barrack I learned from Trinh that one of our group, Linh, not the teller Linh, had lost her luggage. She was a single mother with two young children and they had no spare clothes or toiletries. I took her to the post exchange and helped her resupply her family. Finding clothes for her wasn't easy. She was a size 2, and most of the clothing in the racks was in the 8 to 12 range.

I showed my family where the mess hall was so that they could get some food. It was very different cuisine from what they were accustomed to. After a few years of meat and potatoes they'd probably be buying size 12 dresses too. They'd be able to get fresh fish and steamed rice after they settled in New York, but definitely not while they were here at Clark Air Base.

The map of the base showed everything but a laundromat. I never did discover how laundry gets done on a military base, if it did at all. The only laundry available to us was the sinks at the barracks. Hand soap and tap water was our laundromat. I washed a shirt and a pair of underpants and draped them over a fence in the sun. In the heat they dried stiff in about ten minutes.

*   *   *

Cuong may have noticed my growing reliance on Trinh for administrative matters because he reasserted his authority by establishing some rules for our unusual living arrangements. Among them was lights out at 9:00. I welcomed the early hour. I'd lost a lot of sleep since leaving Bangkok and saw a chance to catch up.

*   *   *

As the crickets took over, I became dejected for having failed to contact the outside world to let someone know where we were. The airman at headquarters had let me down but contacting the world was my responsibility, not his. We'd been safe for twenty-four hours and no one knew. I'd have to go to the *International Tel Center* tomorrow and let Chase New York, Hong Kong, and Manila know where we were. Especially given the alarming news from Saigon, everyone would be very distressed if they thought we were still there. I deserved an unceremonious kick in the butt.

Tuesday, April 29

At breakfast in the mess hall, I got more news about Saigon. The runways at Tan Son Nhut had been bombed at 5:00 p.m. yesterday. Incredibly it hadn't yet been determined whether the attack had been carried out by our North Vietnamese enemies or our South

Vietnamese allies. There was no disagreement about the outcome though; with the runways out of commission, aircraft could no longer take off. The aircraft on the tarmac were stranded, as were the thousands of Vietnamese who had pinned their hopes on evacuation from Tan Son Nhut.

After the bombing of the runways, Americans would have to depart by helicopter, but with their much lower seating capacity, helicopter manifests would have to be far more selective. I doubted that many Vietnamese would get out on helicopters. Also, by the time Tan Son Nhut got bombed, Lanigan's wagon train of barges would have cast off for the South China Sea. If I'd stayed in Saigon just twenty-two hours longer, I'd never have gotten Chase's employees out by air or by sea. I decided never to tell either the employees or head office how narrowly we'd avoided that tragedy.

Even more consequential to our salvation than those slim twenty-two hours was an almost inconceivable sequence of coincidences. What if the first guy to whom John Linker had offered the Saigon assignment had accepted, and he'd evacuated just the priority list employees? What if Jim Ashida hadn't taken off the entire three-day Hung Kings weekend, spurring my evacuation initiatives independent of the embassy? What if the deputy mission warden hadn't been typing Vietnamese names into a flight manifest at the precise moment I visited him, or if he hadn't been called out of the room when I was there? What if Shep Lowman hadn't organized his mutinous back channel, or if I hadn't caught wind of it? What if Ken Moorefield hadn't made the Evacuation Control Center more inclusive, valiantly disregarding the host government's requirement for Vietnamese exit visas? What if the captain who boarded our bus at the gates of Tan Son Nhut had ordered one of our boys off? I'd been a reflex away from murdering him. What if the DC-3 I'd planned on stealing had still been at Tiger Air and I'd attempted to fly a plane for which I was manifestly unqualified? What if Nga hadn't noticed my arrest by the white mice, or if her brother hadn't freed me? Or if Ashida hadn't come up with a second bus when I chanced into him at the air base bathroom, because in that case I'd have left with the priority group and would have abandoned everyone else, including Cuong and his family. Hell, what if General Dao hadn't held at Xuan Loc for ten days, delaying Saigon's ultimate demise? If leaving twenty-two hours before the runways had been bombed made us look lucky, then the entire two-week sequence of events made us look positively blessed.

*　　*　　*

At the *International Tel Center*, I managed to get through to Cor in Hong Kong.

He said, "Thank God. Thank God. And the *people*?"

"The people are all good, Cor. I've got fifty-one of them in this second group. We got out everybody who wanted out. The air force has us comfortably sheltered at Clark Air Base. They're feeding us well. We have toilets and showers. No one's sick as far as I know. Our clothing is getting a little raunchy, but we're out of Saigon. I haven't been able to contact Manila branch but maybe that would be easier for you. I need to divest some currency. By the way I didn't need to pay any bribes."

"So the embassy helped you in the end?"

"There's a long, interesting answer to that question that will have to wait for later. Short answer: Martin and Lehmann turned out to be real sons of bitches. Then I discovered that the Mission Warden was evacuating their people and Shep Lowman and Ken Moorefield risked their careers to help me. They expanded the Evacuation Control Center far beyond what Martin and Lehmann had authorized. An organization called Military Airlift Command, Pacific, in Hawaii, did the heavy lifting, all of it behind the ambassador's back."

Cor said, "How did you figure out who the good guys were in the embassy?"

"Luck and legwork. Legwork and luck. Say, Cor, what happens now? Can you send a plane to fetch us?"

"I sincerely wish it were as easy as that, Ralph. Turns out that we're having a problem with Philippine president Marcos. He wants all Vietnamese refugees removed from the Philippines immediately. This means that the military will be flying you out, so your destination may have more to do with where they want the aircraft to end up."

"Have you located the first group of employees yet? They left two days ahead of us."

"Not yet. We suspect they're in what's being called Tent City, in Guam. It's a fucking hellhole, Ralph. For God's sake, don't let them take you there."

"Cor, what's happening in Saigon? Does anyone know?"

"Not good. Two marine guards were killed in a rocket attack. Then there's the Majestic Hotel . . ."

"I heard about the Majestic. The room where Linker sat me down to explain why we had to keep Saigon branch open was blown up just fifteen days after our conversation. It's a little creepy, though not exactly a close call."

"Linker's a happy guy these days. He owes you."

"He got exactly what he wanted, though not exactly how he drew it up."

"You asked about Saigon. Project Alamo transitioned to Operation Frequent Wind. That's the helicopter evacuation of American personnel we heard about at the Brink."

"So Bing Crosby got his Saigon curtain call? 'I'm Dreaming of a White Christmas' got blared out over Armed Forces Radio? That must have been just this morning."

"Yeah. Your ten-foot-long, handheld wind socks are getting a workout about now. Against Ambassador Martin's orders, a marine major cut down that banyan tree in the embassy parking lot so the navy's biggest helicopters can land there."

"Cor, do you know the U.S. military acronym snafu? It stands for *situation normal, all fucked up*. The helicopter evacuation was ordered too late for it to work. Washington and Saigon were never quite on the same page, so instead of getting the most vulnerable Vietnamese out, the helicopter airlift will only help the ones strong enough to fight their way up the ladders. Suppose I was still there now. Imagine me trying to get my family up those ladders and out by helicopter."

"Sorry Ralph, your *what*?"

"The people, Cor. Chase's people. They would never have gotten out. Martin never understood that the last one thousand Americans had been staying there only to get their dependents and employees out. Shep Lowman and Martin's aide, Ken Moorefield, understood that and loosened up the evacuation protocol for Vietnamese. Lowman and Moorefield deserve medals they'll never see. Shep got them onto the base and Ken got them into the air. Those two guys answer to a higher power. A USAID guy named Bob Lanigan got several hundred out. Makes what I did look like a day at the beach."

Deposit one dollar and thirty-five cents for the next three minutes.

"Cor, I think we're done, right?"

Deposit one dollar and thirty-five cents for the next three minutes.

"Sure, I guess so. Good luck on that next leg. And stay away from that Tent City on Guam. Thanks for everything. *Cam on.*"

Deposit one dollar and thirty-five cents for the next three minutes.

*　　*　　*

I met Chase's country manager for the Philippines, Joseph McGinity, on the deserted sidewalk outside the main gate of Clark Air Base and we'd have looked to bystanders, had there been any, like old friends stopping for a chat.

I unslung my briefcase and took out bundle after bundle of twenties and placed them in a shopping bag he held open for me.

I said, "I didn't count it when I picked it up, so I'm not going to count it now. I'll leave the paperwork to you."

McGinity said, "Your name's all over the wires."

"I was a foot soldier in John Linker's strategy, though I doubted him at the time."

In that conversation with McGinity and in future tellings of the story, I decided to omit the business about the ambassador's dereliction. It was pointless and vituperative. With a little help and multiple dollops of luck, I had bested a United States ambassador, and victors are supposed to be magnanimous.

McGinity said, "David Rockefeller has asked to meet you. You went from being an entry-level credit analyst to being a big deal overnight."

"Shucks."

"Do me a favor. If you get a chance in your meeting with D.R., would you tell him that I could be doing a lot more for the bank in a more important branch. The Hong Kong slot's coming up. I'd love to run that branch. You'll tell him, won't you? You scratch my back and I'll get you a slot in Hong Kong too."

"Sure thing, Joe."

Wednesday, April 30

The air force got us up at dawn and told us to pack. We had a brief stop at the mess hall and carried our egg sandwiches and coffee out to the bus. A Hercules C-130 was waiting for us on the flight line and it gathered all fifty-two of us to its bosom. Webbing seats had been installed for my wards, and I got the jump seat behind the pilot. The crew made me earn the seat with war stories about the fall of Saigon. All five of the crewmembers had been to Saigon, and all five had been to the Tennessee Bar. They inquired about the girls by name.

One asked, "Did you ever meet the ambassador?"

"Yeah, why?"

"He got airlifted out early this morning. The marine guard on the helicopter was authorized to arrest him if he refused to go. That guy must be a piece of work. Reports are he looked dazed."

I said, "Yeah, by the end he'd become fairly disoriented," and left it at that. My new policy.

The flight engineer asked me, "Has anyone told you who's in charge of the refugee operation in Guam?"

"That's where we're headed, Guam?"

"Yeah. The officer commanding the refugee operation there is Rear Admiral Steve Morrison, the father of Jim Morrison of The Doors."

I recalled that the younger Morrison had died in a bathtub in Paris four years earlier. "Formerly with The Doors." I was almost afraid to ask my next question. "Where's the refugee operation in Guam?" I wasn't sure I wanted the answer.

"Formally it's called Operation New Life."

"How about informally?"

"They're calling it Tent City. As an American you won't have to stay there. It's basically a concentration camp for refugees. They'll put you up in a fancy hotel. Worst case, a BOQ."

"I *am* a refugee. Whatever my employees are, that's what I am."

"You may change your mind when you see Tent City, Ralph."

*   *   *

This was my first time in the cockpit of a Hercules C-130, and I was very impressed. It was a quantum leap from a DC-3 and I would never delude myself that I could fly it. It was a four-engine turboprop and looked like a bullfrog with wings. I asked the flight engineer how turboprop engines work and he lost me at *fourteen-stage axial flow compressors*.

My eyes came to rest on a dial on the dashboard labeled *torque*. There were four dials marked *torque*. If the DC-3 exceeded my skill level geometrically, the C-130 exceeded it exponentially.

The captain said, "Would you care to fly her?"

He was as casual as a dinner party hostess asking if I would care for some sage-infused butter.

I tried to sound equally casual. "Love to." I switched seats with the copilot and rested my feet on the rudder pedals and my hands on the yoke that controlled the ailerons and stabilizers. I was able to maintain the heading and altitude reasonably well for a few minutes, but I would not have liked to be in that seat if the cargo shifted or if an engine flamed out. Relieved to be back behind the pilot I said, "Thank you. That was a thrill. I promise not to record it in my pilot's log."

*   *   *

The approach to Andersen Air Force Base in Guam looked terrifying. The runway begins at the precipice of a six-hundred-foot cliff. That's a benefit when a plane is taking off with its maximum load of bombs since, by definition, the plane is six hundred feet in the air when the runway ends. Landing, on the other hand, requires the plane to glide straight toward the edge of the cliff and sacrifice those comforting six hundred feet in the instant before touching down. There is no margin for error at Andersen and it is no place for amateur pilots. Night landings are a test of faith.

My second impression of Guam was of the huge land snails on and alongside the sidewalks of the air base. The cook in me wanted to collect them and prepare escargot. The refugee in me knew that Tent City and escargot didn't belong in the same sentence.

The word *city* was just as telling as the word *tent*, as it extended further than any eye would ever wish to see. I couldn't estimate the size of the facility because I never saw the far borders. Size notwithstanding, Tent City wasn't as disheartening as it was billed. There was no *Abandon All Hope* sign at the entrance. One subtle feature of the place alarmed me, though. The tent stakes were not the usual wooden pegs. They were made from the ribbed steel bar used to reinforce concrete. Using rebar for tent stakes suggested the facility could last for decades if required. A few days here might be endurable. A few months might cause refugees to jump off the six-hundred-foot cliff. After a few years, a refugee might prefer communist Vietnam. I prayed that Chase would locate us soon.

How that might happen was perplexing. There were no road signs. There were no roads. There were footpaths between the tents, but they weren't named or signposted in any way. The tents weren't numbered. Our only address was Tent City. The only people who knew their way around were its residents. It was a vast warren of canvas, cots, rope, and rebar. If a Chase officer were to ask at the entrance where he could find us, the respondent couldn't do much more than point into the mass of tan canvas mounds. Nor was there anything on record that our group had anything to do with the Chase Manhattan Bank. Realistically, locating us would be nearly impossible.

I found a vacant tent large enough to accommodate the Chase contingent about twelve rows deep into the encampment. The tent had fifty cots lined up in rows and we stole two more from another tent so that we could all be together. We preferred being cramped to being separated.

I suppose that if we'd landed in Guam fresh from sleeping on the ground at Tan Son Nhut we'd have considered Tent City a step up. Who knew that three days with real bunks, hot grub, and running water at Clark Air Base would spoil us? Spirits improved when I scrounged an unlimited supply of cold milk for the kids and a carton of Newport cigarettes for the adults.

Dr. An reported illnesses in our group and said that he could treat them if he had access to medicines, so the two of us went out in search of a dispensary. Ultimately we took a municipal bus into the village of Orote Point and found a retail drugstore where he got almost everything he needed.

Tent City also had a tent mess hall, and there were dozens of picnic tables scattered about the place. The latrines were fire base configuration, basically a platform above a cesspool. Despite its amenities, Operation New Life did not have the one thing it needed the most, a lost-and-found for people. It was a people-sequestering operation, not a people-locating one. Admiral Morrison hadn't anticipated that fifty-two of us might want to disengage from his hospitality and stay with friends in Guam. If the first Chase group was still here that would make 113 of us, plus me.

There was no privacy in the Chase tent. At no other place on our odyssey did we feel more like one family than when we were clustered together around our cots in the evening. We became inured to seeing one another in various stages of undress. If anything embarrassed us it was our body odor. There was not one single thing to do.

Someone with a transistor radio picked up a signal from Armed Forces Radio reporting that Big Minh, South Vietnam's last president, had announced an unconditional surrender. Big Minh didn't say to whom he'd surrendered, but the flag flying above the Presidential Palace was reportedly the Viet Cong's gold star on a background of blue and red.

Thursday, May 1

Again I scored several cartons of milk for the kids and another carton of cigarettes for the adults.

Everyone's shins became gashed by the rebar tent stakes.

I stood out in the open trying to look conspicuous in case someone from Chase came looking for a twenty-seven-year-old American with the hair and odor of a gorilla. I found no takers.

Friday, May 2–Saturday, May 3

"Excuse me, sir. Are you Ralph White?" The guy clearly hoped he was wrong. He was faltering with fatigue and had prematurely thinning hair; Stanley to my Livingstone.

"Yes. Hope you're from Chase."

Whatever preconception he had of Ralph White, it wasn't me. It was understandable; I scarcely conformed to my own conception of Ralph White.

He warily extended his hand, contagion clearly on his mind. "I'm Paul Didier. I truly am honored to meet you, Ralph." We shook and he quickly withdrew his hand.

"Did the first group make it out? Are they here?"

"Yes, they're here. Not *here* here, but here in Guam. We've got them in a hotel."

I led Didier to the tent where we were living and he looked as though he might weep at the sight. I'm sure to him we must have looked pitiable, but compared to others in Tent City we were in reasonably good health and high spirits. However bad our situation we'd acclimated ourselves to it. Our misfortunes were communal and they'd overtaken us gradually.

*   *   *

As it was explained to me, Chase had fortuitously come into ownership of the International Trade Center Hotel in Guam through foreclosure on a defaulted loan. I rode up in a crowded elevator to the floor Chase had commandeered, and when the doors opened one of my refugees dashed from the elevator into the arms of her husband. He'd been as surprised to see her as she him. Apparently he had been a major in the maritime police and had been exfiltrated early since he'd have been executed by the new regime. This was the first time they'd seen one another for weeks. Their two little kids cried without knowing exactly why. I was impressed that the major knew where to look for his wife. Tradecraft, I guessed.

*   *   *

That evening I dined with the Vietnam Task Force, as they called themselves, in the hotel's dimly lit restaurant. The Vietnam Task Force, invariably capitalized, comprised Paul Didier, John Mitchell, Mel Anderson, and Cor Termijn. Guam country manager Steve Crytser joined us. The Task Force members, other than Cor, who knew me, outdid one another with their left-handed compliments, the gist of which was that I looked better than expected, all things considered, as disaster cases go. They were kind enough not to mention my still rank, filthy clothing. It took two laundry cycles to bring my hygiene up to American working-class standards. We spent three nights in Guam and I must say that, as repossessed hotels go, the International Trade Center in Guam was excellent.

Chapter Fifteen

THE UNITED STATES OF AMERICA

O n May 4, we flew to Los Angeles and took buses to Camp Pendleton, where all incoming Vietnamese refugees got processed for green cards. What I recall most indelibly was how insistently confused the immigration officials were by the order of Vietnamese surnames and given names. The refugees compounded their confusion when, thinking it would help, they gave their names in the Americanized order, only to have the Social Security clerks reverse them, as they'd been taught, to the incorrect order. It was as entertaining as a comedy routine.

*　　*　　*

On May 6, we arrived in New York to considerable fanfare at One Chase Manhattan Plaza, the bank's world headquarters in the Financial District. All of the refugees were ushered up to the sixtieth floor, where a few international department executives addressed the crowd, and the bank's president, Bill Butcher, welcomed them.

Things started coming into perspective for me when a couple of heavy hitters from the seventeenth floor went out of their way to greet me. The first of these was Frank Stankard, executive vice president for the International Department. When I'd been a credit analyst in that building, about six months earlier, Stankard had been my boss's boss's boss. Now we were shooting the breeze like frat boys at reunion.

It was perfectly fair that Stankard would share some of the glow from the mission's success. He was John Linker's boss, and while I always gave Linker the credit for orchestrating the Saigon evacuation, everything relied on Stankard funding it. In a big corporation the best way to determine who deserves credit is to assess where blame for failure would most likely have fallen. In this case the buck would have definitely stopped on Stankard's desk, so he clearly deserved a little glow. Something else that had stopped on Francis Xavier Stankard's desk was a six-inch-thick, leather-bound Bible. The God of Jesus, Mary, and Joseph might also deserve a bow.

A senior vice president, Tony Terracciano, looked me up and down and said, "You know David wants to meet you, right?"

I didn't have Rockefeller on my calendar, but it wouldn't have surprised me if he wanted to see the refugees for himself. I'd been reminded a few times that Saigon branch had captured his interest, but it would be difficult to exaggerate the chasm separating us, both in the bank's hierarchy and in life. I said, "I'd enjoy that."

Terracciano said, "You aren't going to meet David dressed like that. Go buy yourself a suit and send me the bill." It was an order more than an offer.

True, I was dressed casually even by Bangkok and Saigon standards. But both my shirt and my pants had been freshly laundered and pressed since I slept in them on the ground. I was smoothly shaven and my hair was combed, if a little ratty behind the ears. Few mothers would have minded if I'd shown up to court their daughter looking the way I did. It may have been the bell bottoms that prompted Terracciano's disapprobation.

"Thanks Tony. I'll do that."

After work I went to Barney's and got fitted for a really nice, slim-fitting, dark blue suit. It cost a little more than I'd have typically spent, but it wasn't extravagant. The tailoring wouldn't be complete until tomorrow evening. I hadn't counted on that. I'd just have to evade David for twenty-four hours. I could hardly greet a Rockefeller in my sleep-on-the-ground duds, then charge Tony T for a suit from Barney's. Avoiding Rockefeller for one day shouldn't be that difficult; I'd already succeeded for twenty-seven years.

I asked the clerk, "Any chance of getting it back sooner, say tomorrow morning?"

"Of course, sir. That would be eighty dollars extra."

Would Tony T cover expedited delivery too? Could I even ask him to? God, no; he was being generous enough by paying for the suit. "Tomorrow evening would be fine, thanks."

*　　*　　*

Chase's Vietnam Task Force did most of its work behind the scenes. John Mitchell was with International Personnel, a function that was just starting to be called Human Resources. He was tasked with finding jobs at Chase for the refugees. Paul Didier turned out to be from the Office of the Chairman; he was David Rockefeller's deputy and D.R.'s eyes and ears on the Vietnam Task Force.

Cor Termijn was omnipresent in New York and rarely have I seen a greater transformation in a man than between the dowdy Cor of Saigon and the handsome and dashing gentleman he'd become in New York. He was the quintessential master of ceremonies, never forgetting a name, even those of his employees' spouses and children, and capable of giving inspiring speeches entirely extemporaneously. His Dutch accent had become, if possible, even more endearing. His polished shoes reflected light.

The families of Chase Manhattan Bank officers in New York who took refugees into their homes also deserve enormous credit. Those foster families eased what must have been a traumatic time in the refugees' displaced lives, children and adults alike. By the start of the weekend, May 10, all of the refugees had moved out of hotels and into foster homes in the suburbs.

The allocations to foster families were made in Auditorium A, on the first basement level. It was gratifying to watch my wards being readopted by real families with real houses, fireplaces, and dining room tables. The kids would start going to suburban elementary schools and high schools, possibly as early as Monday. The parents would begin rebuilding their lives, saving, and contributing distinctively to their communities.

I never had a chance to say goodbye to Anh, Linh, and Mai, the three tellers. I heard one relocated to Albuquerque, another to San Antonio. The other just vanished.

Someone in the know informed me that First National City Bank managed to get most of its employees out of Saigon through Ken Moorefield's Evacuation Control Center. One of their young American officers in Hong Kong defied orders and flew in on one of the last Pan Am flights and got Citi's staff out in small groups, a plan I'd considered and rejected. I also learned that Bank of America opted for a limited rescue of eleven of its thirty-seven employees. IBM's experience on the other hand was disgraceful. Their Vietnamese employees and families, 154 in all, were abandoned by their management. On April 30, as the North Vietnamese Army marched into Saigon, they were all still standing in front of the IBM building with their packed suitcases. God knows what happened to them.

*   *   *

After Auditorium A, some of us were ushered upstairs for what was billed as a photo session. I placed a call to Barney's to check my suit's status and because of the call I was a little late for the photos. The room was about the size of a classroom, and the crowd churned, everyone chatting affably as though they were at a cocktail party. From time to time a flashbulb would go off and, irregularly, a bright floodlight signaled a film camera at work. I hardly recognized anyone, and no one took notice of me, which was fine since I was the only male without a suit and therefore camera shy. I shook a few hands and immediately forgot their owners' names.

"Hello, Ralph. I want to thank you very much."

I was taken by the lively gleam in David Rockefeller's blue eyes, and the genuineness of his smile. His handshake was surprisingly soft. I'd been completely unaware that he was in the room. The bright backlighting gave him the aura of a saint healing lepers. The room went quiet and the two of us stood perfectly still, hands clasped, examining one another's faces.

I was too shocked to form a full sentence. "Hi, David."

"You've done something truly exceptional for our bank and I'm very proud of you. John Linker has explained to me how resourceful and creative you were. I will find a way to thank you."

"I'm glad I could help. John deserves credit too. And Cor Termijn."

That was it. He moved on. He chatted with some of the Vietnamese. Then he went back to governing the third largest bank in America.

I picked up my suit that evening but I couldn't bring myself to send the bill to Tony Terracciano. D.R. hadn't noticed my bell bottoms.

*   *   *

May 11 was Mother's Day so I rented a car and drove two hours north to Litchfield, and took my mother to dinner. Her favorite place was the Hopkins Inn, overlooking Lake Waramaug. They had an aquarium filled with trout, and diners could select from the condemned.

Nga hadn't arrived yet and my mother wanted to know all about her. I may have left her with the impression that I'd traveled to Saigon with the sole purpose of helping Nga get out. Nothing would surprise her. Nga would be good company for my mother.

"This girl must be pretty special for you to do so much for her."

"She had a terrible life in Vietnam. I couldn't have forgiven myself if I'd left her."

"She's a charity project?"

"Possibly more, after she graduates from college she can decide what kind of life she wants. I'll see her on home leaves. You too."

*   *   *

I flew back to Bangkok on May 14, thirty days after setting out for Saigon. My Thai colleagues pleaded with me not to close Bangkok branch and relocate them to New York. Oie welcomed me back, demurely at first, then after a decent interval, romantically. I overcame a twinge of guilt about my indiscretion in the barracks at Clark Air Base, partly because it seemed so long ago and so far away, and partly, too, because I claimed grounds for innocence.

*   *   *

Andy Warhol would have called Saigon branch my fifteen minutes of fame, but it was Chase's more than mine. I know of no other commercial enterprise that has ever done anything like what Chase did for its vulnerable Vietnamese employees and their families during the fall of Saigon. John Linker may have selected me for no reason other than my nationality, proximity, and expendability, but with hindsight I understand how the experience straightened and strengthened me.

I worked in Southeast Asia for nearly a decade, and following my eventual extradition back to head office I maintained irregular contact with a diminishing number of my Vietnamese families. I reconnected with the last of them at a wedding of one of Mr. Trinh's children, in about 1999. Eventually, though, I lost contact with everyone from Saigon branch. Fate simply guided us in different directions.

I honored my commitment to support Nga through her schooling. Years later I ran into her entirely by chance and learned that she'd married and had two daughters, and then I lost touch with her as well.

I never did have children of my own, and the 113 wards I adopted on April 24 and 25, 1975, were the only family I would ever know. For half a century I've speculated how their lives changed for having crossed paths with mine. And mine with theirs.

CODA

On February 19, 2022, well after I thought I'd finished this book, I attended the lunar new year festival of the New Jersey Vietnamese American Community Association and chanced to sit next to a friend of My Nga Tran, the former operations officer at the Chase Manhattan Bank's Saigon Branch. I met with My Nga and her husband, Sinh, and through them have established contact with several of the other Chase Saigon refugees. Most have prospered in America, and many have had children and grandchildren. Mr. Cuong and Mr. Trinh have passed, though their families are thriving. Collectively, my adoptive Vietnamese family has generally flourished. I feel blessed.

Sadly, Bach Mai's husband, Cau, died shortly after their arrival in America, and some other Chase employees have suffered heartbreaking losses as well.

Recently a new issue has surfaced for the families of my former Vietnamese colleagues. Some have suffered verbal and physical abuse because of racial bigotry. I developed a profound affection for my adoptive family, and their ill-treatment at the hands of my countrymen sickens me. As I always knew they would, my Vietnamese Chase colleagues have made great Americans!

ACKNOWLEDGMENTS

John Linker, for selecting me for the mission. Cornelis Termijn, for his mentorship. Cuong Vu-Huy, for leadership. David Rockefeller, for his vision. Shep Lowman, for getting us into Tan Son Nhut Air Base. General Dao Le-Minh, for ten days of grace. Ken Moorefield, for administering consular regulations "flexibly." Pacific Air Command, for the planes. Denny Ellerman, Stephen Sossaman, Margaret Van Every, David Gulley, Jack Burger, Bill and Joan Marden, My Nga and Sinh Tran, and Evelyn Ceci for reading, critiques, and images. John DeCicco, for confidential reasons. Laurie Abkemeier for her agency, edits, and guidance. Bob Bender and Frederick Chase for editing. Elizabeth Alleva at JPMorgan Chase Corporate History Collection for archives. Gail Feiner for everything else.

SOURCES

Immediately following the events described here, in the second week of May 1975, I composed and internally circulated an undated nine-page, single-spaced memo to James Bish, the Chase Manhattan Bank's senior vice president for Southeast Asia. It served as a debriefing exercise while the events of the preceding month were still fresh in my memory. It related the complete evacuation story and established a factual report of the evacuation in considerable detail. Twenty years later, in April 1995, I wrote an article based on the Bish memo for the Chase Manhattan Bank Alumni Association newsletter, which was widely circulated.

For a number of years after the events described in the book, I had occasion to meet with a group of Chase's Vietnamese refugees who had settled in New Jersey. We traded stories about the evacuation and these conversations reinforced my memories of the episode. Regrettably, I eventually lost contact with all of the refugees.

From 1977 to 1980, inclusive, I worked in the Chase Manhattan Bank's Hong Kong branch. In that capacity I would have occasion to discuss the Vietnamese evacuation episode with members of senior management, further reinforcing my memory.

In the winter of 1980 I testified as a defense witness for the Chase Manhattan Bank at a trial in the United States Court of Appeals,

Second Circuit in a case dealing with my closure of Chase's Saigon branch. The case is called *Vishipco Line v. Chase Manhattan Bank, N.A.*, and it is easily searched. At issue in the trial was the claim that Chase's closing of the branch prevented our client Vishipco from withdrawing its local currency deposits, which in turn prevented the plaintiff from paying their crews, which in turn resulted in the loss of its ships. Another issue was the applicable exchange rate to be used in calculating remediation. In the course of preparing for that trial, I coordinated with Chase's defense counsel, Milbank, Tweed, Hadley & McCoy, in recreating and documenting the minutest details of the closure and the evacuation of our Vietnamese employees. This exhaustively detailed legal exercise, for which I was flown in from Hong Kong for two weeks, further reinforced my memory of the events of April 1975.

In 2019 I visited the JPMorgan Chase Corporate History Collection and was given unrestricted access to the bank's extensive archives dealing with its former Saigon branch. They provided copies of numerous documents, including photographs and newsletters dealing with the evacuation.

Using modern search utilities, I located five individuals named in the book and I contacted them and set up in-person interviews with two of them and telephone interviews with the other three. I met with former foreign service officers Lucien Kinsolving and Denny Ellerman. Mr. Kinsolving provided me copies of letters he wrote to his family in 1975 and they document details of his activities. Mr. Ellerman provided additional details as well as his appraisal of Ambassador Martin. In three telephone calls, I interviewed former foreign service officer Kenneth Moorefield. He graciously provided several of his own archival photographs. I also spoke with former Chase Manhattan Bank vice chairman Anthony Terracciano, and we took the opportunity to share recollections.

On Independence Day 2021, I spoke with former USAID officer Bob Lanigan, who now goes by his birth name, Russell Mott, by telephone. He doesn't recall how many barges he towed behind his tugboat, or how many refugees were on each one, or how many refugees he rescued in total; he thinks "between five and seven thousand." I think he meant hundred, not thousand. Still, speaking to him was humbling.

Because the primary source for this project is my personal witness to history, I studiously avoided researching or even casually reading any other reporting about the fall of Saigon, Ambassador Martin, or the Vietnamese refugee crisis in order to avoid contaminating my memory and conflating my experiences with those of others. Not until I completed a first draft of the manuscript did I read other accounts. When I finally did, I used others' renditions solely to verify, and in a couple of instances to correct, my own version of events. I freely admit to being gratified to find confirmation of my observations, especially regarding Ambassador Martin's willful delusion. I was disappointed, though, to find no recognition of the clandestine activities of Shep Lowman, Ken Moorefield, and Bob Lanigan, which I believe is original to my work. I rescued 113; each of them rescued multiples of that.

On February 19, 2022, I attended the lunar new year (Tet) celebration of the Vietnamese American Community Association of New Jersey. When the woman seated next to me heard my story, she picked up her phone and called her friend, My Nga Tran, the former operations manager at Chase Manhattan Bank's Saigon branch. I subsequently met with My Nga, and her perspective of the events of April 1975 has been clarifying. With her assistance I've reconnected with a dozen of our fellow refugees, and we have pooled our collective memories.

PSEUDONYMS

In the service of discretion, I have presented some characters pseudonymously. Jackson Dunn has died, but I count his widow a friend and would not want her to become aware that she was his twentieth wife. Similarly, I would not want Nga's grandchildren to become aware of her grim past. There is no telling what the communist secret police would do to Thang were they aware of his early doubts about the revolution. I suspect that Saigon supported numerous black market currency dealers named Raj, though none were my pseudonymous Raj Singh. The Iranian diplomat is also pseudonymous, as are the three tellers.

INDEX

Page numbers in *italics* refer to maps.